THE
Dementia
Care-Partner's
Workbook

A Guide for Understanding, Education, and Hope

A support-group workbook or self-study guide for care partners of a loved one with Alzheimer's disease or another form of dementia

Edward G. Shaw, M.D., M.A.

Foreword by Teepa Snow, M.S., O.T.

THE

Dementia Care-Partner's Workbook

A Guide for Understanding, Education, and Hope

Edward G. Shaw, M.D., M.A.

Companion
PRESS

An imprint of the Center for Loss and Life Transition
Fort Collins, Colorado

Also by Dr. Ed Shaw

Keeping Love Alive as Memories Fade:
The 5 Love Languages and the Alzheimer's Journey

Advance Praise for *The Dementia Care-Partner's Workbook*

"An engaging, informative workbook that encourages dementia care providers to tell their stories as well as become more knowledgeable about the situations they will face. It describes steps to lessen distress while not sugarcoating the challenges that dementia presents."

— Peter V. Rabins, M.D., M.P.H., co-author of *The 36-Hour Day* and emeritus professor of Alzheimer's disease and related disorders, Johns Hopkins School of Medicine

"Being a caregiver is a daunting task, and no one knows this responsibility better from personal and professional viewpoints than Dr. Ed Shaw. This magnificent workbook is based on his years of experience caring for his late wife and working with persons with dementia, their families, and caregivers. The curriculum will be of enormous value to all care partners caring for their loved ones."

— Ronald C. Petersen, M.D., Ph.D., author of *Mayo Clinic on Alzheimer's Disease*, professor of neurology, and director of the Mayo Clinic Alzheimer's Disease Research Center

"When you love someone with dementia, you can feel alone, overwhelmed, scared, and totally misunderstood. This compassionate, experienced care partner, physician, and author knows firsthand why family stories, support, and grieving often-unacknowledged losses are so important for healing. The Dementia Care-Partner's Workbook *offers a structured guide, paring down what is often too much information to present only what's really essential for effective communication and care in family life. Readers will be grateful to have Dr. Shaw's wise counsel in their corner as they read and re-read this workbook. What a gift."*

— Lisa P. Gwyther, M.S.W., L.C.S.W., associate professor of psychiatry and behavioral sciences, Duke School of Medicine and Duke (Alzheimer's) Family Support Program

"The Dementia Care-Partner's Workbook *is written by a medical doctor who has walked the journey and in turn helped others through the challenges of dementia care. An excellent curriculum for care-partner support groups, it can also be used as a personal study guide. Whether you're in a group or on your own, this workbook offers practical information and will help you process your thoughts and emotions on a journey you did not choose. I highly recommend it."*

— Gary D. Chapman, Ph.D., author of *The 5 Love Languages* and coauthor of *Keeping Love Alive as Memories Fade: The 5 Love Languages and the Alzheimer's Journey*

Companion Press is an imprint of the Center for Loss and Life Transition, 3735 Broken Bow Road, Fort Collins, Colorado 80526.

Companion Press books may be purchased in bulk for sales promotions, premiums, and fundraisers. Please contact the publisher at (970) 226-6050 or www.centerforloss.com for more information.

25 24 23 22 21 20 19   6 5 4 3 2 1

ISBN: 978-1-61722-274-0

In loving memory of Rebecca, who lived a grace-filled life and touched the hearts of all who were blessed to know her.

To Erin, Leah, Carrie, Claire, and the millions of dementia care partners around the world who have been or are on their own journey down the path not chosen.

Contents

Foreword

Many people find that after they experience the journey of dementia as a care provider, family member, or partner, they are profoundly impacted and changed as human beings. Few people, however, develop a deep and robust new perspective, let go of their previous career paths, and seek knowledge and skill to focus on a new mission following the loss of a loved one to dementia. Dr. Ed Shaw is one such person. His transformation from caring husband and skilled oncologist to leader of one of the very few university-based dementia research, support, and education programs that serve families and care partners in the United States is a testament to his commitment to making a positive and effective difference in the culture of dementia care.

Others have certainly told their dementia stories and provided care ideas and recommendations, but in this work, Ed has done more. This resource is something different. Ed's workbook provides a full-spectrum approach to helping family members better appreciate the condition of dementia, the changes it will bring into their lives, and the broad array of decisions and situations they will be asked to address during the progression of this life-changing and, ultimately, life-ending condition.

In this text, Ed provides a structured series of sessions based on the process that he uses at Wake Forest Baptist Health to help families and people living with dementia. He assists them in developing the skills they will need to navigate the journey with less distress as well as greater understanding and appreciation for what each other is experiencing. The content and structure of this workbook were created from these programs, which Ed and his colleagues provide at the Memory Counseling Program.

His program and this resource offer what is so needed in dementia care: a combination of practical, emotional, intellectual, social, and spiritual support for those who have to make the journey. This workbook provides individual family members with greater awareness, knowledge, and skill to improve life, relationships, and care throughout the disease process. Its companion leader's manual provides potential support-group leaders with a flexible yet well-structured guide to help families address the very real and important issues that will arise. Together these resources supply essential information to those who are willing to step forward and take an opportunity to learn about their new *normal*, to become comfortable with talking about dementia and the changes it is bringing into all of their lives, and to consider what is working well and what could use some modification.

As the numbers of people living with dementia continue to grow, and knowledge about the various forms and complex nature of dementia remains elusive, more and more families are finding themselves unprepared to become the supporters and advocates people living with this condition need. This workbook can help fill that gap. By preparing support-group leaders and by offering family members a tool they can use, life with dementia can be changed for the better.

My work takes me around the world and into a wide variety of dementia care conditions. In far too many situations, there is simply no one available who has a basic understanding of what is happening when someone is developing dementia. This lack of understanding creates far too many dangerous and painful interactions that result in miserable outcomes and incidents for both the person living with dementia and their care partners. Building bridges to promote different perspectives and new possibilities makes all the difference. This resource supports such change.

Teepa Snow, MS, OTR/L, FAOTA
Lead Trainer and Consultant, Dementia Care and Training Specialist, Positive Approach, LLC
Counseling Associate, Duke University School of Nursing

Introduction

Caregiving, simply put, is a part of life, from raising our children to helping our aging parents. When my mom was diagnosed with terminal colon cancer, her only wish was to live with my wife, our three daughters, and me for the time she had left. We were her caregivers. As an oncologist, I felt pretty comfortable with the day-to-day challenges that arose in Mom's care during the last six months of her life. But a decade later, the girls (then ages 19 to 24) and I again became caregivers when their mom, my late wife, Rebecca, was diagnosed with early-onset Alzheimer's disease, at the age of 53.

> *"There are only four kinds of people in the world: those who have been caregivers, those who are currently caregivers, those who will be caregivers, and those who will need caregivers."*
>
> — Rosalynn Carter

We were confused, overwhelmed, and afraid. How could such a healthy young woman develop an incurable brain disease? Her only symptoms were poor memory and getting lost when driving, yet her doctor told us she'd live eight to ten years, maybe less, and eventually would be in diapers, lose the ability to walk, and need help eating. What lay ahead for us? How would we manage when we all had full-time school and jobs?

Rebecca, understandably frightened by the diagnosis and prognosis, wept as we embraced. "Please, take good care of me," she said. Of course I promised to do that, yet grief-stricken and afraid myself, I wondered who was going to guide us on this caregiving journey, a journey down a path not chosen.

Rebecca lived nine years after her diagnosis. In the last few years, she didn't know the girls and me as her daughters and husband. Indeed, she eventually became incontinent, wheelchair-bound, and incapable of feeding herself. Even though we had excellent providers to care for Rebecca's medical needs, there was nobody to mentor and companion us as her care partners, to understand the challenges we faced.

Discouraged by this lack of support for care partners, I left my job as an oncology doctor, trained as a grief-and-loss mental-health counselor, and in 2011, started a counseling center for those with Alzheimer's disease or another form of dementia and their care

CARE PARTNER

In *The Dementia Care-Partner's Workbook*, I'll use the term "**care partner**" rather than "caregiver" when referring to you, the family member or friend who provides daily care. I've chosen this term because many people with dementia are offended by the term "caregiver," particularly when they are in the early stages of the disease and need little daily assistance. They often find "care partner" more acceptable.

Even for someone with a more advanced stage of dementia, the notion of care partner aligns better with the idea of "doing things with, not for, the person with dementia." I'll reserve the term caregiver to refer to paid healthcare professionals, like certified nursing assistants, who provide care in the home or a residential-care facility for those with later-stage dementia in need of help with basic needs such as toileting, bathing, or eating.

partners, called the Memory Counseling Program at Wake Forest Baptist Health in Winston-Salem, North Carolina.

Over the last eight years, the Memory Counseling Program has grown from two of us working one half-day per week to seven strong, including five counselors, an administrative coordinator, and a social-work graduate student. We have now partnered with hundreds of families who have a loved one with dementia, usually a spouse or parent, to provide support, education, and resources.

In these eight years, we have learned a great deal about the many challenges facing dementia care partners. Based on our extensive counseling experience with individuals, couples, and families, we have identified eight needs central to all dementia care partners. Through its ten lessons, the contents of this book address the eight needs and will help fill the gap in support and information I myself experienced when I first became a care partner to a loved one with dementia.

THE EIGHT CENTRAL NEEDS OF DEMENTIA CARE PARTNERS

CENTRAL NEED 1—*Tell and retell your story.* Being a dementia care partner is a stressful and often lonely, isolating experience. Telling and retelling your story, out loud to others and in writing, helps you vent about the demands and challenges of caregiving, clarify what you're thinking and feeling, and feel heard, less alone, and even validated.

CENTRAL NEED 2—*Educate yourself.* We naturally fear the unknown. Dementia, because it is feared more than cancer or any other disease, is something many of us know very little about. Learning about Alzheimer's and the other forms of dementia, as well as the structure and function of the brain, and the many challenges of caregiving, will give you a better understanding of your loved one's symptoms and make you a more informed, empathetic, and effective care partner.

CENTRAL NEED 3—*Adapt to changing relationships.* Dementia is a progressive disease (in a sense, every day is their best day because of the continual decline) that causes changes in your loved one's behavior, which in turn create challenges in your relationship with them and others. These changes and challenges require you to adapt, and healthy adaptation allows you to stay meaningfully connected to your loved one, and them to you.

CENTRAL NEED 4—*Grieve your losses.* As a dementia care partner, you will experience grief and loss just as someone would who had experienced the death of a loved one. The kinds of losses you will endure as a dementia care partner include personal losses, relationship losses, and the loss of peace of mind. The grief and loss experience will also impact your entire family. Grieving (what you think and feel on the inside) and mourning (the outward expression of your grief) is a necessary part of your caregiving journey and well-being.

CENTRAL NEED 5—*Take care of yourself.* Being a dementia care partner stresses you physically, emotionally, and spiritually, placing you at greater risk for medical problems, depression and anxiety, and social isolation. Being intentional about self-care and wellness will give you the strength and endurance needed for the long journey of dementia caregiving.

CENTRAL NEED 6—*Ask for and accept help from others.* Caregiving is a team sport. Yet most care partners try to do too much themselves and are reluctant to ask for and accept the help of others. Not only is it OK to ask for help, there are many people who want to be part of the caregiving team, and it's not always who you think. Being intentional about forming a team of care partners will help your loved one receive the best care possible and reduce the burden you experience providing for them.

CENTRAL NEED 7—*Prepare for what's ahead.* Dementia is a progressive disease. Once a brain function is lost, it cannot be relearned or regained. As your loved one transitions through the early, middle, and late stages, certain changes, challenges, and transitions can be anticipated and planned for. Among the most difficult of these are the hard-to-manage behaviors of late-stage dementia, such as agitation, aggression, hallucinations, incontinence, resisting care, sundowning, and wandering, because they often require that you get more help at home or even consider a transition to full-time residential care. Being proactive about care needs, as well as related legal and financial issues, will allow you to navigate the ever-changing dementia journey with less stress.

CENTRAL NEED 8 — *Explore existential and spiritual questions to find meaning.* Inevitably, when you or someone you love develops a terrible disease like dementia, you often ask the "Why?" questions – "Why him?" or "Why her?" It is important that we feel the freedom to ask such questions, even if they are unanswerable. Often, wrestling with the why questions allows you to find meaning and purpose in what otherwise seems like a senseless disease.

HOW TO USE THIS WORKBOOK

The Dementia Care-Partner's Workbook has been created as a flexible resource to provide understanding, education, and hope in either a support-group setting or as a self-study guide. The workbook is divided into ten individual lessons that will help you meet the eight central needs of dementia care partners. Let's examine how.

DEMENTIA CARE-PARTNER SUPPORT GROUPS

One of the most effective ways to help yourself address your eight central care partner needs is to participate in a **support group**. Support groups are the backbone of the Memory Counseling Program at Wake Forest Baptist Health. Although many care partners feel hesitant to join a support group, our participants often feel an immediate sense of camaraderie and community from the very first session, relieved that someone else finally understands what they're going through. They consistently rate the program, curriculum, and group leaders very highly, and by the group's end, they also report greater knowledge about dementia and enhanced coping skills.

Our support-group program has two components: an initial weekly classroom experience followed by a monthly maintenance group. The initial classroom experience, offered three or four times yearly, is led by one or two counselors for groups of eight to 16 people who stay together for ten consecutive weekly sessions that are 90 minutes in length. Each week there will be a lesson focused on one or several of the eight central needs. This workbook guides each person through the ten-week experience, offering educational content and providing questions and space to journal responses, all of which serve as the basis for discussion during the weekly sessions.

Here is a listing of the workbook's lessons:

- Lesson One: Telling Your Story from the Beginning
- Lesson Two: Basics of Alzheimer's Disease and Other Dementias
- Lesson Three: Brain Structure and Function, Activities of Daily Living, and Dementia Stages
- Lesson Four: Changing Relationships
- Lesson Five: Coping with Grief and Loss
- Lesson Six: Stress and Self-Care
- Lesson Seven: Getting More Help and Transitioning Care
- Lesson Eight: Legal, Financial, and End-of-Life Issues
- Lesson Nine: Existential and Spiritual Questions
- Lesson Ten: Retelling Your Story Starting Today

In our program, after completing the ten lessons, group members then may choose to transition to a counselor-led, once-a-month 90-minute "maintenance group," which is more unstructured in format. I hope you will be able to participate in a care-partner support group that uses this workbook as an educational guide and expression tool.

If you are a medical or mental-health professional or lay leader in a secular or faith-based organization, you can use *The Dementia Care-Partner's Workbook* to help you establish a sustainable support-group program that includes the initial ten-week classroom experience followed by monthly maintenance groups. I also encourage leaders to purchase *A Leader's Manual for Dementia Care-Partner Support Groups*, a downloadable resource at www.centerforloss.com. It contains step-by-step instructions on how to run the individual weekly lessons, lesson-specific handouts, and general information about establishing and leading support groups, with lots of practical advice based on my

THE BENEFITS OF JOURNALING

Regardless of the setting in which you use *The Dementia Care-Partner's Workbook* (support group or self-study), there is by intention space for you to journal your thoughts and feelings throughout each of the ten lessons. (If you need more room to write, simply use a blank notebook.) This may be unfamiliar and even uncomfortable for you at first. Why is writing so important? Here are just a few reasons:

- The act of writing in and of itself is an exercise in storytelling, which is Central Need 1 for dementia care partners.

- If you are in a support group, or just talking with a trusted family member or friend, journaling in advance will help you clarify what is most important for you to share.

- Writing creates a safe space in which you can fully express yourself, no matter what you're thinking or feeling.

- Journaling will pave the way to greater insight into the problems and challenges you face, helping you become a more empathetic care partner.

If you've never been one to keep a diary or journal, now is a great time to give it a try. Most people become more comfortable with writing over time and may even find their responses to be transformative. The workbook's questions have been written to be thought-provoking, so that even if you decide not to journal, simply reading them will at least get you thinking about important issues confronting you as a care partner.

own experiences as a care partner, doctor, mental-health practitioner, and support-group leader.

SELF-STUDY

I realize that not every dementia care partner has the access, time, or ability to attend a weekly support group, so *The Dementia Care-Partner's Workbook* also serves as a **self-study guide**. You can work through the ten lessons at your own pace, learning the same information as you would in a support group while addressing your eight central needs. I would suggest completing one lesson per week, as if you were in a support group, but you can certainly work at a faster or slower pace. Regardless, it would be ideal if you could complete the written journaling exercises, and I would encourage you to find someone who would be willing to talk with you about the questions and answers you find most thought-provoking in each lesson.

AN UNMET, URGENT NEED

During my counseling training and for a year thereafter, I worked as a grief counselor at our community hospice. We had grief support-groups with many available resources to run those groups. One can go to Amazon.com, search "grief support-group curriculum," and find numerous options.

Yet when I began our Memory Counseling Program dementia care-partner support groups back in 2011, there were no curricula available for leaders and no workbooks for participants. It is still true today. So, having developed and refined a curriculum for Wake Forest's support-group program over the years, I decided to publish it as a resource to others. This is how *The Dementia Care-Partner's Workbook* came to be.

The need has never been greater. At present, there are more than 7.8 million people in the U.S. with Alzheimer's or another form of dementia. On average, each person with dementia has three care partners, so by extrapolation, there are over 20 million dementia care partners. And by 2050, the prevalence of dementia (and the number of care partners) is expected to nearly triple.

The Dementia Care-Partner's Workbook is the resource that was missing when my daughters and I were Rebecca's care partners. So whether you're using it in a support group or for self-study, welcome. My sincerest desire is that it provides understanding, education, and hope to both you as care partner and your loved one with dementia. Godspeed on the long and challenging journey!

Sincerely,

Edward G. Shaw, M.D., M.A.
March, 2019

Telling Your Story from the Beginning

Imagine you and I were meeting in my counseling office for the first time. After introductions, you would sit across from me, and, most likely, I would have a cup of warm coffee. You would as well, if you are caffeine-addicted like me.

"Your story will heal you, and your story will heal somebody else."

— Iyanla Vanzant

My office is a warm and welcoming space. It feels safe. Our time together would begin by you telling me the story of why you've come for counseling. I would learn the name of your loved one who has dementia, his or her diagnosis, and the symptoms they are experiencing. Yes, I could glean this information from the medical chart, but that wouldn't tell me your story. Getting to know you, your loved one, and the challenges you're facing—in other words, hearing your story—is what I love the most about being a counselor.

Since the beginning of time, human beings have been compelled to tell their stories, verbally and in writing, or non-verbally, through art and music. Emotional situations, whether we are sad, mad, glad, or anxious, motivate us to tell our stories. This is why telling and retelling your story is the first of the central needs for dementia care partners.

Recently, the first female Supreme Court Justice, Sandra Day O'Connor, has been in the news. She retired in 2006 to take care of her husband, John, who had been diagnosed with Alzheimer's disease in 2000. Justice O'Connor was very open with the public about the challenges of being a dementia care partner. In a televised hearing before Congress in 2008, she told her story, including the following: "I submit to you that until you have actually stared Alzheimer's in the face, you cannot truly understand the deep sense of frustration, fear, helplessness, and grief that accompany it. Alzheimer's is a family disease. It may directly attack only one member of the family, but every member of that family feels the effects. Every member loses something." Powerful, emotion-laden words, and sadly, she too has just been diagnosed with dementia.

Carolyn Peters found another way to tell her care-partner story. She lost her artist husband, Don, to Alzheimer's disease. After his diagnosis, she took up sculpting stone as a way to express herself, to tell her story, as Don's care partner. In a profile of Carolyn featured on the Family Caregiver Alliance website some time ago, she remarked, "Sculpting ... became both an escape from his illness and a connection to him. Art, always our strong common bond, became... a way to experience some moments of joy even as we plummeted, tethered together, into the black vortex of his disease." Of using stone as her medium, she said, "Stone [is] a material I could chip and grind away at, creating something beautiful, something I could not do with my husband's disease." Her latest sculpture, which shows a swirling spiral, is a vivid representation of the "black vortex" she describes—an aspect of her story told through a piece of white stone.

As you know, and as we can see in Justice O'Connor's and Ms. Peters' words, dementia caregiving is an emotional and stressful journey. For many reasons, which I'll expand on momentarily, you as a care partner have an ongoing need to share with others what you've already been through, what you're experiencing currently, and what you see lying ahead.

Mary and Chris's story also illustrates the importance of storytelling for dementia care partners.

I Want to Go Home

Mary and Chris, both in their mid-80s, had been married for 62 years. A retired pastor, Chris grew up in northern West Virginia, south of Pittsburgh, about a seven-hour drive from Winston-Salem, North Carolina, where they lived.

Chris had been diagnosed with Alzheimer's disease about three years earlier but had many other medical problems causing his dementia to worsen faster than expected. I saw Mary for a counseling session about every three months. Much of each visit was focused on her telling me how Chris was doing. On one particular visit, Mary was very animated and spent an entire hour telling me this story.

Chris, like many people with middle-stage Alzheimer's, was becoming disoriented, including not recognizing his and Mary's house as their home. He would say "I want to go home" over and over and over, such that it was causing Mary to become frustrated and angry. The more she reassured him he was home, the more agitated and insistent he got about wanting to "go home."

So one morning, after her patience had been exceeded for the day, Mary loaded Chris in their car and headed north to the home Chris grew up in. The 350-mile ride was arduous, as Chris continued to tell Mary "I want to go home," even though she now reassured him they were headed there. When they finally arrived, Mary escorted Chris up the front sidewalk and stood at the front door of the family home with him.

Chris looked around for several minutes, at the door, then the yard, and lastly up and down the street. Then he turned to Mary and said with a blank look, "Mary, I want to go home." Mary was dumbfounded. She wasn't sure what to do. This wasn't what she had expected. After a few more minutes, she and Chris got back in the car and started the long journey back to Winston-Salem.

As Mary told me that story, she trembled and had tears streaming from her eyes. "Dr. Shaw, I realized when we stood at the front door of Chris's house, that 'home' to him is not that house, but it's a time, maybe when he was in grade school, where he remembers his mom, dad, brothers, and sisters, a time he felt connected to those he loved and who loved him, rather than the confusing and unfamiliar world he lives in now. I've been viewing his desire to 'go home' only through my eyes, not his. I understand now."

Though Chris continued to repeatedly ask about going home, Mary became much more patient and tolerant with him. She could reassure him that they were home, and that she was there with him, as she had been for the last 62 years. All Mary thought about on the drive back from West Virginia was the need to share her story with me, about what she and Chris had experienced, and what she'd learned from it.

Why was telling her and Chris's story to me helpful to Mary? Please describe.

_____

_____

_____

_____

_____

_____

Do you think telling your story as care partner will be easy or hard? Please explain.

_____

_____

_____

_____

_____

_____

While there are a number of reasons telling your care-partner story is helpful to you, I'll present just a few here.

• Caregiving is often a lonely and isolating experience. Sharing your story in a safe environment, with yourself (journaling) or others (such as in a support group or simply talking to a trusted family member or friend), will help you feel heard, validated, and less isolated.

• Telling your story out loud, or letting others read what you've written, helps them learn from your experience, affecting how they would respond in a similar situation, which gives you a sense of purpose and meaning for what you endure as a care partner.

• Sharing your story, in essence "getting it off your chest," reduces your level of stress, which will improve your physical, emotional, and spiritual health and help you to become more resilient.

• Sharing your story also provides a sense of common experience that connects you with other dementia care partners, creating a feeling of community that you're all in this together. I have seen this connection in many dementia support groups where the diversity of participants—different ages, races, ethnicities, educational backgrounds, and socioeconomic statuses—becomes secondary to why they are there, united as care partners of loved ones with Alzheimer's or another form of dementia.

Even after reading all the reasons why sharing your story is beneficial, you might be thinking or feeling that telling your story will be exceedingly difficult or even impossible. Perhaps you don't have a safe place to share your story due to lack of privacy, or you've been shut down by others when talking openly and honestly about the challenges of caregiving. It might be too hard to tell the story, as it may bring feelings of grief and loss that be emotionally overwhelming. Or maybe you feel some embarrassment, guilt, or shame if, for example, marriage or family dynamics are strained over caregiving roles and responsibilities, or perhaps your loved one is now on Medicaid in a publicly subsidized nursing home.

Whatever the reason, you are not alone, and there are places for you to begin addressing this first central need. I have found through many interactions with care partners, as well as my own journey, that one-on-one counseling or a dementia care-partners' support group can be a vital resource to help you open up and share your story.

MINDFULNESS MOMENT

This is a good time to pause and allow me to teach you an exercise that will be at the beginning and end of each lesson in the book. It is called a Mindfulness Moment, and it is based on the practice of mindfulness-based stress reduction, which you may or may not be familiar with. Whether you are or not, let's jump in!

Mindfulness is a state of mind that you achieve by focusing all of your awareness and attention on the present moment and only the present moment. To do this, you must exclude worries of the past (since you can't change things that have already happened) as well as the future (because you may not have control over some things that haven't happened yet). Mindfulness allows you to take a "brain break" from planning and problem-solving, as well as the negative self-talk associated with being overwhelmed, such as, "I've really screwed up," "What a disaster my life is," or "This is not going to turn out well." With mindfulness, you calmly, non-judgmentally, and compassionately accept your current thoughts, emotions, and body sensations without feeling as though you need to change them. The Mindfulness Moment includes a short breathing exercise that has been shown, through medical research, to reduce your level of stress not only in the moment, but throughout the day.

Having just completed your first journaling exercise, you may be experiencing difficult feelings about your loved one's diagnosis of Alzheimer's or another form of dementia. You may be feeling fear, worry, sadness, or anxiety. For the time being, accept that you have these feelings and that you can coexist with them at least for the brief time of this Mindfulness Moment. Don't judge yourself or blame anyone else for having them. Stay in the present moment without thinking about everything that still needs to be done today, about the past (what he or she was like before their dementia diagnosis) or future (what lies ahead on the dementia journey). Now it's time to breathe your stress away.

This is how it's done.

1. Sit in a comfortable chair, put both feet on the floor (or any other comfortable position), clasp your hands over the middle of your belly, and then close your eyes (if desired).

2. Scan your muscles from head to toe and intentionally relax them. Unclench your teeth, let your shoulders sag, and relax your buttock and leg muscles.

3. Take in a slow, deep breath through your nose (count "one one-thousand, two one-thousand, three one-thousand" to yourself as you do so), then slowly exhale through your mouth to the same count, feeling the rise and fall of your belly. Do a total of ten slow, deep breaths like this. Focus solely on the gentle flow of your breath, in and out. Each time you exhale, consciously blow out the negative feelings and stress you feel about your loved one's dementia diagnosis or symptoms.

4. After the tenth breath, slowly open your eyes.

I hope you feel different when you've finished this exercise. Maybe your heart's beating more slowly, or you feel less tense, in your muscles, chest, and gut. Perhaps you have a sense of peace that at least for the moment, everything is OK. If you don't notice these changes the first time, don't worry, mindfulness takes practice.

Try this exercise in the morning when you get up and at night when you're preparing for sleep. That will provide two minutes in the day that are all about you and your self-care. You can also repeat the Mindfulness Moment whenever you're feeling stressed out, even when you're driving—except you'll need to keep your eyes open!

A SHARED STORYTELLING EXPERIENCE

I would now like to share my story as the primary care partner to my late wife, Rebecca. I'd also like to invite you to tell parts of your story interspersed with mine. Be as brief or long-winded as you'd like. It's your story, so there isn't a right or wrong, better or worse way to write it. Let's get started!

Life before Alzheimer's

Rebecca Lynn Easterly and I began dating in the fall of 1976. We were students at the University of Iowa, where we both were sophomores, she a speech pathology major, I premed. I asked her out on my 19th birthday. One week later we had dinner at the Brown Bottle, an iconic Iowa City restaurant. We talked and talked, as we had so much in common. I walked her home, we shared our first kiss, and we both knew that we were in love. Three weeks after our first date, we discussed marriage and the desire to have three children, all daughters. Three years later, we were married, and within eight years, we had our three daughters!

After college, Rebecca got a master's degree in speech pathology at Iowa, and I went to medical school in Chicago, followed by an internship and residency in radiation oncology at Mayo Clinic in Rochester, Minnesota. I worked for eight years as an oncologist at Mayo, specializing in brain-tumor treatment, then, in 1995, we headed to Winston-Salem, North Carolina, and Wake Forest Baptist Health, where I chaired the radiation-oncology department and started a research program in how brain cancer and its treatments affect the brain in cancer survivors. We thrived as southerners while our daughters Erin, Leah, and Carrie marched through the ranks of elementary, middle, and high school, and then college. Throughout those years, Rebecca was "supermom." Navigating with her Day Planner notebook, kindness, and grace, she organized, fed, and nurtured our family while I was busy at work.

How and when did you and your loved one meet? Please tell the story.

_____

_____

_____

_____

_____

Before the onset of your loved one's dementia, what were some of the highlights of your life together? Please tell your story.

_____

_____

_____

_____

_____

Early symptoms and diagnosis

In the spring of 2005, Erin, who was engaged to be married, noticed something odd: her "supermom" was struggling to keep up with the details of wedding planning. A year later, one of Rebecca's sisters died, and during most of 2006 and 2007, she was sad, distant, disorganized, forgetful, and occasionally got lost driving to familiar places. I attributed it to grief and an empty nest until one Saturday morning when Rebecca was reading the latest issue of *U.S. News and World Report,* she said, "I've read this article three times and I can't remember a thing about what it says." At her age, 53, I knew this was not normal.

Wake Forest Baptist Health, the hospital where I work, is well known for both geriatric research and care. In mid-2007, Rebecca was diagnosed with depression and prescribed an antidepressant after her symptoms failed to improve. Blood tests, a magnetic resonance imaging (MRI) scan of the brain, and cognitive-function tests were also obtained. The MRI showed mild shrinkage of Rebecca's brain, especially in the regions that control memory and spatial skills, definitely abnormal for a 53-year-old. The cognitive assessment confirmed abnormal loss of short-term memory and difficulties with problem-solving and spatial skills. She was diagnosed with mild cognitive impairment (MCI), a condition that often leads to Alzheimer's disease.

A year later, we traveled back to Mayo Clinic for a second opinion. There, Rebecca had an even more extensive evaluation to find the cause of her memory loss, but unfortunately, despite our earnest hopes and fervent prayers, the diagnosis was definitive: early-onset Alzheimer's disease. The prognosis: eight to ten years' life expectancy, progressive decline in all brain functions, the need for professional caregivers, and possibly nursing-home placement.

After receiving the news, Rebecca and I drove in silence to the Minneapolis airport. We wept, exchanging glances filled with sadness, fear, and uncertainty. At one point, I pulled over so we could talk. She had already forgotten what the doctor said. We embraced, speaking our love for one another in silence, reaffirming the vows we had made to each other 28 years earlier. Her voice full of sadness, Rebecca said,

"I don't want to be a burden. I want Erin, Leah, and Carrie to live their lives, pursue their dreams, and not let this get in the way. I will be OK. I know God loves me and that you love me. Just promise that you will take care of me." This was the only time we would ever directly speak about her Alzheimer's.

How and when did your loved one begin to experience symptoms of dementia? What were the steps involved in the diagnosis, and how did you and your loved one feel and react to the diagnosis? Please tell your story.

_____

_____

_____

_____

_____

_____

Progression of symptoms

In the years that followed, Rebecca's dementia progressed relentlessly through the stages of Alzheimer's disease. By mid-2010, her driving skills had deteriorated to the point that she was no longer safe on the road, and her keys had to be taken away. She was hurt and traumatized by this, as she'd never had a ticket or car accident. Shortly thereafter, while Rebecca and I were out of town on a driving trip, Rebecca lost her purse. "I hate my f***ing my brain," she said, teary-eyed, as we drove home. I had never heard her say the f-word before!

For me, the most difficult and challenging day of Rebecca's Alzheimer's journey occurred in August of 2013. It was a beautiful day, and Rebecca and I were sipping our coffee on the back porch, part of our morning ritual. As I was pouring cream into her cup, with the sun illuminating her beautiful blonde hair, Rebecca looked at me and said, "I have no idea who you are." Her blank stare confirmed that she really meant it. "But sweetie, I am your husband, Ed. You are my wife. We've been married for 33 years." This clue, more like a plea, didn't help. She didn't know me, and as I was soon to find out, she no longer knew Erin, Leah, and Carrie as her daughters anymore.

In the four months that followed that awful day, Rebecca became very agitated, especially from dusk into the early evening (known as "sundowning"). "I want to go home," she'd say, marching around the house from door to door, trying to escape. "But you are home, sweetie," I would tell her. "This is our home." She could not be comforted. Rebecca was yearning for her childhood home, a small bungalow in her hometown of Cedar Rapids, Iowa, where she had lived in the mid-to-late 1960s. I would have to physically block her attempts to exit as she punched and kicked at me, behaviors that were so atypical for gentle Rebecca. Eventually, she required medication to reduce her agitation.

After Rebecca no longer

AN UNANSWERABLE QUESTION

Many times I've reflected back on that terrible morning, asking myself the same unanswerable question: how could 37 years of a loving relationship disappear from Rebecca's mind overnight? It is a mystery of the human brain. As advanced as medicine currently is, there will be things that happen in your loved one's journey with dementia that neither doctors nor other healthcare providers will be able to explain, and that's frustrating. In Lessons Two and Three, you will learn a great deal about the brain's structure and its different functions, which I hope will answer some of your questions about memory loss and other symptoms of dementia.

DEMENTIA AND THE LOVE LANGUAGES

Keeping Love Alive as Memories Fade: The 5 Love Languages and the Alzheimer's Journey, written by Ms. Deborah Barr, Dr. Gary Chapman, and me, describes five ways that people express and receive emotional love: quality time, words of affirmation, physical touch, acts of service, and gifts. Even though a person with Alzheimer's disease has progressive difficulty expressing themselves emotionally during their journey, the ability to feel loved is preserved all the way until the end. The five love languages are simple tools to facilitate the expression of love to a person with any type of dementia. You'll learn more about them in Lesson Four: Changing Relationships.

recognized me as her husband, we continued to sleep in the same bed, but she turned her back to me and stayed on the very edge of the bed, as far away as she could be without falling out. One night she became very agitated and told me she didn't want me sleeping with her, so I set up a twin daybed in the corner of our bedroom. Those first few nights apart I was sleepless, grieving. We were only separated by a few feet, but it felt as though she were a million miles away. I would lie awake at night, literally aching with the desire to touch Rebecca, to lie in bed with her, to hold her. This was when I began my own journey of loneliness and celibacy.

By early 2014, Rebecca had no concept of the day, date, month, season, or year. She was unable to read or write, even to sign her own name, or add two plus two. Another challenge was spatial orientation. She had lost the ability to center her bottom over a chair or couch and required assistance just to sit, including sitting on the toilet. She already had a daytime paid caregiver, and with these further declines, evening and nighttime caregivers were added. This meant that Rebecca and I would never again have an evening alone at home together. There didn't seem to be any part of our lives that Alzheimer's disease hadn't taken away or changed. Rebecca and the girls and I experienced one loss after another.

Despite the challenges her disease presented, everyone on Rebecca's team of care partners, which at this point included family, friends, and paid caregivers, were focused on the same goal: to make each day the best it could be for Rebecca. On weekdays when I returned home from work, and on weekends, my time was devoted to her. Guided by the five love languages, one way I could show my love to her was to make supper and help her eat. Whenever I gave her an ice cream cone for dessert, her smile brought as much joy to me as it did to her. Afterward, we'd sit on the couch and watch old musicals. Her favorite was *The Sound of Music*, which we watched hundreds of times together. For Rebecca, the familiarity of each song was comforting. For me, it was a time when we were physically close, perhaps holding hands, being present to one another.

In the spring of 2016, Rebecca had transitioned into late-stage Alzheimer's. She lived only in the moment, with no remembrance of the past and no thought of the future. Her days were spent coloring at the kitchen table, putting simple puzzles together, and breaking twigs into small pieces. She initiated no conversation, spoke unintelligibly, and often needed to hear something repeated multiple times to understand. She walked slowly and unsteadily, always at risk for a fall. Because of this and her brain's difficulty processing visual information, someone had to accompany and hold onto her at all times. Due to unpredictable incontinence, she wore pull-up adult diapers. She needed help using the toilet, taking a shower, and getting dressed. Her medicines had to be crushed and mixed into food, as she was no longer able to swallow pills.

Despite all this, Rebecca was happy most of the time. Though she wasn't able to acknowledge me as her husband, at some level I knew that I was familiar to her, and at the very least, I was the nice man who lived in the same house that she did. We were always able, in a magical and mysterious way, to maintain some degree of emotional intimacy.

How and when did your loved one's symptoms progress or change over time? What was this experience like for you? Please tell your story.

_____

_____

_____

_____

_____

_____

_____

What are some ways you've been able to stay connected with your loved one? Please tell your story.

_____

_____

_____

_____

_____

_____

_____

The end of the journey

In August of 2016, Rebecca awoke one day unable to get out of bed and refusing to eat or drink. Ten days later, she was gone. The girls and I were present, piled into a hospital bed, when she took her last breath. She died with the same grace with which she lived her life. I know that if the situation had been reversed, me with dementia and Rebecca as my care partner, she would have taken care of me with the same level of commitment that I did caring for her. I also know that if I could have somehow carried this burden for her, traded her diseased brain for my normal one, I would have done it without a moment's hesitation. If I had known before we married that she would develop early-onset Alzheimer's, I still would have married her "in a heartbeat." The life we had—40 years together, 36 of them married, three children, a son-in-law, and two grandsons—was more than we could have ever dreamed of when we spoke those vows of for better or worse, in sickness and in health, till death do us part.

When you think about your loved one's future and your life together, what comes to mind? Please tell your story.

_____

_____

_____

_____

_____

_____

_____

_____

_____

PRETTY MAMA

After losing Rebecca, my middle daughter, Leah, a singer-songwriter similar to Jim Croce and John Denver in style, mourned her mom's death by telling a story about their relationship in a song she wrote. Here are the lyrics, which speak for themselves:

1.
Hey pretty mama
Pretty mama how you be

Hey pretty mama
Are you watching over me?

Well I hope you turned away last night
Cause I wasn't who you raised me to be

Oh pretty mama
I just wanna make you proud of me

2.
Hey pretty mama
Pretty mama how you be

Hey pretty mama
Are you watching over me?

If you are, that is good
Just know that I did the best I could

Oh pretty mama
I just wanna make you proud of me

3.
Hey pretty mama
Pretty mama how you be

Hey pretty mama
Are you watching over me?

If you are, let me know
Cause I've been worried I'll end up alone,

Oh pretty mama
I just wanna make you proud of me

Pretty mama, I just want to make you proud of me

When Leah was growing up, she played many different instruments, mainly piano and bassoon. Whenever she was going to perform, Rebecca always encouraged her by saying "play beautifully." The song "Pretty Mama" is featured on an album of Leah's songs dedicated to her mom, called *Play Beautifully* (song and album are available for download/ purchase via BandCamp and are streamable on Spotify, Amazon, YouTube, SoundCloud and other platforms, as well as Leah's website http://www. leahshawmusic.com).

A FINAL REFLECTION AND LOOKING AHEAD

In this first lesson of *The Dementia Care-Partner's Workbook*, we focused on Central Need 1—Tell and retell your story. You've received information on the importance of telling your story, read my story, and have written about your own story. Thank you for sharing that. It is a hard but important part of your journey as a care partner.

You will have an opportunity to respond to questions and continue writing your story in the lessons ahead. In addition, if you are journaling on your own, formally or informally, and/or if you have a trusted family member or friend with whom you talk on a regular basis, I'd encourage you to continue these things, as they're an important and necessary part of your self-care.

Of all the thoughts and emotions you've processed in this lesson, what is the one thing that stands out the most? Don't overthink what that one thing is—just let it float to the top. Maybe it's already there, and in the spirit of mindfulness, don't judge it as good or bad, right or wrong. Just write it down for personal reflection or to talk about with someone, perhaps in your support group. Please share.

_____

_____

_____

_____

_____

_____

In the next two lessons, you'll be learning a great deal about the human brain. Lesson Two: The Basics of Alzheimer's Disease and Other Dementias, covers what dementia is and how to diagnose it, as well as the symptoms of Alzheimer's disease and the other common forms of dementia. Lesson Three: Brain Structure and Function, Activities of

Daily Living, and Dementia Stages, covers the three areas described in the lesson title as well as medications used to treat dementia. Both Lessons Two and Three focus on Central Need 2—Educate yourself. Before you know it, you'll be a brain expert!

Anticipate being tired the next couple of days, and even having mixed feelings about continuing on in the support group or with self-study. These reactions are normal. Telling your story can be mentally exhausting, as can the thought of going through nine more lessons that require you to confront the reality and challenges of being a dementia care partner.

If you are participating in a support group, experience has taught me that the second session is almost always the hardest one to return to.

IF YOU'RE FEELING OVERWHELMED

Besides feeling overwhelmed with emotion, you might also be overwhelmed by the roles and responsibilities you have as a care partner. This is understandable! Sometimes the help of a mental-health professional becomes necessary. If you are feeling depressed, anxious, or stressed beyond what you can handle (for example, needing to use alcohol or drugs to calm yourself, or are having feelings of harming yourself or your loved one with dementia), contact your medical doctor or a counselor or therapist, or call one of the following resources available 24/7 to you:

- 911 (or go to your local hospital's emergency department)

- Alzheimer's Association Helpline at 1-800-272-3900
  www.alz.org

- National Suicide Prevention Lifeline at 1-800-273-TALK
  or 1-800-273-8255
  www.suicidepreventionlifeline.org

- IMAlive, a live online instant messaging crisis line
  www.imalive.org

That little voice in the back of your mind might be saying, "I can do this on my own," or "I don't want to be vulnerable in front of all those strangers." My response is something I learned in counseling graduate school: sometimes you have to "trust the process"! So hang in there and stick with the group or your commitment to independent study. You are on the pathway to understanding, education, and hope.

Basics of Alzheimer's Disease and Other Dementias

According to a recent poll, Alzheimer's disease is the most feared illness in America, more so than cancer, strokes, heart attacks — even brain tumors. If you're a dementia care partner, chances are you are afraid not only for your loved one, but for yourself as well.

> *"The oldest and strongest emotion of mankind is fear, and the oldest and strongest kind of fear is fear of the unknown."*
>
> — H.P. Lovecraft

It's normal and understandable to feel this way. This is why Central Need 2 focuses on education, which literally means to train and prepare for something. What you will learn in this lesson, and *The Dementia Care-Partner's Workbook* as a whole, has been written to train and prepare you to be a more knowledgeable, better-equipped, and more confident care partner.

No doubt you are aware of the dementia epidemic ravaging the United States. I mentioned this statistic in the Introduction but will repeat it here because it is so staggering: there are 5.8 million people in the U.S. who have Alzheimer's disease, and another two million who suffer from other forms of dementia, the most common being vascular, frontotemporal, and Lewy body dementia, as well as the dementia of Parkinson's disease.

Alzheimer's and the other dementias are considered neurodegenerative diseases, meaning they affect the brain ("neuro"), causing the cells of the brain, called neurons, to get sick and die, which results in gradual shrinkage of the brain ("degenerative"). Other common neurodegenerative diseases include Parkinson's disease, amyotrophic lateral sclerosis (also called ALS or Lou Gehrig's disease), and Huntington's disease. When neurons die and the brain shrinks, someone with a neurodegenerative disease progressively loses both brain and body functions, functions that cannot be relearned or regained, making them more and more dependent on others for their day-to-day care over time.

In this second lesson of *The Dementia Care-Partner's Workbook*, we will cover some basic information about what dementia is as well as how it is diagnosed. Even though your loved one likely already has a diagnosis, many care partners find it helpful to better understand the tests and other procedures that led to the diagnosis, and perhaps why some things were not part of the diagnostic process. We will also review the common forms of dementia. Although there are some shared features among all the dementias, for the most part they are quite distinct from one another, especially early on. Above all, you want to make sure your loved one's diagnosis is correct, for your confidence and their proper care.

Before we jump into the lesson, let's take time for some journaling then a Mindfulness Moment. If you're experiencing a lot of emotion right now, that's normal and healthy. Feelings are the outward expression of what's on your mind and heart, and writing about them is part of telling your story!

UNDERSTANDING OUR EMOTIONS

Human beings have four basic emotions: happiness, sadness, fear, and anger. Other emotions are variations of these core emotions.

How you express your emotions depends on a number of different factors, such as your personality, how your childhood family shared feelings, your culture, and the life experiences you've had.

Over the years of leading dementia care-partner support groups, I have often asked participants to complete the following statement:

More than anything else, right now I feel _____.

I have listed below the most common responses. Pick the one you are feeling the most right now, and in the space below the list, describe why you selected this particular emotion. If what you're feeling isn't on the list, that's OK. Write about what you are feeling, and why.

Abandoned	Desperate	Frantic
Afraid	Devastated	Frightened
Angry	Disbelieving	Frustrated
Anxious	Disgusted	Furious
Ashamed	Disorganized	Grief-stricken
Betrayed	Distraught	Guilty
Bewildered	Embarrassed	Happy
Bitter	Empty	Hateful
Confused	Encouraged	Heartbroken
Crazy	Envious	Helpless
Crushed	Fearful	Hopeless
Defeated	Fed Up	Horrified
Depressed	Flustered	Hurt
Desolate	Fragmented	Irritable

Jealous	Powerless	Surprised
Joyful	Rageful	Terrified
Lonely	Regretful	Terrorized
Lost	Relieved	Trapped
Loveless	Resentful	Unwanted
Mad	Sad	Weak
Numb	Scared	Worried
OK	Shameful	Worthless
Overwhelmed	Shocked	Yearnful
Panicked	Stunned	Zoned Out

_____

_____

_____

_____

_____

_____

_____

_____

_____

_____

_____

_____

MINDFULNESS MOMENT

As you'll recall from Lesson One, mindfulness is a state of mind that you achieve by focusing all of your awareness and attention on the present moment and only the present moment, excluding worries of the past as well as the future. The practice of mindfulness gives you a "brain break," calmly, non-judgmentally, and compassionately accepting your current thoughts, emotions, and body sensations without feeling as though you need to change them. The Mindfulness Moment includes a short breathing exercise that may provide a sense of peace that at least for the moment, everything is OK.

Having just completed this lesson's first journaling exercise on emotions, you likely chose a negative one to write about: sadness, fear, or anger, or something closely related. For the time being, accept that you have this and other emotions you may be feeling, and that you can coexist with them at least for the brief time of this Mindfulness Moment. Don't judge yourself or blame someone else for having difficult feelings. Stay in the present moment without thinking about everything that needs to be done still today, about the past, or the future. Now it's time to breathe your stress away.

Here's how it's done.

1. Sit in a comfortable chair, put both feet on the floor (or any other comfortable position), clasp your hands over the middle of your belly, and then close your eyes (if desired).

2. Scan your muscles from head to toe and intentionally relax them. Unclench your teeth, let your shoulders sag, and relax your buttock and leg muscles.

3. Take in a slow, deep breath through your nose (count "one one-thousand, two one-thousand, three one-thousand" to yourself as you do so), then slowly exhale through your mouth to the same count, feeling the rise and fall of your belly. Do a total of ten slow, deep breaths like this. Focus solely on the gentle flow of your breath, in and out. Each time you exhale, consciously blow out the negative

feelings and stress you feel about your loved one's dementia diagnosis.

4. After the tenth breath, slowly open your eyes.

Remember, mindfulness takes practice, so if you don't notice much change in your stress level after this Mindfulness Moment, repeat it later today or sometime this week.

UNDERSTANDING THE BASICS OF ALZHEIMER'S DISEASE AND OTHER DEMENTIAS

By way of introduction to this section of the lesson, I want to share the story of Laura and Devin with you, as it is pretty typical for a couple facing a new diagnosis of early stage-Alzheimer's disease.

When Answers Bring More Questions

Laura is a 72-year-old woman whose primary-care doctor referred her to a geriatrician specializing in memory disorders due to slowly worsening short-term memory loss over the last two to three years. She had some other symptoms too, even though Laura thought these were normal for her age. In fact, Laura thought she was "just fine" and was miffed that Devin and her two adult children were even making her go to a specialist.

Though she had always been an energetic person, Laura had begun napping almost every afternoon, yet she still slept well at night. She was finding certain tasks more difficult, like following a recipe, writing checks, organizing her pill holder, and even making a short shopping list for the grocery store. She got lost driving home from her son's house, a route she'd taken many times in her role as babysitter for her four-year-old granddaughter.

Laura and Devin had just celebrated their 45th wedding anniversary. Devin had noticed that he and Laura had seemed to grow apart, even though they'd always been a close couple. They didn't hold hands and cuddle like before. And to him, Laura seemed a bit depressed and less interested in doing things they'd always enjoyed, like a Friday evening dinner date or going out to lunch after church. Like the kids, Devin was worried Laura was not "just fine."

At their initial visit to the clinic, the specialist spoke with Laura and Devin about her symptoms then performed a neurological exam and brief test of Laura's memory and thinking skills, called the Montreal Cognitive Assessment (MoCA). She then had Laura return for a second visit to get some blood tests, a brain scan, and more extensive tests of her memory and thinking skills administered by a special doctor called a neuropsychologist. Laura returned for yet a third visit, during which the doctor shared all of the test results with her and Devin. Here is a reconstruction of what she told them. I'm sure the information was actually conveyed in more of a back-and-forth conversation than the monologue I am presenting here.

"Laura, you came to me because of the short-term memory loss you've been experiencing over the last couple of years. In addition, you've had some change in your personality, mostly a lack of interest in usual activities, and you're having trouble with some of your day-to-day duties like shopping and cooking, bill paying, managing medications, even driving. When I first saw you in clinic, your neurological examination was normal, but your score on the MoCA test was below normal and confirmed you had short-term memory loss and some other cognitive abnormalities.

"The neuropsychologist who saw you observed a significant decline in your ability to learn and remember information to a much greater degree than we'd expect for your age and level of education. Furthermore, tests of your executive function—the ability to plan, problem-solve, and multitask—were also significantly impaired.

"Your MRI scan of the brain showed some shrinkage—also more

than we'd expect for your age, especially in the part of your brain responsible for memory and learning, the hippocampus. The blood tests didn't show deficiencies in your thyroid hormone or B12 levels to explain your symptoms, and neither the neuropsychologist nor I think you are significantly depressed.

"Based on all of this information, I am diagnosing you with dementia. Specifically, I believe you have early-stage Alzheimer's disease. Alzheimer's isn't a curable disease, but there is a medicine I can prescribe that might help your memory. There are clinical trials available to you that are testing promising drugs that might slow disease progression or reverse some of the damage that's already occurred in your brain. And, there are a couple of things you yourself can do to try and accomplish these goals, too: exercise between 90 and 150 minutes a week, and keep your blood pressure down, so the top number is 120 or below. I'm providing you some information about these and other lifestyle modifications you can also make for brain health.

"I will see you back in three months to see if the medicine is helping without too many side effects, and we'll talk more then about research studies, if you and Devin are interested in pursuing this option. In the meantime, I'm going to refer you and Devin to our counseling center. A diagnosis of dementia can be very emotionally challenging in a number of ways. Please don't hesitate to contact me if you have questions."

Although both Laura and Devin were relieved to finally have an answer to explain Laura's memory loss, they were also overwhelmed. Some of what they heard was "doctor speak," a language they didn't fully understand. All Devin could think about was what this meant for their future. Were they not going to grow old together now? What were they going to tell their kids, the rest of the family, and friends? Wasn't there something they could do to slow down the disease? Did they need a second opinion? They even wondered about the answer to simple questions such as: Could they still have a glass of wine together before supper? Yes, they were hopeful the medicine would help Laura's memory, but beyond that, they felt confused, uncertain, and discouraged about their present and future.

Let's pause so you can journal any thoughts or feelings brought up by reading Laura and Devin's story. What aspects of Laura and Devin's story do you relate to? Which are different than your experience? Please share.

_____

_____

_____

_____

_____

_____

Now let's jump into the educational portion of this lesson to see if it may answer some of your questions, realizing it may also raise some additional ones, and that's OK. If some of the topics or journaling questions don't seem relevant to your loved one's situation, please feel free to skip over them. As with any of the lessons in *The Dementia Care-Partner's Workbook*, I want you to feel free to pick and choose the information and exercises that are most helpful to you.

WHAT IS DEMENTIA?

When people talk about a loved one having Alzheimer's disease, I've noticed they often say he or she has "Alzheimer's and dementia." Technically, this is incorrect. Dementia is the umbrella term referring to a medical condition in which a person has significant difficulty with memory, multitasking, language, or other thinking skills, causing them to require assistance or be dependent in their day-to-day activities. The most common cause or form of dementia is Alzheimer's dementia (not Alzheimer's and dementia), usually referred to as **Alzheimer's disease**.

About 70 percent of people with dementia have Alzheimer's, but there are many other causes. The second most common form of dementia is **vascular dementia**, accounting for 15 to 20 percent of cases. The other more common forms, including **frontotemporal dementia, Lewy body dementia**, and the **dementia of Parkinson's disease**, make up the remaining 10 to 15 percent. There are also some other causes of dementia, but they are quite rare.

Because of the fear associated with the diagnosis of dementia, most people don't like to say "the A-word" (Alzheimer's) or "the D-word" (dementia). It's understandable. These words often bring thoughts of losing one's mind, a spouse or parent no longer knowing who we are, being a burden, or winding up in some awful nursing home. If you or your loved one with dementia are having any of these thoughts, be encouraged that times have changed and progress is continually being made.

Doctors are now able to make an early and accurate diagnosis of Alzheimer's and other forms of dementia 90 percent of the time. There is now an understanding of the important role of lifestyle choices, particularly exercise and blood pressure control, in preventing and slowing the progression of the disease. Standards are higher than ever for assisted-living, memory-care, and nursing-home facilities. And researchers have discovered drugs now being tested in clinical trials that show more promise than ever before. I hope *The Dementia Care-Partner's Workbook* will empower you as a care partner to face what's ahead on the journey armed with knowledge and an action plan.

HOW IS DEMENTIA DIAGNOSED?

Over the last several decades, tremendous strides have been made in diagnosing dementia earlier and more accurately. The first step in the process is to have a knowledgeable doctor perform a **thorough**

and detailed history, to understand which symptoms are and are not present, and a **complete physical** that includes a neurological examination. The person's **mental-health history** is also very important, since short-term memory loss can be due to depression, which may be reversible with counseling, medication, or a combination of both.

Blood tests are also an important part of the diagnostic process, including a complete blood count (CBC), complete metabolic panel (CMP), thyroid function tests, and vitamin B12 and D levels, among others. While none of these blood tests are dementia-specific, they can rule out other reversible causes of memory loss such as hypothyroidism, which is an abnormally low level of thyroid hormone.

In order to see the structure of the brain, a **magnetic resonance imaging (MRI) scan** is often obtained. The MRI can identify shrinkage of the brain or evidence of a stroke, and it can rule out other causes for memory loss such as a brain tumor or a condition called **normal-pressure hydrocephalus,** in which the normal fluid drainage pathways of the brain become blocked.

There is also a special kind of scan called a **fluorodeoxyglucose positron emission tomography (FDG-PET) scan**, which looks at how sugar, one of the brain's main food sources, is absorbed by the brain's neurons, also known as **brain metabolism**. Normally, all parts of our brain are using sugar, even when we're asleep. However, if certain parts of our brain are inactive, due to damaged or dead neurons, those portions will not process sugar. A FDG-PET scan shows pictures of the brain with the sugar uptake (brain metabolism) superimposed on them. Imagine you are a doctor seeing a person with short-term memory problems and difficulty multitasking. If their MRI scan shows shrunken temporal and parietal lobes (you'll learn about the brain lobes in the next lesson), and their PET scan indicates a lack of sugar absorption in the same lobes, this would be consistent with a diagnosis of Alzheimer's disease.

A different kind of PET scan can also determine if someone is accumulating **amyloid** in their brain. Amyloid PET scans are not paid for by insurance yet, whereas in many instances, FDG-PET scans are. PET scans for tau are being developed. We'll talk more about amyloid and tau later in the lesson.

Another test that can be performed, which is more invasive than the others mentioned, is a **spinal tap**, which is most helpful in the diagnosis of Alzheimer's disease and can rule out other disease processes that might cause memory loss, such as autoimmune diseases (like multiple sclerosis) and cancer. A spinal fluid analysis that shows decreased amyloid and increased tau protein levels is consistent with an Alzheimer's diagnosis.

To make a diagnosis of dementia, doctors must take all of the above information into account and even then, sometimes a firm diagnosis of Alzheimer's or another form of dementia cannot be made. To add to the challenge, doctors are recognizing with increasing frequency that one person can have more than one type of dementia, such as Alzheimer's and vascular dementia together. In such cases, the possible diagnoses can be narrowed down to several things, but it may take time for the correct diagnosis to "declare itself," which is to say, sometimes **diagnosis is more of a process than an event**. Remaining patient can be a real challenge during the diagnostic process!

What do you feel you understand and don't understand about your loved one's diagnosis of dementia and how the diagnosis was made? Please share.

_____

_____

_____

_____

_____

Based on your loved one's current diagnosis and everything you've read thus far in this lesson, what questions do you have for the doctor or medical provider? Please write them down for the next time you take your loved one to see them.

_____

_____

_____

_____

_____

_____

_____

WHAT ARE THE RISK FACTORS FOR DEVELOPING DEMENTIA?

It's natural to wonder why your loved one developed dementia. At the present time, the cause of Alzheimer's disease is unknown. The same is true of the other forms of dementia. We can diagnose dementia accurately, and we understand a lot more about the disease than we used to, but when it comes to understanding causes, there is still much research that needs to be done.

While we can't pinpoint the causes of most dementia, we do know there are a number of risk factors. Having an Alzheimer's risk factor doesn't mean you will develop the disease. It just means your chances are higher than if you didn't have that particular risk factor. Below are some of the common risk factors for developing Alzheimer's disease.

The most common risk factor for Alzheimer's is **age**. Only five percent of people with Alzheimer's are younger than 65 years old (so-called early-onset Alzheimer's). The risk of being diagnosed with Alzheimer's is one in 25 by age 65 to 70, one in eight by age 75 to 80, one in three by age 85 to 90, and one in two if one lives to be 100.

The vast majority of cases of Alzheimer's disease are "**sporadic**," meaning they occur at random for unknown reasons and are not inherited. Only two to three percent of those with Alzheimer's have the "**familial**," or inherited, form. Genetic tests can be performed to determine if a person is at higher risk of developing Alzheimer's disease. The most common one tests for a gene called APOe4. The challenge is in the interpretation and utility of the result. Having one or two copies of the APOe4 gene is associated with an increased chance of developing the late-onset (after age 65) type of Alzheimer's disease. However, having the gene doesn't automatically mean that a person will develop Alzheimer's, and its absence doesn't mean the disease cannot occur. As such, at this time, routine APOe4 testing is not routinely recommended.

Gender is the next biggest risk factor. Women are twice as likely to develop Alzheimer's disease as men. Age may partially explain this difference, since women live about five years longer than men on average, but age alone doesn't account for the entire difference. Hormones, specifically the loss of the female hormones estrogen and progesterone during menopause, are thought to play a role.

Other health factors are also related to developing Alzheimer's disease. Individuals who have had a **heart attack** are at increased risk, whereas those who have experienced a **stroke** are at increased risk of both Alzheimer's and vascular dementia. Similarly, both high blood pressure and diabetes increase the risk of Alzheimer's. **African-Americans** are two to four times as likely to develop Alzheimer's disease as Caucasians, which is at least in part related to an increased likelihood of having high blood pressure and/or diabetes. Those who are Hispanic or Latino are intermediate in risk between Caucasians and African-Americans. Head trauma also increases the risk of Alzheimer's, as well as an Alzheimer's-like condition called **chronic traumatic encephalopathy** sometimes experienced by football players, boxers, and others with repeated brain injury.

While there are other risk factors for Alzheimer's disease, those I've listed above are the most common.

What questions do you have about the causes of your loved one's dementia? Which if any of the risk factors we've reviewed does your loved one have?

_____

_____

_____

_____

_____

You may have found reading this section on risk factors scary. Many care partners, particularly adult children and siblings, are worried about developing the same kind of dementia their parent, brother, or sister has been diagnosed with. Please share your thoughts and feelings about your own risk of developing dementia.

_____

_____

_____

_____

_____

WHAT IS HEALTHY COGNITIVE AGING?

Have you ever had the experience of seeing someone at the grocery store whom you've met before, perhaps even gone to church or volunteered with for some time, and not remembered their name? This brain skill is called **confrontational naming**—that is, when you're confronted by someone (or something) you're familiar with and you can't remember their (its) name. When this happens, you might even think or say, "I'm getting Alzheimer's!" Having some difficulty retrieving the names of people and objects is actually a common experience that most people encounter starting in their 50s, and it's perfectly normal.

Other features of **healthy cognitive aging** include slowing down of your thought processes, decreased attention span, mild short-term memory loss (particularly remembering and recalling recently learned information), more difficulty multitasking, and needing to focus on one thing at a time. You may also have some subtle changes in personality (for example, becoming more serious). In addition, occasional lapses in judgment, changes in mood (moodiness and/or irritability), and a reduced energy level can occur with age.

However, more serious problems with the brain that warrant medical evaluation to consider the possibility of dementia include things like forgetting the year you were born or the names of grandchildren, getting lost while driving, not being able to follow a recipe or prepare a meal, a dramatic change in personality (for example, saying or doing socially inappropriate things) or mood (severe depression or anxiety), loss of interest in or lack of motivation to do usual activities, and excessive napping or sleeping.

How is your brain working these days? Do you have any concerns about your own brain's aging process? Please describe.

_____

_____

_____

_____

_____

_____

_____

WHAT IS MILD COGNITIVE IMPAIRMENT?

Mild cognitive impairment (MCI) is an intermediate state of brain function between normal brain aging and early-stage dementia. A diagnosis of MCI is made when a person's memory (or some other aspect of their cognitive function) is worse than you would see with normal brain aging. When memory loss is present with MCI, the term used is "**amnestic**" (literally meaning, "without memory") MCI. Someone with MCI is able to function independently in their day-to-day activities. In contrast, those with early-stage Alzheimer's require some assistance, or even depend on others for daily activities such as driving, shopping, cooking, taking medication, or paying bills. Half to three-quarters of people diagnosed with amnestic MCI will go on to develop Alzheimer's disease (or another dementia) within five years of diagnosis, while others will remain stable, and some may even show improvement in their memory if the underlying cause of their memory loss is reversible.

Is your loved one's diagnosis MCI? If it is, please describe the symptoms they are experiencing that are consistent with that diagnosis. Which symptoms do they not have? Please share.

_____

_____

_____

_____

_____

_____

WHAT ARE THE DIFFERENT TYPES OF DEMENTIA?

Following are brief descriptions of the common forms of dementia. While your loved one may have been diagnosed with a certain type of dementia, I invite you to read about all of the types. Understanding the sometimes nuanced differences among them may help you clarify a diagnosis or advocate for a different treatment. In addition, if you are participating in a dementia care-partner support group, learning about the various forms of dementia will help you be a more informed and supportive friend to others.

ALZHEIMER'S DISEASE

Alzheimer's disease is the most common form of dementia. It was first discovered over a hundred years ago by the German psychiatrist and neuropathologist Dr. Alois Alzheimer, who identified two abnormal structures, known as **plaques and tangles,** in the brains of people who died of the disease.

ALL TANGLED UP

A helpful analogy to understand what amyloid plaques and neurofibrillary (tau) tangles do to the brain is that of adding sugar to the gas tank of a car. If you poured a five-pound bag of sugar into your gas tank, that sugar would make its way into the car's gas line, causing the engine to sputter and backfire, eventually preventing it from running at all. The car would no longer be operational. Plaques and tangles have a similar effect on the brain. The affected parts of the brain don't function as well at first (for example, short-term memory loss), then stop working altogether (inability to remember anything, short- or long-term).

Plaques, or more specifically **amyloid plaques**, are accumulations of a "bad" protein called amyloid-beta or just amyloid. Amyloid is normally eliminated as brain waste. For unknown reasons it accumulates and forms clumps or plaques in those with Alzheimer's. The plaques, located in between the brain's neurons, lead to inflammation, sickness, and death of the neurons as well as shrinkage of the brain. This process is what causes the symptoms of Alzheimer's disease, which we'll talk about shortly.

Tangles, or more specifically **neurofibrillary tangles**, are accumulations of a different protein, called **tau**, inside neurons rather than in between them, as with amyloid-beta. When tau proteins over-accumulate inside neurons, they disrupt their ability to communicate with one another, which also causes symptoms. It is unknown whether neurofibrillary tangles occur independent of amyloid plaques or are caused by them.

Normally, our brain has billions and billions of neurons. With the normal brain-aging process, some neurons die and parts of our brains will shrink, but just a little bit, one percent or less. However, with Alzheimer's disease the brain can shrink by ten percent or more due to the loss of millions upon millions of neurons. Fewer neurons means less function. For example, short-term memory loss, the most common and usually the first and worst symptom of Alzheimer's disease, is caused by shrinkage of the part of the brain that is responsible for memory, the hippocampus, which is located in the brain's temporal lobe. This is why a person with the disease asks the same question over and over. It's not that they choose not to remember they've already asked the question, or refuse to remember, **they can't remember**. That part of the brain is damaged or gone. The figure at left compares a normal adult brain to that of someone with severe Alzheimer's disease.

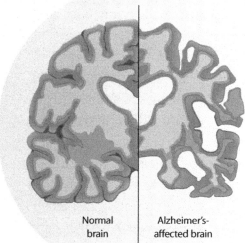

Normal brain | Alzheimer's-affected brain

The same is true for all dementia symptoms—it's not that the person won't do certain things, it's that they simply can't. For many care partners, knowledge of this simple fact helps them be more understanding, empathetic, and patient.

Some describe the symptoms

of Alzheimer's disease as the four A's": amnesia (memory loss), aphasia (difficulty speaking or understanding language), agnosia (trouble recognizing familiar objects and/or people), and apraxia (impaired purposeful movement like using a fork and knife to eat). Besides the four A's, other symptoms of Alzheimer's disease include:

- difficulty multitasking, organizing and planning, and problem-solving

- poor judgment (such as with financial matters)

- spatial function challenges (such as getting lost while driving, difficulty navigating stairs or curbs, and falling)

- changes in mood (usually depression and often anxiety)

- personality changes (social withdrawal, suspicion, or even paranoia), delusions (believing something that isn't true, such as infidelity or theft), obsessive/compulsive tendencies, and doing/saying inappropriate things

Lifespan after diagnosis of Alzheimer's is usually eight to ten years, but it can be shorter, especially for early-onset Alzheimer's, or longer.

Is your loved one's diagnosis Alzheimer's disease? If so, please describe the symptoms they are experiencing that are consistent with that diagnosis. Which symptoms do they not have? Please share.

_____

_____

_____

_____

_____

_____

_____

_____

VASCULAR DEMENTIA

Vascular dementia, sometimes called "multi-infarct dementia," is a type of dementia caused by strokes or mini-strokes. A stroke occurs when there is a blockage (infarct) or rupture (hemorrhage) of an artery supplying blood to the neurons in a specific part of the brain. When those neurons are affected by a stroke, they become inflamed, sick, and may die, resulting in symptoms.

The symptoms of vascular dementia are usually similar to those of Alzheimer's disease with one difference—short-term memory may or may not be impaired with vascular dementia. In addition, depending on the location and severity of the stroke(s), there may be other symptoms too, for example:

- drooping or numbness on one side of the face
- weakness in an arm and/or leg on one side of the body
- speech difficulties (not understanding what is being said, or spoken words not coming out correctly)
- impaired vision

When an MRI scan of the brain is obtained in someone with vascular dementia, evidence of one or more strokes, as well as shrinkage of the brain, may be present.

Vascular dementia may or may not be progressive like Alzheimer's disease, so prognosis and life expectancy are more variable.

Is your loved one's diagnosis vascular dementia? If it is, please describe the symptoms they are experiencing that are consistent with that diagnosis. Which symptoms do they not have? Please share.

_____

_____

_____

_____

_____

FRONTOTEMPORAL DEMENTIA

Frontotemporal dementia (FTD), also referred to as frontotemporal lobar degeneration, is actually a group of disorders caused by the loss of neurons located in the frontal lobes (the brain areas behind your forehead) and temporal lobes (the brain areas beneath your temples and ears). The brain of someone with FTD shows accumulated clumps of the tau protein (or a related protein, called **TDP43**), known as Pick bodies, named for the doctor who first identified them years ago, and hence the older label "**Pick's disease**" for what we now know as FTD.

The damage and brain shrinkage caused by frontotemporal dementia causes symptoms primarily related to behavior and judgment, emotions, and speech and language.

The most common form of this disease is called **behavioral variant FTD.** The most prominent symptoms in this subtype are socially inappropriate behavior in conjunction with poor judgment, such as saying or doing things, even to strangers, that are considered unacceptable (for example, sexually oriented comments, inappropriate touch, poor manners, and even reckless behavior without regard to consequences).

Other symptoms are related to the declining or lost functions of the frontal and temporal lobes, such as:

- lack of initiative or motivation (apathy)
- loss of sympathy and empathy
- development of obsessive, repetitive, and/or ritualistic behaviors or speech
- carbohydrate craving (especially candies, cookies, and desserts)
- binge eating, drinking, and/or smoking
- loss of insight
- difficulty planning, problem-solving, and multitasking

Memory is usually normal, especially in the early stage of the disease, as opposed to Alzheimer's, in which short-term memory loss is usually the first and most prominent symptom. Mental-health and personality changes and challenges, such as depression, anxiety, and being emotionally flat or unexpressive (or just the opposite, being overemotional) may also occur.

The next most common subtype of FTD is called **primary progressive aphasia (PPA).** Aphasia means "without speech," so the most prominent PPA symptoms include difficulties with and eventual loss of expressive language (saying or writing what you want to say) and receptive language (understanding what others say to you, including reading difficulties). Some individuals who are diagnosed with PPA may later develop behavioral variant FTD or Alzheimer's disease. Behavioral variant FTD and PPA tend to occur in a younger age group than Alzheimer's, with diagnosis usually in someone 45 to 65 years old. However, they can occur at younger as well as older ages.

Life expectancy in someone diagnosed with FTD is usually a year or two shorter than Alzheimer's, with average life expectancy in the range of six to nine years, but this too can vary.

Is your loved one's diagnosis frontotemporal dementia, either behavioral variant frontotemporal dementia or primary progressive dementia? If so, please describe the symptoms they are experiencing that are consistent with that diagnosis. Which symptoms do they not have? Please share.

_____

_____

_____

_____

_____

_____

LEWY BODY DEMENTIA

Lewy body dementia (LBD) is a neurodegenerative disease distinct from Alzheimer's, vascular dementia, or FTD. From the standpoint of symptoms, it can be thought of as a cross between Alzheimer's and Parkinson's disease, since both cognitive function and movement are affected. The brain of someone with LBD accumulates clumps of the abnormal protein **alpha-synuclein**, which is visible inside the neurons (called Lewy bodies, after the doctor who discovered them).

The symptoms of LBD are related to damage and shrinkage in multiple areas of the brain, causing problems in four distinct areas of brain function: cognitive, physical, behavioral, and autonomic.

The most common symptoms of LBD include:

• Cognitive: impaired attention span, judgment (but insight usually normal), and spatial function and balance (increased fall risk). Short-term memory may or may not be impaired.

• Physical: slowness of movement, especially walking, shuffles feet while walking, often hunched over and looking down, unsteadiness with frequent falls, tremulousness of the hands, blank expression on face (also referred to as facial masking), and muscle stiffness or rigidity. Later in the disease, loss of the gag reflex and aspiration (inadvertently swallowing liquids or solids into the lungs, which can cause choking and even pneumonia) can occur.

• Behavioral: apathy, depression, delusions, hallucinations (seeing things that aren't there, sometimes hearing things too, which may or may not be frightening), nightmares (aggressive acting out of dreams or nightmares, referred to as rapid eye movement or REM sleep disorder), and compulsive behaviors (such as repetitively taking things apart and putting them back together).

• Autonomic: The autonomic (or what I like to call the automatic) nervous system of the brain and body regulates things that are largely unconscious, such as degree of alertness and wakefulness, body temperature, blood pressure, the heart beating and lungs breathing, digestion, sexual function, and bladder and bowel control. Autonomic symptoms of LBD may include body-temperature changes (feel hot and sweaty or cold and shivering), irregularities of blood pressure (usually too low, with dizziness or fainting), irregularities in heart and breathing rates (usually too fast, may include a heart condition called atrial fibrillation), digestive issues (bloating or indigestion), bladder or bowel problems (difficulty urinating, frequent urination at night, urgency to go, incontinence), impotence, and a decreased or fluctuating level of alertness and wakefulness.

A characteristic somewhat unique to LBD is the rapid cycling of good and bad days. On good days, the brain and body of someone with LBD may function nearly normally, and on bad days, they can't think or move. Sometimes a person with LBD will even alternate good hours and bad ones within a given day.

The diagnosis of LBD can be difficult, particularly early on, since it may resemble Alzheimer's if the first symptom is memory loss, Parkinson's disease if tremor is the initial symptom, or even schizophrenia if delusions and hallucinations occur first.

LBD typically develops in the 70s, and lifespan is similar to that of FTD (six to nine years on average, but is variable).

Half or more people with Parkinson's disease will eventually develop dementia. The symptoms and prognosis of Parkinson's disease dementia are similar to LBD, and Lewy bodies are also present in the brain.

Is your loved one's diagnosis Lewy Body Dementia or Parkinson's disease dementia? If so, please describe the symptoms they are experiencing that are consistent with that diagnosis. Which symptoms do they not have? Please share.

_____

_____

_____

_____

_____

_____

_____

A FINAL REFLECTION AND LOOKING AHEAD

Wow! You may be feeling overwhelmed about all the information you've been given, and this is only Lesson Two. Your brain has worked hard learning about itself. With the content covered in this lesson and the associated journaling, you've told some more of your story (Central Need 1), and begun to educate yourself about the brain and dementia (Central Need 2). Before telling you about the next lesson, let's pause for a brief journaling exercise.

What are the most important things you learned from this lesson on the basics of Alzheimer's disease and other dementias?

_____

_____

_____

_____

_____

_____

Up next is Lesson Three: Brain Structure and Function, Activities of Daily Living, and Dementia Stages, which discusses these three interrelated topics. Specifically, you will learn how the lobes of the brain work and about the five cognitive functions, which will help you understand why your loved one with dementia does or doesn't say or do things normally. You'll also learn about the instrumental and basic activities of daily living (ADLs), which are the simple to complex activities that you perform on a day-to-day basis that require brain function. A discussion about the stages of dementia (early, middle, and late) and the different medications used to treat dementia will also be provided.

Finally, I invite you to take a minute and repeat the Mindfulness Moment we opened today's lesson with. And once again, please "trust the process" as you continue on the pathway to understanding, education, and hope.

Brain Structure and Function, Activities of Daily Living, and Dementia Stages

As a care partner of someone with dementia, you have likely experienced times when your loved one said or did something that made you say, "Where on earth did THAT come from?" Well, it came from their brain! Of course, everything we think, feel, say, and do comes from our brains. Similarly, when people with dementia can't express themselves or do something they want to do, it's also a result of a problem in the brain.

"Everything we do, every thought we've ever had, is produced by the human brain. But exactly how it operates remains one of the biggest unsolved mysteries, and it seems the more we probe its secrets, the more surprises we find."

—Neil deGrasse Tyson

One of the most common brain hiccups in dementia—and one of the most challenging to care partners—is **repetitive questioning**. Has some version of the following happened to you?

What Time is Dinner?

Stephanie and Ray are a couple in their mid-70s who have been married for sixteen years. When Stephanie was diagnosed with Alzheimer's five years ago, they weren't too surprised, as her two older sisters, mother, and maternal grandmother also had the disease. Her main symptom was short-term memory loss, and in the last year, it had worsened considerably. One afternoon, Ray decided he would take Stephanie out for a special dinner. He told her they would go at six o'clock. About an hour before, Stephanie asked Ray, "What time is dinner?" Ray replied, "Six o'clock." A minute or two later, she repeated the question as if she'd never asked it before. "Six o'clock," Ray said, this time with a bit of stiffness in his voice. Not five minutes later, she asked again. He yelled back, "Like I said two times in the last ten minutes, six o'clock. Don't ask me again, Steph." Stephanie looked at Ray with tears in her eyes. Ray immediately felt guilty about losing his temper and apologized to Stephanie. It wasn't the first time he'd run out of patience. In fact, the worse Stephanie's memory got, the more impatient he had become. As he promised himself he'd do a better job, he heard Stephanie say, "Honey, what time are we going out to dinner tonight?"

What experiences have you had with repetitive questions (or behaviors) from your loved one with dementia? Please describe.

_____

_____

_____

_____

_____

_____

As you learned in the last lesson (and perhaps experienced firsthand from the person in your life who has dementia), the first and most prominent symptom of Alzheimer's disease is short-term memory loss. That's because it starts in the temporal lobes, the parts of the brain responsible for memory. And when the temporal lobes shrink from the disease process, memory function is lost.

If I apply a principle from the last lesson to Stephanie and Ray's predicament, it's not that Stephanie *won't* remember what time dinner is—it's that she *can't*. She just doesn't have enough neurons in her temporal lobes to remember things anymore. Once Ray came to appreciate this, he became a more patient care partner to Stephanie.

Patience is one of the most important skills you can have as a dementia care partner. If you are not a naturally patient person, or if, understandably, your patience has been wearing thin due to repetitive questioning, repetitive behaviors, or any number of other challenging dementia symptoms, the good news is that patience is indeed a skill. And a skill is something you can improve with awareness, intention, and practice. To illustrate what I mean, let's go back to Stephanie and Ray.

When Stephanie asked Ray what time dinner was for the third time and he lost his temper, he was probably thinking something like, "Why does she keep asking me that same question over and over again? I can't take it anymore!" However, he could choose to think differently. Armed with an understanding of what is happening in Stephanie's temporal lobes and the awareness that she *can't* remember, he could instead reply, "Honey, we're going at six. Do you need any help getting ready? I'm really looking forward to our date." Stephanie wouldn't have felt hurt, and Ray would not have felt guilty about snapping back at her—all because Ray drew upon both his dementia education—his learning about the biology of the brain and what happens to it in dementia—and his relationship-building skills, which we'll discuss in Lesson Four: Changing Relationships .

Describe a situation in which you lost patience with your loved one. Please share.

_____

_____

_____

_____

_____

_____

Regarding the above situation, how could you have responded
differently? Please share.

_____

_____

_____

_____

_____

Now let's transition to the first part of this lesson, in which you'll
learn more about the structure and function of the different parts
of the human brain. As you saw with Ray, knowledge of how the
brain works—and begins to stop working in dementia—can help you
understand why your loved one with dementia may no longer say
or do things normally. The information will also provide a basis for
responding as often as possible with acceptance and patience.

In this lesson you will also learn about **activities of daily living** (ADLs),
which are the things we all do, with the help of our brains, on a day-
to-day basis—things like grocery shopping, driving home from the
drugstore, and getting dressed. As the brain continues to deteriorate,
people with dementia become less and less able to perform their ADLs.
You'll also learn about the stages of dementia (early, middle, and late
stage), which is a window into understanding the progressive nature
of the disease. The lesson will wrap up with an overview of the most
common medications used in those with dementia and a sneak peek

at a new class of drugs being tested for Alzheimer's prevention and treatment. But before we talk about lobes, ADLs, and stages, let's pause for a Mindfulness Moment.

MINDFULNESS MOMENT

The introduction to this lesson has covered several weighty topics, including repetitive questions and impatience. In the process of self-reflection, you may be experiencing some strong emotions about this and perhaps some stress. Times of emotion and stress, however you experience them, are good opportunities to take a Mindfulness Moment.

Remember, mindfulness is a state of mind that you achieve by focusing all of your awareness and attention on the present moment and only the present moment, excluding worries of the past as well as the future. The practice of mindfulness gives you a "brain break," inviting you to calmly, nonjudgmentally, and compassionately accept your current thoughts, emotions, and body sensations without feeling as though you need to change them. The Mindfulness Moment includes a short breathing exercise that I hope provides you with a sense of peace that, at least for the moment, everything is OK.

As a reminder, here's how it's done.

1. Sit in a comfortable chair, put both feet on the floor (or any other comfortable position), clasp your hands over the middle of your belly, and then close your eyes (if desired).

2. Scan your muscles from head to toe and intentionally relax them. Unclench your teeth, let your shoulders sag, and relax your buttock and leg muscles.

3. Take in a slow, deep breath through your nose (count "one one-thousand, two one-thousand, three one-thousand" to yourself as you do so), then slowly exhale through your mouth to the same count, feeling the rise and fall of your belly. Do a total of ten slow, deep breaths like this. Focus solely on the gentle flow of your breath, in and out. Each time you exhale, consciously blow out the negative

emotions and stress you feel about your loved one's dementia symptoms and your care-partnering challenges.

4. After the tenth breath, slowly open your eyes.

THE BRAIN LOBES AND HOW THEY FUNCTION

For an organ that controls everything you think, feel, say, and do, the human brain is remarkably small. It is the size and weight of two large grapefruit, about three pounds, and firm, more like rubber than a sponge. Even though it only accounts for two or three percent of your total body weight, at any given time about twenty percent of the blood circulating in your entire body is inside your brain.

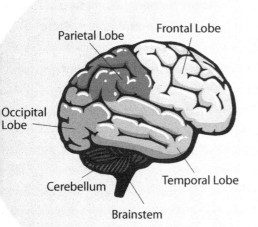

The brain is divided into lobes, as shown in the figure at left. Each side of the brain has the same four lobes. The brain lobes are deeply connected to one another on the same side of the brain as well as across sides. As you learned in the last lesson, the cells inside the brain are called neurons, and you have billions upon billions of them. In addition, individual neurons are connected to a thousand to ten thousand other neurons. Therefore, there are trillions and trillions of neuronal connections in the brain. An old myth says that you only use ten percent of your brain at any given time, and yet, just the opposite is true. You use more than 90 percent of your brain 90 percent of the time, whether you're awake or asleep! In other words, the human brain is always "on." What follows is

A COSTLY SCAM

Vernon was an elderly widower with early-stage vascular dementia who lived alone in the same house he had spent his married life in. He had worked hard his entire life as a school custodian, was able to pay off his house right before retiring, and with a small pension and Social Security, was able to live comfortably. He even had a small nest egg in the bank. When a nice young man called him one day with a plan to double his retirement savings, Vernon thought he'd hit the jackpot. All he had to do was provide his account information. By the time Vernon's son discovered the scam, all the money had been withdrawn from Vernon's financial accounts. The "nice young man," whom Vernon defended as trying to help him until his son interfered, was long gone. Recognizing his dad had lost insight and judgment, and was in denial about this, Vernon's son took appropriate steps to safeguard his dad's finances.

---

a simplified description of each of the brain lobes and their functions, but please understand that all parts of the brain work together in very complex ways to allow you to think, feel, and do as you want to.

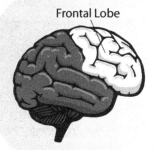

Frontal Lobe

THE FRONTAL LOBES

The frontal lobes, which are located just behind the forehead, are the largest of your brain lobes, making up 40 percent of the brain's volume. Here's a list of what your frontal lobes do, and it's a lot. The frontal lobes:

- Are where your **thoughts, feelings, and behaviors** (what you say and do) originate.

- Determine your **personality**.

- With the temporal lobes, play a role in determining your **mood** (sad, mad, happy, or anxious), including your ability to be **emotionally expressive** and have sympathy and **empathy** for others.

- Are where your **morals and values** are instilled.

- Help you be **social**, desire relationships.

- Provide **insight and judgment**, including helping you understand risks, benefits, and consequences of the choices you make.

- Are responsible for **planning, problem-solving, and multitasking**.

- Help you **pay attention** and concentrate; also involved with **orientation** to the day, date, month, and year.

- Along with the temporal lobes, are responsible for **expressive language** function, the ability to say what you want to say.

- Are where voluntary (that is, intentional) **movements** of your arms, legs, and body are controlled.

- Play a role in your **balance** when walking, as well as keeping your bladder and bowel **sphincters** in the closed position without having to think about it.

Wow! No wonder the frontal lobes are said to do the "heavy lifting" of your brain. Go back to Lesson Two and read through the symptoms of Alzheimer's disease, frontotemporal dementia, and Lewy body dementia, or whichever diagnosis is applicable to your loved one. You will see just how many of these symptoms come from degeneration of the frontal lobes.

Read back through the list of frontal-lobe functions. What are the symptoms your loved is experiencing that seem to be coming from problems with the frontal lobes?

THE TEMPORAL LOBES

Temporal Lobe

The temporal lobes are located just beneath your temples and behind your ears. They have functions that are very different than those of the frontal lobes. Your temporal lobes:

• Are where your memory is located, both **short- and long-term memory**. (There are many different types of memory besides

---

THE RHINESTONE COWBOY

In 2017, world-renowned country singer Glen Campbell died of Alzheimer's disease. Even with severe memory loss, he was able to sing all his old favorites during his final tour, as shown in the documentary *I'll Be Me*. With the help of a teleprompter, Glen could link the words of his familiar songs to the musical notes on his guitar, and perform the tune flawlessly, accessing a special type of memory called **procedural memory**. This is part of your long-term memory that allows you to do rote activities, things you never or almost never forget, like tying your shoes, riding a bicycle, or making the family recipe of chocolate chip cookies. We sometimes call procedural memory "muscle memory," even though it originates in the brain, not the muscles. This is an encouraging example of how amazing the human brain is, even in the face of a difficult disease like Alzheimer's.

short- and long-term, but we won't be reviewing all of them in this workbook.) Memory is located in a peculiarly named structure inside the temporal lobes called the **hippocampus** (which is the Greek word for "seahorse," although it's quite a stretch to see the seahorse when looking at a human hippocampus!). A temporal lobe function related to memory is **learning**. If you can't retain information in your short-term memory, you can't learn or store it in your long-term memory.

A helpful way to understand the relationship between learning and memory is the cup and sieve analogy. When you hear or read new information you want to remember, imagine that it is held in a cup (short-term memory) that empties into a larger receptacle for storage (long-term memory). Sometimes, a few repetitions are necessary for learning, which is why, for example, you study for a test. For those with Alzheimer's or another form of dementia that affects memory, the short-term memory cup becomes more like a sieve. New information in short-term memory drains right through the sieve, leaving nothing to empty into long-term memory storage. In the context of Ray and Stephanie's situation, each time she asked Ray what time dinner was, her short-term memory cup was empty; she had absolutely no recollection that she had already asked the question.

- Process the words and sentences you hear into **speech and language,** and help you form your thoughts and words into sentences. This is done in conjunction with an area in the frontal lobes called Broca's area, and an area in the parietal lobes called Wernicke's area.

- Are involved in **emotional memory**. For example, most of your childhood memories associated with strong emotions, positive and negative, are in your temporal lobes, linked to a small structure at the front of the temporal lobe called the **amygdala**. Emotional expression is controlled by very complicated brain circuits involving the amygdala, other parts of the frontal and temporal lobes, and deeper structures in the brain, which together are called the **limbic system**.

- Help you with **facial recognition**. You identify people by looking at their face and remembering the shape and appearance of their face.

Though not as big as the frontal lobes, the temporal lobes have a lot of functions too. Read through the list of temporal lobe functions again. What are the symptoms your loved is experiencing that seem to be coming from problems with the temporal lobes?

_____

_____

_____

_____

_____

_____

_____

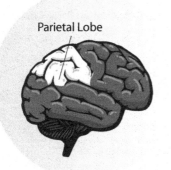
Parietal Lobe

THE PARIETAL LOBES

The parietal lobes are located behind the frontal lobes and above the temporal lobes, just beneath the upper-back part of your skull. As with the frontal and temporal lobes, the functions of the parietal lobe are unique and include:

- **Sensory perception**, which is the interpretation of information that comes through your senses, including touch, pain, and temperature.

- **Spatial function**, sometimes called visuospatial function, which is a brain function that allows you to judge distance and know where your body is in three-dimensional space. This is important for safely navigating when walking, going up and down stairs, and navigating curbs, as well as for safe driving. Spatial tasks while driving include maintaining position in the center of a lane, moving from one lane to another correctly, turning, and judging distances when coming to a stop sign or light.

- **Math skills**, including the basics of adding, subtracting, multiplying, and dividing, math-related games like Sudoku, and interpreting mathematical information, such as judging distances and understanding the correct shapes (and colors) of objects. The frontal, temporal, and occipital lobes are also involved in math skills.

THE FALLOUT FROM A FALL

One of the greatest challenges a person with dementia and their care partners face is falling. There are many reasons someone may fall, but spatial function problems are high up on the list. Most falls occur on the way to or from, or in, the bathroom. Nearly all hip fractures are the result of a fall. Three of four falls occur in women. Only half of those with dementia will recover the ability to walk after a hip fracture, and one in five will die related to complications from the fracture itself, surgery, or the post-operative recovery.

Although fall prevention is at the top of the safety checklist for family and professional dementia care partners alike, falls are not completely preventable. Sadly, the reality for those with dementia is, "It's not if they will fall, but when."

Having learned about the functions of the parietal lobes, what are the symptoms your loved one is experiencing that seem to be coming from problems with the parietal lobes?

_____

_____

_____

_____

_____

THE OCCIPITAL LOBES

Occipital Lobe

The **occipital lobes** are located at the very back of the brain. Their main function is to process **vision**. Your eyeballs are like the cameras for the things you look at, whereas the occipital lobes are more like the computer that processes the visual information. Nerves from your eyeballs travel all the way back through your brain, traversing and integrating with the temporal and parietal lobes until they reach the occipital lobes. Any type of dementia can affect vision, particularly in the later stages. Indeed, there is a rare form of dementia, called **posterior cortical atrophy**, that primarily affects vision.

OTHER STRUCTURES OF THE BRAIN

The other two structures of the brain we'll discuss are the **cerebellum** and the **brainstem**. The cerebellum's main function is to help with **balance**. The brainstem is the deepest structure in the brain, and it connects the brain to the rest of the body. It is involved in some of the **autonomic functions** we discussed in Lesson Two, including the control of heart rate and breathing. The brainstem also regulates our level of alertness, the sleep-wake cycle, appetite and hunger, sexual desire, and swallowing. In people who are in the late stage of dementia, the neurodegenerative disease process can involve the brainstem (see End-of-Life Issues discussion, below).

END-OF-LIFE ISSUES

There are many difficult decisions care partners must make on behalf of their loved one with dementia, especially if certain issues weren't discussed when the person was able to provide input. The main end-of-life decisions involve questions related to brainstem function, such as whether or not to shock the heart if it stops, use a breathing machine or ventilator if the lungs don't work, and administer intravenous fluids or insert a feeding tube into the stomach if the person can't swallow liquids or solids. If someone with dementia is still able to be involved in their own end-of-life decisions, as difficult as this may be, it removes a great burden from you and other family members. Lesson Eight will cover these and other end-of-life issues.

THE COGNITIVE AND RELATED FUNCTIONS

Now that you've learned what the different lobes of the brain do, let's look at how the brain works in a different but related way by understanding what **cognitive function** is. Cognitive function is what your brain does when you are thinking. There are five cognitive functions, and I've already described them in the prior section in the context of brain lobe structure and function. Here's a brief description of each:

THE FIVE COGNITIVE FUNCTIONS

1. **Attention and concentration** is the first of the cognitive functions. It's sometimes called "the gateway to the brain" because if you're

not paying attention, you're not going to be in tune with your environment or take in new information. Children with attention deficit disorder, or ADD (if they're also hyperactive, it's called attention deficit hyperactivity disorder, or ADHD), don't learn because they cannot pay attention to their teacher. Attention deficit and difficulty concentrating can also occur in those with dementia.

2. In the prior section describing the functions of the temporal lobe, you learned about the second cognitive function, **memory and learning**, including the relationship between short- and long-term memory and learning new information.

3. The third cognitive function is called **executive function**—not executive in the sense of the president of a company, but rather the need to execute a series of steps in order to accomplish a task. Executive function requires planning, problem-solving, multitasking, and judgment. Most things you do in a day require the use of your executive function.

4. Your **language** and speech skills include the ability to express your thoughts in words and sentences, called **expressive language**, and being able to understand what others say to you, referred to as **receptive language**. Language is the fourth of your cognitive functions.

5. The fifth cognitive function is **visuospatial function**, which helps your body analyze and understand where it is in three-dimensional space, helps with judging distance and depth perception, and gives you your sense of direction, like an "internal GPS." Visuospatial function helps you navigate from here to there safely, without falling and hurting yourself. Situations where you use visuospatial function include sitting down properly on a chair, walking down the middle of a sidewalk (or driving in the middle of your lane), and going up and down stairs or a curb.

Now that you've learned about the cognitive functions, please describe any dementia symptoms your loved one may be having related to attention and concentration, memory and learning, executive function, language, and visuospatial function.

RELATED BRAIN FUNCTIONS

There are several functions of the brain that are technically not one of the five cognitive functions but are often affected by dementia and warrant brief description. They include personality, mood, and orientation.

Your **personality** refers to your unique characteristics—how you think, feel, and behave about and toward yourself and others. How people describe you is often a summary of your personality: "She's so cheerful" or "He's really serious." Personality is influenced by your culture, the family you grew up with, and your life experiences. Changes in personality can occur with dementia, ranging from very subtle to some of the most challenging symptoms of the disease.

Another is **mood**, or how you feel, particularly related to your emotions. The most common disturbances of mood in those with dementia, as well as care partners and the general population, for that matter, are depression and anxiety. Emotional expression is also affected by dementia. I'll talk more about these things in the next lesson on changing relationships.

The third is **orientation**, which is knowing the day, date, month, and year, your location (city and state), distinguishing day and night, and the capacity to have a plan for the day. Orientation is a brain function you take for granted, and like personality changes, orientation challenges do occur with dementia and range from very subtle to complete confusion and disorientation.

With that quick introduction to related brain functions, please describe the dementia symptoms your loved one may be having related to their personality, mood, and orientation.

_____

_____

_____

_____

_____

_____

_____

COGNITIVE FUNCTION TESTING

Now that we've covered brain structure and functions, let's talk about how physicians and other healthcare providers go about assessing the cognitive function of someone suspected of having or diagnosed with dementia. Long before your loved one's diagnosis, you probably noticed a number of changes, subtle or pronounced, in their cognitive function. You were able to see these changes because you know them and spend time with them. But providers can't observe people with possible dementia as they go about their daily lives, so they must rely on cognitive function tests designed to be quickly and effectively administered in the clinic setting.

The simplest and quickest way to test cognitive function is with a paper-and-pencil test. The two most commonly utilized brief assessments are the **Mini Mental Status Exam (MMSE)** and **the Montreal Cognitive Assessment (MoCA). A third, called the St. Louis University Mental Status or SLUMS is very similar to the MoCA and won't be described herein**. The MMSE and MoCA are screening tests that give a bird's-eye view of how the brain is working but cannot in and of themselves yield a diagnosis of dementia. Both have 30-point scales. The lower the score, the more impaired the person's cognitive function is.

Sometimes more sophisticated cognitive function tests are required and are administered by a specially trained professional called a **neuropsychologist**, a doctor who is an expert in understanding brain structure, cognitive function, and dementia diagnosis.

The figure below shows the initial portion of the MoCA, which tests the cognitive skills of executive function and visuospatial function, as completed by a person with middle-stage Alzheimer's disease. The test on the left is a connect-the-dots exercise. The test-taker is asked to start with the number 1, alternating between numbers and letters, and going in ascending order. A common error of executive function is to just connect the numbers (as shown) or the letters. The middle test is an assessment of spatial function, which is simply copying the drawing of the cube. Often a person with visuospatial impairment will see the cube only in two dimensions or flat, looking more like a picture frame.

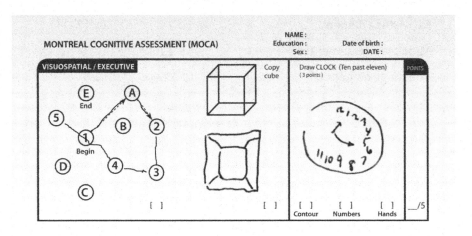

Last is the so-called "clock-draw" test. The instructions are straightforward: draw a clock face, put all the numbers on it, and show the time 11:10. The clock draw assesses both executive and visuospatial function. The person who completed this clock draw couldn't draw a circular face or put the numbers in the right place, or draw the short and long hands correctly. Inability to complete the clock draw properly, especially when coupled with MMSE or MoCA scores in the dementia range, suggests that a person may be unsafe to drive. If this test result was obtained in someone who was still driving, further assessment of their driving safety with a more thorough evaluation conducted by an occupational therapist is recommended, something you'll learn more about in Lesson Eight on legal issues.

WHAT'S THE SCORE?

The maximum number of points on the MMSE and MoCA is 30, but the MoCA is harder and tests more brain functions than the MMSE, so MoCA scores are usually lower than MMSE scores. Here are the scoring categories:

	MMSE	MoCA
Normal	28-30	26-30
Mild cognitive impairment	25-27	18-25
Early-stage dementia	20-24	11-17
Middle-stage dementia	13-19	6-10
Late-stage dementia	0-12	0-5

Several things are important to note when testing an individual and interpreting their scores on the MMSE or MoCA. First, they must be able to see the test sheet and hear the instructions. Second, the results are strongly influenced by one's education level, so, for example, a score of 26 on the MMSE might be a normal score for a person with an eighth-grade education. This is why cognitive tests like the MMSE and MoCA are just one piece in the puzzle of assessing an individual person's overall cognitive function, and would never be used alone to make the diagnosis of mild cognitive impairment or dementia.

ACTIVITIES OF DAILY LIVING (ADLs)

The activities of daily living, often called ADLs by healthcare providers, are tasks that you do in day-to-day life that require the cognitive functions of paying attention, remembering, multitasking, listening and speaking, and spatial orientation. They are divided into the more complex ADLs, called **instrumental ADLs**, and the **basic ADLs**.

The degree of ADL impairment is directly related to the stage of dementia. In the early stage, the instrumental ADLs begin to be affected first because they are the more complex tasks. By the late stage, the instrumental ADLs are a thing of the past, and the basic ADLs become impaired. In other words, people normally perform both their instrumental and basic ADLs independently, but after the onset of dementia, over time (usually years), they will require more and more assistance, first with their instrumental ADLs and then with their basic ADLs, eventually becoming wholly dependent on family care partners and paid caregivers.

INSTRUMENTAL ADLs

- **Cooking** – planning a meal, following a recipe, preparing and serving it
- **House cleaning** – keeping living space neat and clean
- **Taking medication** – taking meds as prescribed, including organizing pill bottles or filling pill holders
- **Laundry** – washing clothes, sheets, and towels properly
- **Shopping** – grocery and other shopping to meet needs such as food and clothing
- **Managing finances** – budgeting, financial planning, and timely payment of bills
- **Communication** – making and receiving phone calls, listening to voicemail (cell phone, smart phone, and computer use for email)
- **Transportation** – driving a car, using a car service (taxi, Uber, Lyft, and the like), or public transportation

Describe any challenges you've observed in your loved one's ability to perform their instrumental ADLs.

_____

_____

_____

_____

_____

_____

_____

BASIC ADLs

- **Bathing** – showering or taking a bath
- **Dressing** – selecting clothes and putting them on properly
- **Transferring** – getting up or down from a lying, sitting, or standing position
- **Toileting** – being able to urinate and have a bowel movement in the toilet as well as clean oneself afterward
- **Feeding** – conveying food and drink to the mouth

Describe any challenges you've observed in your loved one's ability to perform their basic ADLs.

_____

_____

_____

_____

_____

_____

STAGES OF DEMENTIA

Dementia is a progressive disease. That means it worsens over time. Brain functions that are lost cannot be relearned or regained. Doctors have divided the disease into stages as a way of understanding and measuring where patients are in the progression and what to expect next.

There are several different staging systems in place. For this section, I will blend them together, integrating cognitive and other symptoms, instrumental and basic ADLs, MMSE and MoCA scores, as well as personality, mood, and orientation. Note that while staging systems have been primarily used for Alzheimer's disease, they apply to other dementias as well.

As you read through the description of the stages, you will naturally try to figure out which stage best fits your loved one. It's likely they will have symptoms in several stages rather than fitting neatly in one specific stage. This could be due to the normal variation in symptoms that occurs among those with dementia, or your loved one could be transitioning from one stage to the next.

MILD COGNITIVE IMPAIRMENT (MCI)

MCI is sometimes referred to as the "pre-dementia" stage, though technically this is not correct because not everyone with MCI goes on to develop dementia (see below). When a person has MCI, one or more of their cognitive functions is worse than predicted in comparison to someone of similar age and education.

With MCI, the person is able to perform their instrumental and basic ADLs well enough that to the casual observer, they may seem quite normal. But to the person affected by MCI and to those who know them well, it seems that cognitive function may be slipping.

What might you notice in someone with MCI? They may, on occasion:

- Be forgetful.
- Have difficulty retaining recently learned information.

- Repeat questions or stories.
- Lose their train of thought.
- Enter a room but forget why.
- Misplace keys.
- Have a noticeable change in performance at work or home (less focused, more disorganized, indecisive, and easily overwhelmed).

As you'll recall from the chart on page 81, the MMSE score for someone with MCI is 25-27; the MoCA score is 18-25.

Memory is the most commonly affected cognitive function. More subtle changes in personality and/or mood may be evident as well, such as decreased motivation, irritability and moodiness, even some depression and anxiety. Orientation is normal.

Over time, some people with MCI remain stable or even show improvement in their cognitive function, but half to three-quarters will go on to develop early-stage dementia within five years of diagnosis. The transition from MCI to dementia becomes apparent when the person begins to display more cognitive symptoms, such as worsening memory and/or more difficulty multitasking. They may start needing assistance with some of their instrumental ADLs, and/or they may experience a decline in MMSE and MoCA scores. Mild cognitive impairment lasts five years on average, but this is variable.

EARLY-STAGE (MILD) DEMENTIA
The early stage of dementia is characterized by impairment in one or more cognitive functions such that the person needs assistance with multiple instrumental ADLs, though they are still able to perform their basic ADLs independently. Toward the end of the early stage, the person becomes fully dependent in one or several of their instrumental ADLs. The person can often maintain their independence throughout the early stage but may not be able to be home alone safely at the end of the early stage.

What might you notice in someone with early-stage dementia?

They may:

- Frequently repeat questions and stories, forget recent conversations or events, and frequently misplace things (most true with Alzheimer's; less so with other dementias).

- Have difficulty with cooking, house cleaning and laundry, getting bills paid on time and/or correctly, and taking pills properly or remembering them at all.

- Get lost while driving, especially to unfamiliar places.

- Be disorganized when grocery shopping and forget items, even with a list.

- Experience difficulty finding the right word at times.

- Have trouble planning, problem-solving, and multitasking to the degree that this is very apparent, both at work and at home.

In early-stage dementia, the MMSE score is 20-24, whereas the MoCA score is 11-17.

Changes in personality and/or mood may be even more evident than in someone with MCI. You may notice decreased concentration, more irritability and moodiness, overt depression and/or anxiety, and less interest in socializing, activities, and trying new things. The person may deny there is anything wrong with them. Some aspects of orientation, such as consistently knowing the day, date, and month, may begin to get fuzzy, but orientation is mostly intact in early-stage dementia. The early stage lasts two years on average, but this is variable.

MIDDLE-STAGE (MODERATE) DEMENTIA

Middle-stage dementia is characterized by impairment in multiple cognitive functions such that the person becomes progressively dependent in all of their instrumental ADLs. Toward the end of the middle stage, they begin needing assistance in one or several of their basic ADLs as well.

Typically, the person in the middle stage cannot be left home alone safely and will require one or even several care partners. They will quite likely stick very close to those who are most familiar to them, although the middle stage is where wandering or even getting lost may occur.

What might you notice in someone with middle-stage dementia? They may:

- Repeat questions over and over, show little interest in or recall of current and recent events, and not remember their personal details (such as address and phone number).

- Recall long-term memories (such as knowing their own name and remembering some childhood memories), but they may no longer recognize grandchildren and infrequently seen family or friends.

- Become unable to cook, clean house, pay bills, take medication, or drive.

- Require some assistance in picking out clothes as well as require a reminder to change clothes (and underwear) daily, but they are usually still able to dress themselves.

- Go to the toilet on their own, but hygiene may be poor. They might experience occasional episodes of incontinence, may need reminders and possibly some assistance bathing or showering, and might require some help eating (for example, cutting meat).

- Require assistance getting out of bed or up from a chair.

- Find expressing themselves verbally very difficult.

- Seem apathetic and unmotivated, experience afternoon and evening confusion and agitation, be paranoid (about infidelity and theft, most commonly), experience delusions and hallucinations, and exhibit obsessive thoughts and compulsive repetitive behaviors (these challenging behaviors will be discussed in more detail in Lesson Four).

- Sleep up to 12 hours a day but can have long stretches without sleep if agitated. Normal sleep patterns may be disrupted (such as being awake during the night and sleeping during the day).

In middle-stage dementia, the MMSE score is 13-20, whereas the MoCA score is 6-10.

Personality and/or mood changes are likely to be very apparent in this stage. The person is often apathetic and unmotivated, even withdrawn and socially isolated, and may have little to no insight into their condition. They will likely have some confusion and disorientation to the day, date, month, and/or year. This stage lasts four years on average, but this is variable.

LATE-STAGE (SEVERE) DEMENTIA

Late-stage dementia is characterized by severe impairment in multiple cognitive functions. The person becomes progressively dependent in all their basic ADLs (remember, they're already dependent in their instrumental ADLs). By the end of the late stage, the person is dependent in all of their ADLs. They require total care.

What might you notice in someone with late-stage dementia? They will:

- Be unable to cook, clean, do laundry, shop, pay bills, take medicine on their own, use the phone, or drive.

- Need progressively more help and eventually require full assistance getting dressed, showering, going to the bathroom, eating, and getting up from bed or a chair.

- Be incontinent.

- Be mostly unaware of and unresponsive to their surroundings.

- Be unable to talk intelligibly, walk, or swallow by the end.

In late-stage dementia, the MMSE score is 12 or less, whereas the MoCA score is 5 or less. At some point, the person with late-stage dementia becomes unable to complete either the MMSE or MoCA at all. Personality and/or mood changes are similar to those seen with middle-stage dementia but even more pronounced. The person is confused and disoriented. The late stage lasts two-and-a-half years on average, but this is variable.

Based on the descriptions of the stages of dementia, what stage would you say your loved one is in? How do you feel about this?

_____

_____

_____

_____

_____

_____

_____

Having just answered the above question, let's pause for a moment. If you are like most of the support-group participants I've had answer this question in the past, you're now realizing that your loved one is farther along in their journey than you thought. On the one hand, you might feel like the clock is ticking, and you have fewer years left together than you thought. On the other hand, you might be wondering how you'll be able to endure the stress of caregiving for several more years. Whatever your thoughts and feelings, I would encourage you to share them, either in your support group, or with a family member or friend. You might even want to pause for a Mindfulness Moment. And when ready, you can transition to the last part of the lesson.

MEDICATIONS TO TREAT MCI AND DEMENTIA

A full discussion of the medications used to treat mild cognitive impairment (MCI) and the different forms of dementia could be an entire lesson in and of itself. So in this section, we'll briefly cover the basic three categories of medications used to treat dementia — memory-enhancing drugs, experimental drugs for preventing and treating Alzheimer's disease, and drugs for mood and behavioral challenges.

MEMORY-ENHANCING DRUGS

There are two types of prescription drugs that have medical evidence to improve cognitive function in those with Alzheimer's disease and, to some extent, those with other dementias.

The first type are the **cholinesterase inhibitors**. These drugs increase a brain chemical called acetylcholine, which is important for memory and learning as well as the other cognitive functions. The three available cholinesterase inhibitors include the pills **donepezil (Aricept®)** and **galantamine (Razadyne®)**, and **rivastigmine (Exelon®)**, which comes in patch, pill, and liquid forms. They are usually used in the early and middle stages of Alzheimer's and are generally well-tolerated, though side effects such as fatigue, headaches, dizziness, appetite loss, nausea, vomiting, weight loss, more frequent and urgent bowel movements, muscle cramps, bruising, and vivid dreams do occur.

The second type are the **NMDA receptor antagonists**. These drugs block the effects of a brain chemical called glutamate, which interferes with memory, learning, and other cognitive functions. The main drug in this category is the pill **memantine (Namenda®)**. It is usually used in the middle and late stages of Alzheimer's, often in combination with a cholinesterase inhibitor (a pill that combines donepezil and memantine is now available too, called **Namzaric®**). Also generally well-tolerated, memantine does have some side effects, which include headaches, dizziness, drowsiness, confusion, irritability, and constipation.

Neither of these types of drugs are a cure for Alzheimer's disease. They usually help symptoms on average from six months to several years, but are usually continued for life since stopping them may cause cognitive decline, and they may reduce some of the challenging behaviors seen in late-stage Alzheimer's. Some people don't benefit from the drugs, or they can't take them because of side effects. There is evidence that they also are helpful in Lewy body dementia, but less so for vascular and frontotemporal dementia. The cholinesterase inhibitors and NMDA receptor antagonists have been available for many years. New medications to improve cognitive function are definitely needed.

DRUGS FOR PREVENTION/ TREATMENT

At the present time, there are no FDA-approved drugs that prevent, slow the progression of, or cure Alzheimer's disease or other dementias. Because of this, I encourage those with dementia to consider participating in a clinical trial—that is, a research study testing new drugs that we hope can effectively prevent and treat dementia. While many drugs are being tested, there is one in particular I'll briefly discuss.

FINDING CLINICAL TRIALS

The Alzheimer's Association (www.alz.org) has a free service called TrialMatch®, which allows you to input information about your loved one's dementia. The service will notify you if your loved one is a match to a specific clinical trial somewhere in the United States.

At the time of this writing, one category of drugs under investigation in Alzheimer's disease clinical trials shows great promise: **monoclonal antibodies**. These types of drugs work through our immune system to attack, disable, and/or eliminate "bad guys" in our body that cause diseases like cancer. A wide range of highly effective monoclonal antibodies drugs is already the standard of care for many different cancers.

Monoclonal antibodies may show promise in the fight against Alzheimer's disease, too. Clinical trials with the first of these drugs, **aducanumab**, a monoclonal antibody that targeted amyloid to try to prevent amyloid buildup and reduce amyloid plaques, did not show benefit, but others are being tested.

For the time being, until the "magic bullet" is found to prevent and cure dementia, lifestyle modification is something you can do that will make a difference. For your loved one with dementia, lifestyle modifications can sometimes slow the progression of their disease. For

BRAIN-HEALTHY LIFESTYLE MODIFICATIONS

It's true, there is no "magic pill" to prevent or cure dementia. However, there are lifestyle changes your loved one can make that may help prevent or slow the progression of the disease. These same things will also help your brain and body age more healthfully. Many of these seem like heart-healthy tips. In geriatrics, we often say, "What's good for the heart is good for the brain."

- Exercise your body. Exercising regularly, 90 to 150 minutes of aerobic (breaking a sweat) minutes per week, is the most important and effective lifestyle modification you can make. If 90 to 150 minutes is too much, do the best you can. Some exercise is better than none. Even moderate to brisk walking makes a difference.

- Keep your blood pressure in check. Recent research suggests maintaining a systolic blood pressure (the top number) of 120 or less reduces your chances of developing mild cognitive impairment and dementia.

- Be good to your body. Don't smoke, drink only in moderation (a glass of red wine or the equivalent amount of alcohol daily) or not at all, keep your cholesterol and triglyceride levels in the normal range (with medication, if necessary), maintain a normal weight, and if you're diabetic, aim for an A1C value of 6.5 to 7.0. Most importantly, team up with your primary-care provider to focus on disease prevention.

- Exercise your brain. Keeping your brain active is important, just like physical exercise. Reading, crossword puzzles, Sudoku, word searches, sewing, woodworking, watching TV or movies, time on the computer (looking things up, playing games, and brain training programs), going to a museum, even learning a new language—anything that challenges your mind helps. And note that it's better to vary the activities rather than do the same thing all day long.

- Eat a brain-healthy diet. In recent years, research has shown that following a Mediterranean-style diet, either the DASH (Dietary Approaches to Stop Hypertension) diet or the MIND (Mediterranean-DASH Intervention for Neurodegenerative Delay) diet, can slow the cognitive changes associated with aging. And don't take most supplements. Besides vitamin B12 and D supplements for those whose levels are low, no other supplements are medically proven to be beneficial to brain health, including coconut oil (which is a very heart-unhealthy dietary fat) and Prevagen.

- Stay socially active. Being with family and friends, and getting out and doing things—even routine, day-to-day errands like grocery shopping or going to the drugstore—may be as important as physical exercise for brain health.

- Manage stress. I know this is easier said than done, but excessive stress negatively impacts your medical and mental health. You've already learned about one approach to stress reduction: the Mindfulness Moment. You'll hear a lot more about stress and how to keep your stress level down in Lesson Six, which focuses on self-care.

- Wear hearing aids if you need them. Decreased hearing reduces mental stimulation because you are less likely to be socially active if you can't hear. If you find it difficult to hear others in group conversation or have to turn the television volume up quite loud, seek an audiologist to have your hearing tested.

- Get a good night's sleep. Last but not least, poor sleep—whether from the pain from arthritis, medications, frequent urination, sleep apnea, or any other cause—has now been linked to a variety of adverse health conditions in seniors, ranging from obesity to heart disease, high blood pressure, depression, and, yes, dementia. Aim for seven to nine hours a night, and see your doctor if sleep is a struggle.

you as care partner, lifestyle modifications may prevent mild cognitive impairment and dementia.

MEDICATIONS FOR MOOD AND BEHAVIORAL CHALLENGES

Mental-health medications play an important role in the care of those with dementia in a number of different settings, which I'll focus on in this section. Mental-health challenges in care partners, particularly depression, anxiety, and stress, are also covered in detail in Lesson Six.

For the person with dementia, **antidepressants** (there are too many for me to mention specific ones) are frequently prescribed at the time of diagnosis, particularly if there is uncertainty about whether depression may be contributing to memory loss, and continued throughout the dementia journey, since depression commonly coexists with dementia. In general, depression is best treated by counseling, medication, or a combination of both. Depending on the stage of dementia, however, counseling may be of limited effectiveness. Lifestyle modification, particularly exercise, can also be effective for the treatment of depression, in addition to or as an alternative to medication.

Stress and anxiety, as well as related challenging behaviors, such as agitation and aggression, can occur in those with dementia. The latter are discussed in Lesson Seven: Getting More Help and Transitioning Care. Sometimes **benzodiazepines**, such as lorazepam (Ativan®) and alprazolam (Xanax®) are used in this setting. While they may be effective at reducing anxiety in the short-term, these medications can be addicting, increase fall risk, and cause drowsiness and confusion with worsening of cognitive function. Similar concerns exist for many common sleeping pills, with the exception of mirtazepine (Remeron®).

The drugs used to treat severe agitation and aggression as well as delusions and hallucinations include the **antipsychotics** (such as risperidone/Risperdal® and quetiapine/Seroquel®) and **mood stabilizers** (for example valproate/Depakote®). They may be effective, and are sometimes necessary, but they also have inherent risks, such as drowsiness, increased fall risk, infections, blood clots, stroke, abnormal heart rhythm, and even sudden cardiac death. In Lesson Four, you will learn about a number of strategies to manage challenging behaviors that can be used as alternatives to or in conjunction with antipsychotic or mood-stabilizing drugs.

Which medications, if any, is your loved one currently taking? Do you have questions or concerns about medication? Are there medications listed that your loved one isn't taking that you think might be helpful? Please write down your medication questions and thoughts so you have them handy for the next healthcare provider appointment.

_____

_____

_____

_____

_____

_____

_____

A FINAL REFLECTION AND LOOKING AHEAD

Congratulations! Having completed the last lesson and this one, you are now an expert in the brain! That being said, there may still be things you don't understand about your loved one's dementia and lingering questions about what is really going on inside their brain.

The truth is, despite lots of progress in recent years, there are still things that are not understood about the brain and dementia. Many questions, such as the very basic one of what causes dementia, remain unanswered. A couple of things really encourage me right now. The pace of scientific discoveries about the brain and dementia is faster than ever, and there has never been more money spent on research by our government and the pharmaceutical industry than there is presently. Many years ago, one of my mentors told me "coping is hoping," and hope that we'll soon find the cause and cure for dementia is a hope you can have right now.

What did you learn from the lesson that stands out the most? Please share.

_____

_____

_____

_____

_____

_____

You're probably wondering about the topic for the next lesson. We'll be shifting gears again as we move to Lesson Four: Adapting to Changing Relationships. You'll learn about a number of common behavior changes that are caused by dementia, the impact these behaviors have on relationships, and ways to adapt. Adapting to changing relationships is the third central need of dementia care partners.

Take a minute now and repeat the Mindfulness Moment we opened today's lesson with, and consider it the first step in recharging before continuing your support group or self-study.

Adapting to Changing Relationships

In Lesson Three, we reviewed all the ways the brain can change when affected by dementia, including changes in cognitive (thinking) functions, personality, mood, and orientation, as well as in the capacity to manage activities of daily living. In Lesson Two, we learned about the symptoms of Alzheimer's disease and the other forms of dementia, many of which were behavioral changes.

"Even though behaviors have changed, the person you remember is still in there."

— Roxzan Sukola

When your loved one's cognition and behavior changes, your relationship with them naturally begins to change as well. The most typical relationship change is an increase in the emotional distance between you as care partner and the person with dementia. In psychological terms, there is a weakening of what are referred to as **attachment bonds** between the two of you. And ironically, this distancing in turn tends to promote a number of additional behavior changes, which many caregivers respond to by pulling away yet further from the person with dementia. It's a vicious cycle.

To understand why this happens, let's put on our psychologist hats and learn a bit about something dating way back to the 1950s called attachment theory.

ATTACHMENT THEORY

Attachment is the process by which two human beings develop a long-lasting emotional connection to one another. In other words, it's how one person comes to like or love another, to experience the joy of being together and avoid the dislike or distress of being apart.

Attachment theory says our very first attachment is in infancy, when we bond to our first caregiver, usually our mother, for nourishment, comfort, safety, and security. Children who feel **secure in their parental attachments** are able to interact with strangers and not feel threatened, separate from parents without feeling anxious, and explore new situations without being fearful. Securely attached children are confident, have positive self-esteem, and are more socially connected, forming numerous long-lasting bonds with attachment figures throughout their lifetimes, including parents, siblings, extended family members, friends, coworkers, spouses or partners, and eventually children of their own.

On the other hand, children who are **insecurely attached** feel threatened by strangers, anxious when not with their parents, and fearful in new situations. They lack confidence, have low self-esteem, are more isolated, and struggle with forming relationships in childhood and adulthood. They are more likely to experience emotional distress when separated from attachment figures; this is referred to as **separation distress**, and in children it might manifest as crying, clinging, and calling out because they feel abandoned.

What does this have to do with dementia, you rightly ask? We're getting there. Thanks for bearing with me. You see, dementia, by its very nature, creates insecurely attached adults. It causes people with dementia to feel disoriented, overstimulated, fearful, and anxious in many environments, feeling unattached to those who are closest to them, and even detached from reality. The damaged and dying neurons in the brain are in essence mimicking or creating the illusion of insecure attachment, and in doing so, cause separation behaviors that may further widen the emotional divide between you and your loved one.

A person with dementia who feels insecurely attached may respond in ways that are similar to how a child would behave if separated from their parent—with overt anxiety, worry, fear, panic, anger, aggression, and/or distressing vocalizations (such as "Help, help!"). This is called the **seeking response**. On the other hand, the person with dementia may have a more **withdrawn response,** characterized by feelings of sadness, depression, grief, loneliness, and even helplessness.

As a result of these insecure attachment behaviors, many care partners can become put off. It's common and understandable for care partners to withdraw and feel helpless themselves when they encounter the behaviors of separation distress due to insecure attachment. But the more a care partner withdraws, the more insecure their loved one may feel. This is the vicious cycle I referred to!

And by the way, it's not fair that your loved one may experience this

THE DOWNSIDE OF TOO MUCH DOPAMINE

When a person with dementia feels insecurely attached or totally unattached and experiences separation distress, there is an increase in a brain chemical called dopamine. Perhaps you've heard of dopamine. It is called the "feel-good hormone" because under normal circumstances dopamine levels increase when you have a pleasurable experience (dopamine does lots of other things in the brain too). In the setting of separation distress, the brain over-produces dopamine in anticipation of being reattached and feeling good as a result. But here's the rub: too much dopamine causes the challenging emotions and behaviors that are part of the seeking response. This is also why antipsychotic drugs, which block the effects of dopamine, are often effective at lessening anger, aggression, and other seeking-response behaviors.

insecure attachment, especially when you are likely going above and beyond to provide loving care, security, and companionship to them, with the best of intentions. But I am hopeful that understanding what's going on "beneath" their separation-distress behaviors will help you respond with empathy and love.

Attachment theory also helps explain another experience that is common in people with dementia: They often think that their parents are still alive—speaking of them in the present, even talking aloud to them, when they have been long deceased. This adaptation may actually be mentally healthy, the reflection of secure attachment in childhood and a strategy to cope with feelings of insecurity, perhaps loneliness, or even abandonment that occur in those with dementia. Suppose an older woman with Alzheimer's disease frequently talks to her mother, even though the mother passed away three decades earlier. It may be that bringing her mother into the present through conversation gives the person with dementia the same feelings of safety and security she had as a child when the mother was present.

Has your loved one had any behaviors that might stem from dementia-related separation distress, such as crying, clinging, calling out, sadness, depression, grief, loneliness, helplessness, anxiety, worry, fear, panic, anger, aggression, distressing vocalizations, or talking to their deceased parents? How have these behaviors affected your relationship? Please describe.

_____

_____

_____

_____

_____

_____

_____

In the remainder of this lesson we will discuss common behavioral changes and challenges that occur in those with early- to middle-stage dementia that erode and alter the very nature of your relationship with them. But first, a Mindfulness Moment to center you.

MINDFULNESS MOMENT

So far in this lesson we've reviewed something that may not have been familiar to you, attachment theory, but that may explain some of the behaviors you have observed in your loved with dementia. In the process of reflecting about these things, you may be experiencing some strong feelings or stress. This is a good opportunity to turn all of your awareness and attention on the present moment, tuning out worries of the past and future, for a stress-reducing Mindfulness Moment. I hope it will allow you to experience a "brain break" in which you calmly, nonjudgmentally, and compassionately accept your current thoughts, emotions, and body sensations without feeling as though you need to change them. So, let's begin the short breathing exercise that frames the Mindfulness Moment.

1. Sit in a comfortable chair, put both feet on the floor (or any other comfortable position), clasp your hands over the middle of your belly, and then close your eyes (if desired).

2. Scan your muscles from head to toe and intentionally relax them. Unclench your teeth, let your shoulders sag, and relax your buttock and leg muscles.

3. Take in a slow, deep breath through your nose (count "one one-thousand, two one-thousand, three one-thousand" to yourself as you do so), then slowly exhale through your mouth to the same count, feeling the rise and fall of your belly. Do a total of ten slow, deep breaths like this. Focus solely on the gentle flow of your breath, in and out. Each time you exhale, consciously blow out any negative emotions and stress you're feeling.

4. After the tenth breath, slowly open your eyes.

BEHAVIORAL CHANGES AND CHALLENGES IN EARLY- AND MIDDLE-STAGE DEMENTIA

Several years ago, a nurse I knew approached me in confidence. "There must be someone else," she said of her high school sweetheart and husband of 40 years, with tears in her eyes. "He no longer seems interested in spending time with me. There are no more compliments. Sweet, loving gestures, even hand holding, have gone away. We haven't made love for years." After questioning my colleague further, I became suspicious that his personality changes, in combination with some forgetfulness he was experiencing, might represent Alzheimer's disease. Unfortunately, this proved to be the case. Changes in behavior, personality, and mood, as well as the more typical loss of short-term memory, can be the first signs of any of the dementias.

In retrospect, what are the very earliest changes you saw in your loved one's behavior, mood, and memory or other cognitive functions that turned out to be mild cognitive impairment or dementia? How long ago did they occur?

_____

_____

_____

_____

_____

_____

Following are eight changes in behavior that most commonly begin in the early and middle stages of dementia and often continue throughout the journey. (In Lesson Seven, I'll describe behavior changes that are more typical of late-stage dementia). Your loved one may have some of these behaviors now, and they could develop others in the future, but they won't necessarily experience all of them. Every person with dementia is unique in terms of which behaviors occur, as well as their severity and duration. Some may even come and go. After describing these eight behaviors, I'll discuss five things you can do to adapt to the relationship challenges that accompany them.

APATHY

One of the earliest and most subtle personality changes that may occur in those with dementia is **apathy**. Apathy literally means "without feeling." Apathetic individuals are unmotivated and lack interest in doing most anything, ranging from basic activities like getting dressed, showering, or even eating, to more enjoyable activities. They often seem uninterested in engaging socially with family and friends, being involved with their faith community, or actively participating in leisure or hobby groups. Gratitude for things you do for them may go unrecognized. Apathetic loved ones may even resist you caring for them.

Apathy can be extremely angering and frustrating for you as care partner as it may make you feel your loved one is being lazy or even resisting your care on purpose. While this is possible, it's unlikely. Apathy, like all of the behaviors we'll review in this lesson, is caused by the disease and is a symptom your loved one is most likely unaware of.

Has your loved one experienced apathy as one of the behavioral changes of their dementia journey? How has this affected your relationship? Please describe.

_____

_____

_____

_____

_____

_____

_____

LACK OF INSIGHT, IMPAIRED JUDGMENT, AND DENIAL

Insight is the ability to understand a person, situation, or thing. Insight is required for judgment. In my experience, about half of those with dementia will **lack insight** into their disease and have **impaired judgment**. They are simply unaware of their changes in cognitive function, personality, mood, or orientation (just as they are unaware of their behavior changes). On the one hand, not recognizing one's limitations can be liberating for the person with the disease and ease the frustration of cognitive disability and emotional changes. On the other hand, those with **preserved insight** are typically frustrated by what they can't do correctly, which will often generate negative emotions directed at themselves and others, including you as care partner and even medical and mental-health providers.

Lack of insight, particularly when your loved one is in **denial** about their symptoms and diagnosis, can be extremely challenging to care partners. It can be exasperating to try to provide help to someone with early-stage dementia who needs assistance with their instrumental activities of daily living (like taking their medications or paying bills properly, for example) yet refuses your assistance. Here's a common scenario in which lack of insight, denial, and impaired judgment all play a role.

On the Road to Danger

Jack was an 82-year-old man who was brought in for counseling by his wife, who wanted me to "make him stop driving." He had been diagnosed with vascular dementia following a stroke three years earlier, and he had been told by his doctor that it was unsafe for him to drive. Jack would not comply. He had been involved in three major motor vehicle accidents in the prior six months, amazingly without significant injury to himself or anyone else. In each instance, he was ticketed for being at fault, and following the third accident, his license was even taken away. He had no insight into his accidents and tickets ("It was their fault!") or driving challenges ("I've been driving since I was 14 years old!"). For that matter, he didn't even believe his diagnosis ("I don't have Alzheimer's!").

As I'll discuss in the latter part of this lesson, when it comes to issues of safety, sometimes you as care partner find yourself doing some difficult things to make sure your loved one, you, and others are out of harm's way. In this case, I suggested to Jack's wife that she either take his car keys away, or better yet, somehow remove the car from Jack's sight—take it to an adult child's house, sell it, give it away, anything so that he could no longer see the car and want to drive it. Though he protested at first, eventually Jack did forget about the car and wanting to drive.

Has your loved one experienced a lack of insight, poor judgment, and/or denial during their journey with dementia? How has this affected your relationship? Please describe.

_____

_____

_____

_____

_____

_____

CHANGES IN EMOTIONAL EXPRESSION

Remembering that the brain controls everything you think, feel, say, and do, it shouldn't surprise you that emotional expression changes in a person with dementia as the disease progresses. The change typically begins with a decrease in the amount of time the person with dementia spends with their spouse (or another close family member or friend), as well as less physical touch such as hugging, kissing, and hand holding, fewer expressions of affection like "I love you" or "thank you," less interest in helping out around the house with indoor and outdoor chores, and less inclination to give gifts like flowers, chocolate, or a card.

All of this probably feels like the person with dementia is **emotionally withdrawing** and becoming more **emotionally isolated** from you as care partner. Whether you are the person's spouse, adult child, sibling, friend, or coworker, this emotional distancing erodes emotional intimacy. For couples, it also affects sexual intimacy, a topic we'll discuss more in Lesson Five: Coping with Grief and Loss.

A somewhat unique kind of emotional withdrawal—**loss of empathy**— is one of the hallmark features of behavioral variant frontotemporal dementia, though it can occur with other dementias too. Empathy is the ability to experience another person's pain (or any emotion, really) through their eyes, not yours. In contrast, sympathy is the ability to understand and care about, at an intellectual level, what another person is experiencing, but not necessarily in a way that you internally feel it as they do. Sympathy is probably lost along with empathy in frontotemporal dementia. Here is a story that illustrates this loss of empathy.

He Doesn't Care Anymore

Scott and Cindy were in their early 70s and had married young, right out of high school. Scott was the third-generation owner of a replacement window business; Cindy was a successful realtor. Scott began having difficulty organizing his business, relying more and more on his business partners for sales, scheduling, marketing, and overseeing operations. Cindy noticed that he stopped showing appreciation for things she did to make their life easier, such as shopping, cooking, and doing the laundry. Unexpectedly, Cindy suffered a heart attack and had to be hospitalized for several days while she underwent tests and eventually placement of two heart stents. Scott showed no concern for Cindy. He never visited her in the hospital and was even unwilling to help her get to doctors' appointments after her driving was restricted for several weeks following hospitalization. In the months that followed, Cindy began noticing several seemingly unrelated changes in Scott, such as difficulty expressing himself verbally and a craving for sweets, which led them to a visit with their family doctor and then a neurologist. Sadly, Scott was in the early stage of behavioral variant frontotemporal dementia.

Has your loved one experienced emotional withdrawal, loss of empathy, or other changes in emotional expression as part of their dementia journey? How has this affected your relationship? Please describe.

_____

_____

_____

_____

_____

_____

MOOD CHANGES

About half of people with dementia experience major changes in mood, particularly depression, anxiety, or both. You may also hear these changes referred to as "mood disorders."

The most common **symptoms of depression** you might notice in the person with dementia include feeling sad or down, **irritable and/or moody**, and **uninterested** in usual activities, like being around family and friends. The latter is indistinguishable from the apathy of dementia discussed previously. Other depressive symptoms may include fatigue, changes in sleep and/or appetite (up or down), low self-esteem, difficulty focusing, and lack of motivation (or being restless and fidgety).

The most common **symptoms of anxiety** include restlessness or feeling edgy, worry, irritability, muscle tension, insomnia, fatigue, and difficulty concentrating. The coexistence of depression, anxiety, or both with dementia further strains the relationship between you and your loved one. It is important to assess for both depression and anxiety in someone suspected of having dementia, since untreated or inadequately treated anxiety is also associated with worsening cognitive symptoms, especially memory and executive function (planning, problem-solving, and multitasking) as well as judgment and decision-making ability.

Has your loved one experienced depression or anxiety in their dementia journey? What have their symptoms been? How has this affected your relationship? Please describe.

_____

_____

_____

_____

_____

_____

Another pair of personality changes that can further challenge the relationship between you and the person with dementia is obsessions and compulsions. Obsessions are **recurring thoughts**, whereas compulsions are the **repetitive behavior**s that result from obsessions. The challenge of this is illustrated in the following story.

An Obsessed Sister

Theresa and Vanessa were sisters, the two youngest in a family of nine. After Theresa's husband passed away, she decided to move in with Vanessa, already a widow, who lived in the same old home they were raised in decades and decades earlier.

Early on, Vanessa noticed some things that just weren't quite right with her sister. Theresa wasn't really able to help prepare meals, and despite being an accountant for nearly 40 years, she didn't have a good understanding of monthly expenses and splitting the bills.

But more than anything else, Theresa obsessed about all sorts of things around the house. She constantly checked the stove to make sure the burners and oven were turned off. Even though they lived in a small town and knew practically everybody, Theresa kept locking and relocking the doors and windows to make sure nobody broke in.

Historically a very fun-loving and spontaneous person, Theresa became very rigid about the schedule she adhered to, and was insistent that Vanessa do the same. Coffee and breakfast were at 8 a.m., lunch at noon, and supper at 6 p.m. If they got off schedule, Theresa became hypercritical of Vanessa, driving her to tears.

Their relationship deteriorated such that they began having independent lives despite living in the same place. Vanessa knew things couldn't continue as is, but she also had come to realize that Theresa would never function on her own. She began pursuing options to have Theresa evaluated for dementia.

In Vanessa and Theresa's situation, Theresa had obsessive thoughts that the house was unlocked and therefore not safe. Her checking and rechecking to make sure the doors and windows were locked were the compulsive behaviors. This, in combination with Theresa's other personality changes, ultimately resulted in a diagnosis of behavioral variant frontotemporal dementia. This is the most common form of dementia to demonstrate obsessions and compulsions, though they can occur with any form of dementia.

Hoarding is a form of obsessive-compulsive thinking and behavior. It usually involves gathering and saving (sometimes hiding) ordinary objects, and may include anything from money to garbage. Hoarding is most common in Alzheimer's disease and behavioral variant frontotemporal dementia. It occurs in people with dementia for several reasons. Often it is a reflection of paranoid thoughts that someone is stealing their money or other possessions (to be discussed further in the upcoming section on delusional thinking). Sometimes the person may save "stuff" because they feel an emotional attachment to it. For example, a widow may keep everything associated with her late husband, including his clothes, other personal effects, mail that had his name on it, and even food that was in the pantry when he was alive, because ridding herself of it would make her feel disconnected from him.

Has your loved one demonstrated any obsessive-compulsive thoughts and behaviors (or hoarding) during their dementia journey? If so, what has this been like for you? Please share.

_____

_____

_____

_____

_____

_____

REPETITIVE AND PERSISTENT BEHAVIORS

Some of the most exasperating and relationship-challenging behaviors your loved one with dementia may demonstrate are the repetitive and persistent ones. **Repetitive questioning**, which we introduced in Lesson Three with Stephanie and Ray's story, is one consequence of short-term memory loss. It's not that the person *won't* remember they just asked the same question or said the same thing, they *can't* remember. Another is **repetitive vocalizations**, a common one being, "I want to go home," which may be a manifestation of attachment loss and separation distress related to feeling disconnected from one's childhood home and family growing up (described in Mary and Chris's story in Lesson One). **Repetitive behaviors** also occur in those with dementia. Examples include sorting mail, tearing tissues apart, and breaking twigs into small pieces. These behaviors may seem overly simple or pointless to you, but for your loved one, there is comfort in routine and being able to start and finish a task.

Another common behavior you may experience is something referred to as **shadowing**, what I call "being velcroed at the hip." This is when your loved one follows you around, usually at a close distance, everywhere you go. Over time, it may feel annoying if not stifling. Shadowing is a behavior best explained by attachment theory. Those with dementia almost always feel most settled by being close to the care partners they know and love best, whom they feel the most connected to, so much so they literally try to attach themselves to that person. This helps them minimize separation distress and the behaviors that accompany it.

Repetitive questioning, vocalizations, and behaviors, as well as shadowing, test the tolerance of even the most resilient care partners. Learning to become more patient in these situations will reap big relationship rewards, but this is definitely a process, not an event!

Has your loved one exhibited repetitive questions, vocalizations, and/or being velcroed at the hip as part of their dementia journey? How has this affected your relationship? Please describe.

_____

_____

_____

_____

_____

_____

LOST IDENTITY

When someone with dementia becomes confused about or totally forgets the identity of their spouse, adult children, other family members, and friends, this can be one of the most heartbreaking events you experience as your loved one's care partner. **Lost identity** is another example of an attachment loss. When I share the story of Rebecca no longer knowing the girls and me as her daughters and husband, people often respond with a great deal of emotion for our loss. For Rebecca, the loss was devastating. It was like a child had been taken from her parents and home. She struggled with sadness and depression, agitation and even aggression, and wanting to "go home." It is a reminder that lost identity, like other challenging behaviors, must be viewed from the perspective of both the person with dementia as well as their care partner.

Some time ago, while I was speaking to an audience of dementia care partners on the topic of relationship changes, including lost identity, an older man in the back of the auditorium raised his hand and asked whether it was possible for a wife of many years to no longer recognize her husband. I gave a short answer (yes) then sought him out after the event, which is when he shared this story.

What's She Doing With That Other Man?

Nathan and Pamela were a couple in their early 90s, married for nearly

70 years. Pamela's Alzheimer's had entered the late stage. She could no longer perform her basic activities of daily living independently (getting dressed, going to the toilet, and showering). When Nathan was unable to help her, she voluntarily went into a local nursing home. Nathan would visit Pamela faithfully every day, from late morning through supper time. One day Nathan found Pamela sitting on a bench with another older gentleman, holding his hand and conversing with him. He watched them, tears streaming down his face. As time went on, Pamela no longer recognized Nathan and spent more and more time with her gentleman friend. Devastated, Nathan sought counseling to help him understand how this could have happened.

In my experience, lost identity occurs in about half of people with Alzheimer's disease as well as the other dementias when memory is affected. Typically, the more distant the relationship is in terms of the family tree, and the more recent the relationship is chronologically, the sooner it is lost from the person's memory (for example, adult friends, coworkers, and in families, cousins and grandchildren are forgotten first). In contrast, closer and long-term relationships, such as spouses, adult children, and parents, are often preserved to the end.

Has your loved one lost your identity or that of other loved ones during their dementia journey? What aspects of their own identity have they lost? How has this affected your relationship with them? Please describe.

_____

_____

_____

_____

_____

DELUSIONAL THINKING

About 70 percent of those with Alzheimer's disease, even more common in Lewy body dementia, will have **delusions**. When someone has a delusion, they believe something is true even though there is evidence to the contrary. It is a false belief. **Paranoid delusions** are the most common and include the following:

- The delusion that you, or another family member, are stealing money or valuables. This will often compel the person with dementia to hide things such as cash, jewelry, or an item of sentimental value.

- The delusion of infidelity, which can be a devastating accusation to a faithful spouse or long-term partner and damaging to the marriage relationship or partnership.

- The delusion of persecution, that someone is trying to hurt or kill them. Often they involve people, animals, or even demons. Persecutory delusions can be frightening, even psychologically disabling to the person with dementia who experiences them. They can also make you feel helpless as a care partner.

Although your tendency may be to deny, defend yourself against, or ignore a delusion expressed by the person with dementia, for them, the delusions are real and should generally be acknowledged. Later in this lesson you'll learn a strategy that will help you deal with paranoid delusions and other challenging behaviors.

Has your loved one experienced any delusions as symptoms of their dementia? How have you responded to them? How have they affected your relationship? What has been your response to them? Please describe.

_____

_____

_____

_____

_____

_____

BEHAVIORAL DISINHIBITION

I'm sure you've had the experience of thinking about saying or doing something that didn't feel exactly right, so you decided not to say or do whatever it was. Essentially, you weighed the pros and cons, and using your judgment, decided not to proceed. This is a frontal-lobe function (executive function) that you learned about in the last lesson. It's called behavioral inhibition, or simply put, our "brain brakes." About a third of those with Alzheimer's disease, and virtually all those affected by behavioral variant frontotemporal dementia, have lost the ability to suppress behaviors that may be harmful to self or others, or are socially unacceptable.

Examples of **behavioral disinhibition** vary widely and include rudeness, insensitivity, **socially inappropriate comments and behaviors** in private and public settings, uncontrollable crying or laughing, and excessive eating (especially sweets). Suggestive comments and socially unacceptable behaviors in men may be particularly challenging, especially in this era of heightened awareness of inappropriate or unwanted remarks and touch. The very nature of most disinhibited behaviors often drives a wedge between people with dementia and their loved ones, pulling them apart and making them more emotionally distant.

Has your loved one exhibited behavioral disinhibition? Describe the behaviors, how they made you feel, and what your response was. Please share.

_____

_____

_____

_____

_____

_____

You may be feeling quite overwhelmed by the diversity of behavior changes your loved one with dementia may experience. Perhaps you now know some things that you wish you had known earlier, things that might have helped your and your loved one's relationship. If so, now is as good an opportunity as ever to make some changes in how you think and respond. The remainder of the lesson will focus on a number of "win-win" ways you can adapt to behavioral challenges.

ADAPTING TO CHANGING RELATIONSHIPS

You have now learned about eight common areas of behavior change that begin most often in early- and middle-stage dementia. Some of these changes challenge the relationship you have with your loved one with dementia, perhaps testing your patience. Other changes, particularly those due to attachment loss, are distressing for you as well as your loved one, resulting in them feeling unsafe, insecure, and unloved, and you emotionally removed from them. How can you adapt to these changes? What can you do to maintain and even strengthen the love you have for them, enhance your own resilience, and cope with the behavioral changes and relationship challenges? Let's look at some general strategies designed to equip and empower you to help accomplish these goals.

PATIENCE

Being patient is easier said than done! The general principle that motivates patience is the need to stay calm and keep the drama level down in a given situation in which you're inclined to lose your temper, (which increases the drama level). You accomplish this in several ways. First, do not take what your loved one says or does personally. Their behavioral expression is not about you, it's a reflection on what's going on inside them. Second, think about how you're going to respond *before* you say or do something in response to the situation. Be intentional about responding in a caring, compassionate, respectful, and empathetic way, providing your loved one the gifts of grace and mercy.

Let's go back to the story about Stephanie and Ray in Lesson Two. She kept asking him the same question about what time dinner was, over and over. Ray had two options—either respond quickly with anger, or think about the importance of keeping the drama level down by not losing his cool and calmly replying that dinner was at six o'clock. An intentionally patient approach may be effective for anything your loved one does or says that is repetitive, either behaviors or vocalizations.

AFFIRM, ACKNOWLEDGE, AND REDIRECT

Another strategy that is helpful when the drama level increases involves three easy-to-remember steps: affirm, acknowledge, and redirect, or AAR for short.

For example, when the person with dementia experiences paranoid delusions, especially regarding infidelity or being harmed by someone or something else, they can become extremely upset, saying or doing things that raise the drama level, often leaving you as care partner uncertain how to manage the situation. Rather than feeling paralyzed by uncertainty, you can turn to AAR as a way to reduce the drama level and make everyone calmer.

Here's a real-life example. There was a couple I counseled who had been married for over 60 years. One day, while shopping together in the grocery store, an older gentleman passed by them, prompting the husband to say to his wife, in a rather loud voice, "You're having an affair with him, aren't you! I saw the way you looked at him!" Of course, the man was a stranger, but in her husband's mind, there was infidelity. The wife, taken completely by surprise, responded impulsively in a very offended manner: "Of course I'm not having an affair with him. How could you even suggest such a thing?" Both she and her husband were angry at this point, and she wasn't sure what to do.

After this incident, I met with the wife and had her consider how the AAR approach might be applied to the situation if it were to happen again. Here was my advice. Stop where the situation occurs, gently put

FIBLETS

There are times as a care partner when it is easier not to tell the truth. In the world of dementia care partnering, these are called **fiblets**, and some people are more comfortable with them than others. A fiblet may be for your loved one's benefit. Let's say they need to go to the doctor for a check-up, something they usually resist. You might say, "Let's go out to lunch today" and just happen to stop at the doctor along the way. Fiblets may be for your benefit, too. If your loved one is velcroed at the hip and you need some down time, you could say, "I'll be gone the next few hours running errands" when really you're on your way to a workout or coffee with a close friend, thus avoiding the potential for words of conflict or confusion if you were to be truthful.

your hand on his, look him in the eye, and calmly say, "Honey, I'm not having an affair with that man. I don't even know him." This statement acknowledges the situation rather than just ignoring it, which is what I find most care partners do when they're not sure how to respond. But ignoring doesn't bring any resolution to the situation and may even escalate it.

Then share a comforting statement, something like, "You and I are married. See our wedding ring? You gave this to me over 60 years ago. I wear it for everyone to see because I love you and only you." These words affirm their relationship. You can also add words of praise. A simple compliment such as, "You have been the best husband a wife could have" is both affirming and reassuring.

Lastly, she could then say, "Let's go to the ice cream aisle and pick one of our favorite flavors to bring home and share for dessert tonight." This is a statement of redirection, shifting his thoughts to something more positive and pleasant, away from the inciting situation.

Like patience, AAR is something you can use effectively across a broad range of challenging situations, and it's also a skill you can improve with practice. If your loved one's cognitive function is severely impaired, or they have limited insight, the AAR strategy can be difficult to use successfully.

KEEP IT SHORT, SIMPLE, AND SAFE

Benjamin Franklin once wrote, "An ounce of prevention is worth a pound of cure." This proverb is good advice for you as a dementia care partner, too.

Care partners often ask me if I think their loved ones with dementia will be able to handle a certain situation, like going out to eat or on an overnight trip. A simple yet effective way to manage such situations is to have realistic expectations for what your loved one can do and try to prevent them from getting too tired, emotional, and/or overwhelmed. Strive to keep the activity short, simple, and safe, hence the "keep it short, simple, and safe" principle, or KISSS.

One activity many of us enjoy is going out to restaurants, yet the whole restaurant experience can present a series of challenges. For example, if your favorite restaurant has limited handicapped accessibility, formal dress and etiquette, and an extensive menu, it might be difficult to make this particular restaurant experience KISSS-friendly for your loved one with dementia.

A better choice might be a more casual restaurant that's easier to navigate, has a family-friendly restroom, and provides the freedom to interact more freely with your loved one without worry, for example if they are messy when eating. You yourself can also help simplify the experience by offering your loved one two entrée choices in lieu of the entire menu, or even order for them. As a person's dementia gets progressively worse, their ability to make choices diminishes.

Another common situation is whether or not to travel or vacation with your loved one. People with dementia tend to like routine, not only what they do but where they do it. Being away from home for multiple days requires some advanced planning. If you're uncertain how your loved one will do, think about the KISSS principle when planning. Try just an overnight trip not too far away at first, with familiar friends or family members at your destination as well as short, simple activities. Set realistic expectations that are achievable, be prepared to go home early if the trip doesn't work out well, and realize that there will come a point in time when overnight travel will no longer be possible.

RELATIONSHIP BUILDING WITH THE FIVE LOVE LANGUAGES
When your loved one's behavior changes due to attachment loss and separation distress, and they are feeling unsafe, insecure, and unloved, one approach I recommend to help them feel safe, secure, and loved again is called the five love languages. These are ways to communicate emotional love to another person based on the book *The 5 Love Languages: The Secret to Love That Lasts,* by pastor and marriage counselor Dr. Gary Chapman.

Dr. Chapman says **the deepest emotional need we have as human**

beings is to love and be loved. As such, life's deepest meaning is found in relationships. And, as a consequence, life's deepest pain is found in fractured relationships. The love languages concept uses the metaphor of literal languages to help you and those you are in relationship with understand which language you prefer to be loved with.

According to Chapman, there are five unique love languages:

• *Words of affirmation*: The unsolicited compliments and words of kindness and appreciation you receive from others, such as "I love you" and "You're doing a great job."

• *Quality time*: Time spent with someone in which you receive their full, undivided attention.

• *Gifts*: Gifts that are given to you as visible symbols of love, whether they are purchased, made by hand, or even found.

• *Acts of service*: Meaningful, helpful acts performed by someone else to lighten your load.

• *Physical touch*: The touch of another that conveys their presence, love, and appreciation for you.

Dr. Chapman says that for your relationships to be successful—for both you and the other person to feel loved—you must each communicate love to your partner in their primary love language, and each of you must give one hundred percent effort toward loving one another.

Our natural tendency is to love others using our own language—the one that makes us feel loved—instead of speaking the other person's language—the one that makes them feel loved. Even when both people go to great lengths to express love to the other, if they are each speaking in their own love language instead of the other person's, neither of them will feel sufficiently loved.

For example, if your primary love language is gifts, giving your loved one flowers may not make them feel loved if their primary love language is physical touch. Rather, you should hug them! Similarly, if they hug you, the physical affection might not convey love as much as the gift of a card, especially a handmade card that says, "I love you."

You can identify which of the five love languages is your primary language, and how the others rank (many of us have a primary and a secondary love language), by taking the free love language quiz at www.5lovelanguages.com. You can have your loved one with mild cognitive impairment or early-stage dementia do the same, perhaps with your help. If they are unable to take the quiz, the text in the box below suggests some alternative ways to assess their primary love language.

FIGURING OUT YOUR LOVED ONE'S PRIMARY LOVE LANGUAGE

If your loved one can't or won't complete the love languages quiz, another way to determine their primary or preferred love language is by asking yourself the following three questions about them. Before they developed mild cognitive impairment or dementia:

1. How did your loved one naturally or most often express love to you?

2. What did your loved one complain about that you didn't do to express your love or appreciation for them?

3. What did your loved one request of you to make them feel more loved or appreciated?

For questions 1 and 3, was it affirming words, quality time, gifts, acts of service, and/or physical touch? For question 2, was it the lack of one or more of these five love languages? Thinking back to specific memories will help you identify their primary and secondary love languages. If it helps, discuss your thoughts with someone else who has or had a close relationship with the person with dementia.

What is (are) your primary love language(s), and how do the others rank? Please describe. Are you surprised by your results? Please explain.

_____

_____

_____

_____

_____

What is (are) your loved one's primary love language(s), and how do the others rank? Please describe. Are you surprised by their results? Please explain.

_____

_____

_____

_____

_____

In Rebecca's nine-year journey with Alzheimer's, my daughters and I were able to maintain a very meaningful degree of **emotional intimacy** with her despite progressive memory and cognitive loss. The five love languages framework provided us with a simple yet effective toolkit to help us love Rebecca, and it can help you, too. However, there are three important things to remember when applying the five love languages to relationships in the setting of dementia.

First, **the deep human need for love does not disappear with a diagnosis of dementia.** It remains a part of the person with the disease for as long they live. Even though memories fade, other cognitive functions decline, and personality changes, the ability to receive emotional love and **the feeling of being loved persists through all the stages of dementia to the very end.**

40 WAYS TO SHOW SOMEONE WITH DEMENTIA YOU LOVE THEM

Here are 40 ways you can show love to someone with dementia based on the five love languages. Keep in mind that the further along a person is in their disease, the simpler your expressions of love must be.

WORDS OF AFFIRMATION

- Tell them, "I love you."

- Answer each repeated question as if it were being asked for the first time.

- Talk to them (even if they can't talk back)—about their life growing up, marriage, children, grandchildren, work, and hobbies.

- Tell them they look handsome/ beautiful (even if it's the same outfit they wore yesterday and it's dirty).

- Help them write a card or letter and sign it.

- Sing them to sleep.

- Tell them that you have taken care of everything.

- Tell them you are proud of all the things they have accomplished in life.

- Brag about them to others while they are present.

QUALITY TIME

- Read to them or, if they can, have them read to you or a grandchild.

- Reminisce about old times and important events of history as you look at a photo album or family movies.

- Watch a favorite movie over and over.

- Go for a ride in the car.

- Bake some cookies together.

- Laugh and giggle—they may join in.

- Color in a coloring book or do a puzzle with them.

- Tell stories.

RECEIVING GIFTS

- Give them a piece of chocolate, an ice cream cone, a chocolate chip cookie, or whatever they love.

- Give them a surprise package to open.

- Send a card to them in the mail.

- Give them an iPod loaded with music from their teen and young adult years.

- Bring them a coloring book with some markers or crayons.

- Be generous with the gift of your time.

ACTS OF SERVICE

- Look them in the eye when they speak to you, no matter what they say or how they say it.
- Include them in conversations (rather than talk about them as if they are not present).
- Let them help in the kitchen, around the house, wherever and whenever they want to contribute (remember the principle of "do with, not for").
- Help them groom (makeup, shave, comb hair, pick out clothing).
- Advocate for them.
- Smile at them as you come and go.
- Simplify their choices (for example, reduce menu options in a restaurant or clothing possibilities to just two options)
- Use the Acknowledge, Affirm, and Redirect (AAR) strategy when they experience a behavior change that is challenging to you.
- Let them be right.

PHYSICAL TOUCH

- Hold hands and take a walk together if they're able.
- Give a hug (and kiss, if appropriate).
- Sit close by or hold them if they're afraid, angry, or agitated.
- Rub their feet or their back or gently stroke their cheek.
- Let them hold a baby, puppy, or doll.
- File and/or put polish on their fingernails and toenails.
- Dance or move to music with them.
- Massage their hands and arms with lotion.

Excerpted and modified with permission from *Keeping Love Alive as Memories Fade: The 5 Love Languages and the Alzheimer's Journey*

Second, **the depth and breadth of the connection lies almost entirely in your hands as care partner,** and this is one of the greatest challenges you will face on the journey.

Third, **how you use the five love languages to communicate emotional love should change as the disease progresses**. In the mild cognitive impairment or early stage, speak their primary love language. However, in the middle and especially the late stage, use all five love languages to show your love for them.

With these three things in mind, and knowledge of the five love languages, you can maintain a meaningful relationship, even share relational intimacy, with your loved one with dementia, but it is going to require intentional and sacrificial effort on your part. As care partner, you will have to make repeated efforts—what my *Keeping Love Alive* coauthor Deborah Barr described as **"love by choice" decisions**—that exceed what is required of you in any of your relationships that are unaffected by dementia.

What are some of the "love by choice" decisions you have already made as care partner to your loved one with dementia?

_____

_____

_____

_____

_____

_____

The notion of love by choice decisions, and the use of the five love languages by a dementia care partner, is illustrated in the story of Pastor Ellen. She came to see me for a counseling visit that I will never forget!

Why Should I Visit?

As an assistant pastor of a large church, Pastor Ellen visits hospitalized, nursing-home, and shut-in parishioners, including older adults and those with dementia.

"Ed," she said to me one day, "I have to confess, there is one lady I see who is in a nursing home with late-stage Alzheimer's. When I visit, she doesn't acknowledge my presence. After five minutes sitting by her bed, I get fidgety, check my phone for e-mails and voicemails, then get up and leave, usually without interacting with her in any way."

Pastor Ellen's story, perhaps surprising for a member of the clergy, is all too common. Family members, particularly teens, will say, "If Grandpa doesn't even remember who I am, why should I go visit him?"

After I talked through the situation with Pastor Ellen, she realized that unlike most hospital or home visits, in which she could dialogue with the person she was visiting, she and the nursing-home resident were on different levels as far as their ability to contribute to the relationship. In other words, the person with dementia didn't have anything she could actively contribute to the conversation. We discussed the giving and sacrificial nature of her role in this setting, and I made the following suggestions to Pastor Ellen for her next visit to with this person.

"Plan to spend 30 minutes with her (quality time). Bring a small gift, maybe a single red rose in a small vase (gift). When you enter the room, greet her out loud, tell her you're glad to see her (words of affirmation), put the rose on her bedside table, and sit by her. Place a hand on her shoulder or elbow (physical touch), perhaps telling her what a beautiful day it is, or asking her how she's been. Read to her from your Bible, perhaps a favorite psalm or proverb, and/or sing a hymn (more words of affirmation). If she opens her eyes, ask about her family, or share some news from the church or a current event that might be of interest to her. Whether or not she responds, pray for her (act of service). The time will pass faster than you realize."

I'm sure you noticed that my advice to Pastor Ellen included easy ways she could reach out to her parishioner with dementia using all five love languages in a short visit. With your loved one, just being mindful of the five love languages whenever you are with them provides an opportunity to try one or more languages to intentionally connect on an emotional level and help them feel the love.

REMINISCENCE APPROACHES

If your loved one is experiencing separation distress due to attachment loss, it may be helpful to try and strengthen their attachment bonds through **reminiscence approaches**, or simply put, to bring their past (people, places, and events) into the present. Because they help the person with dementia feel more grounded and connected to something familiar, reminiscence approaches like the ones described next may reduce the separation-distress-related behaviors we talked about at the beginning of this lesson.

First, encourage your loved one to **talk about their past**, which they will be much more likely to successfully remember and discuss than the present. The list of topics to prompt them are endless—stories of their family growing up, when they were in school, marriage and raising family, military service, occupations, places lived or traveled to, interesting life experiences, and the like. Photographs or other familiar items from the past may be useful props to facilitate the discussion. You can even be creative by triggering memories through smell (a whiff of a favorite cologne or perfume) and taste (a favorite childhood candy).

Music is another incredible tool that facilitates reminiscence. Many of us find joy and comfort in music we listened to in the past, especially during our adolescence and young adulthood. Think about the music you tend to listen to now; it's often from this period of time. Also, music that is spiritual in nature can be especially joyful and comforting, like favorite hymns.

For the person with dementia, music can help improve mood, reduce stress and agitation, encourage social interaction, help memory, and even encourage movement, especially when music is combined with dance. For a wonderful example of the benefits of music, watch the story of Henry on YouTube (go to www.youtube.com and search "Henry Alive Inside"), a long-term nursing-home resident with late-stage dementia who "comes alive" when he's connected to an iPod with music from his past (part of the *Alive Inside* documentary, www.aliveinside.us).

Other things that may help your loved one feel more safe and secure include the love of a companion animal, like a dog or cat, a baby doll or stuffed animal like a teddy bear, or some other inanimate object. During Rebecca's agitated phase, when she wanted to "go home," she had two things that comforted and calmed her, things she clung to like security blankets. One was her "clothy," a small piece of fabric from her childhood blanket given by a favorite aunt, and the other was a swimming suit, which connected her to the security of her past because she was a competitive swimmer in high school.

A rocking chair can also be calming as it may remind your loved one of an earlier time in their life when an important care figure, such as mom or grandma, rocked and sang to them or rocked them to sleep.

Reminiscence approaches, along with patience, AAR, KISSS, and the five love languages, can be helpful ways for you as care partner to respond to the common changes in your loved one's behavior described in this lesson, as well as the even more challenging behaviors we will cover in Lesson Seven. These tactics will make the dementia journey a little easier and more pleasant for both you and the person with dementia. This is a wonderful reason to use them! But more than that—they will help your loved one continue to feel, as much as possible, safe, secure, cared for, and loved. They will help keep your love for one another alive.

And as the disease progresses and the responsibilities of loving fall increasingly on your shoulders alone, they will help you feel assured that you continued to love as well and as deeply as you could, right till the end.

A FINAL REFLECTION AND LOOKING AHEAD

This was another lesson with lots of information and practical tips to help you address Central Need 3 of dementia care partners, Adapt to Changing Relationships.

What is the one thing we reviewed in this lesson that stands out the most to you?

_____

_____

_____

_____

_____

As you studied this lesson, you may have experienced some feelings of grief and loss as a result of the emotional distance between you and your loved one due to changing relationships. This topic will be the focus of Lesson 5: Grief and Loss on the Journey. You'll learn about the nature of grief, which is what you think and feel on the inside in response to loss, and mourning, the outward expression of your grief, and why they are both necessary parts of your caregiving journey that address Central Need 4—Grieve your losses.

Once again, repeat the Mindfulness Moment from earlier in the lesson as a way to help prepare for your next support-group meeting or self-study lesson.

Coping With Grief and Loss

Being a dementia care partner might be one of the loneliest and most isolating experiences of your life.

Feeling **desolate**—that no one else can (or wants to) understand what you are going through—is common. There is also the sense of a **shrinking world** as the disease progresses through its stages. For one, the person with dementia becomes less aware of and interested in the world around them, including people, places, and things. Plus, because of this disinterest as well as the many challenges that come with taking the person with dementia on errands or visits outside of the home, care partners often become literally bound by the walls of their home. In addition, relationships among family members and friends change. People with whom you and your loved one were once close may become more distant or even fade away. These are just some of the many losses you and your loved one with dementia are facing on the journey, and with these losses you will naturally grieve.

> *"One of the hardest things you will ever have to do is grieve the loss of a person who is still alive."*
>
> — Jeannette Walls

Describe the feelings of isolation, or of a shrinking world, that you have experienced so far as a care partner. Who among family and friends has faded away or is uninvolved (or minimally involved) in the dementia journey you're on with your loved one? Please share.

_____

_____

_____

_____

_____

_____

Over the last seven years, I have been privileged to hear hundreds of stories from care partners in counseling sessions and support groups. Some stories stand out because of what people taught me or from things I learned when they shared their experiences. When it comes to understanding the grief and loss endured by dementia care partners, Katie and Jack's story comes to mind.

Missing More Than Class

Katie and Jack were an amazing couple. He was a university professor with three master's degrees and a Ph.D. Jack had taught at the undergraduate and graduate levels in two different areas of study. For a time he was the university president's right-hand man, making most of the operational day-to-day decisions.

Katie was a successful financial planner. They lived busy parallel lives with thriving careers as they raised five children together.

The concern for dementia started when Jack, in his mid-60s, began teaching the same lesson two or three times in a row. He also came to class on the wrong day or time, and on several occasions failed to show up for class at all. He was diagnosed with early-stage Alzheimer's, but his disease progressed rapidly. Within a couple of years, he'd completely lost his ability to remember anything, was disoriented to the point that he no longer knew or cared about the day or date, and had a frustrating apathy that led him to sit in a chair from morning to night and read the same book over and over, excluding Katie and their children and grandchildren from his life.

Exasperated and lonely, with tears in her eyes, Katie said, "There isn't a single aspect of our relationship, or for that matter of our life as a family, that dementia hasn't stolen from us. I'm an Alzheimer's widow." Not long after, feeling trapped since she couldn't leave Jack safely home alone, Katie transitioned him to a memory-care unit in the retirement community where they lived.

Do you relate to Jack and Katie's story? What thoughts and emotions are you experiencing right now? Please describe.

_____

_____

_____

_____

_____

Jack and Katie's story, especially the sad, heartfelt words she expressed in the support group, is consistent with what grief experts say about the grief and loss associated with dementia care partnering: it is indistinguishable from that experienced with the physical death of a loved one.

In this lesson, we will review grief, mourning, and the kinds of losses care partners of loved ones with Alzheimer's or another form of dementia experience, including family grief and loss. But first, let's pause for a Mindfulness Moment.

MINDFULNESS MOMENT

The introduction to this lesson has forced you to think about the loneliness and isolation—as well as other losses—you are probably experiencing as a result of your loved one's dementia journey. In the process of self-reflection, you may be experiencing some strong emotions about this. This is a good opportunity to turn all of your awareness and attention on the present moment, tuning out worries of the past and future, for a stress-reducing Mindfulness Moment. I hope you can experience a "brain break" as you do this, calmly, nonjudgmentally, and compassionately accepting your current thoughts, emotions, and body sensations without feeling as though you need to change them. So, let's begin the short breathing exercise that frames the Mindfulness Moment.

1. Sit in a comfortable chair, put both feet on the floor (or any other comfortable position), clasp your hands over the middle of your belly, and then close your eyes (if desired).

2. Scan your muscles from head to toe and intentionally relax them. Unclench your teeth, let your shoulders sag, and relax your buttock and leg muscles.

3. Take in a slow, deep breath through your nose (count "one one-thousand, two one-thousand, three one-thousand" to yourself as you do so), then slowly exhale through your mouth to the same count, feeling the rise and fall of your belly. Do a total of ten slow, deep breaths like this. Focus solely on the gentle flow of your breath, in and out. Each time you exhale, consciously blow out any negative emotions and stress you're feeling.

4. After the tenth breath, slowly open your eyes.

WHAT IS CARE-PARTNER GRIEF?

In this section, I want to familiarize you with the definition of some basic words that will help you understand the grief and loss experiences that occur when caring for a loved one with dementia.

They are adapted from the writings of Dr. Alan Wolfelt, a world-renowned grief counselor, educator, and author of numerous books, including *Healing Your Grieving Heart When Someone You Care About Has Alzheimer's: 100 Practical Ideas for Families, Friends, and Caregivers.*

DEFINITIONS OF GRIEF AND MOURNING

Grief refers to the internal thoughts and feelings you have related to your loved one's diagnosis of dementia, your role as care partner, and the journey you both are on with the disease. Your grief is everything you think and feel about the experience. The disbelief you may have had about your family member's dementia diagnosis—that's grief. The anger and sadness you may feel because the disease is incurable and terminal— that's grief too. And when you physically hurt on the inside because you're so worried about how you're going to meet the needs of everyone who depend on you—that's also grief.

Though it's painful and difficult, grief is normal and natural. It's the result of having loved, which is life's greatest gift.

There are two grief-related experiences that are important to mention here: anticipatory grief and ambiguous loss.

Anticipatory grief refers to the awareness that your loved one has a progressive, incurable disease, so at some level you are anticipating their progressive cognitive and physical decline as well as their eventual death and the grief associated with it. In other words, you are both grieving the losses you are already experiencing, and you are anticipating more grief to come.

Ambiguous loss, on the other hand, is the experience of having your loved one physically present yet absent in mind and perhaps spirit. For example, if and when your loved one has lost your identity and no longer knows you as husband or wife, son or daughter, brother or sister, relative or friend, the loss feels ambiguous. They're right in front of you, yet they have no idea who you are and how your lives are connected. It is a **paradox**, which occurs when two things that seem to be in conflict

A TEARFUL GOOD NIGHT

The dementia journey is full of anticipatory grief, ambiguous loss, and paradoxes. Here's a story that hit close to home.

My middle daughter Leah's guitar music and singing were a great comfort to her mom over the years of her journey with Alzheimer's disease. Leah's music was especially effective at calming Rebecca when she was agitated. One particularly challenging evening, when it seemed nothing would settle Rebecca, Leah offered to put her mom to bed and sing her to sleep. It worked, but Leah emerged from the room in tears. Rebecca had told her, "I have a daughter who looks just like you and she sings beautifully just like you do." This story is a heartbreaking example of ambiguous loss.

with one another, that both can't be simultaneously true, actually are both true. (For example, a daughter caring for her mom with dementia as well as her spouse and children might say, "I need to spend more time caring for my mom" as well as "I need to spend more time with my family." This is a paradox).

While grief is the inward experience of your losses, **mourning** is the outward expression of your grief. It's how you show what you're thinking and feeling on the inside, or as Dr. Wolfelt says, it's "grief inside out." When you talk to a trusted family member or friend about the stress of being a care partner—that's mourning. The writing you've been doing for this workbook or in your personal journal—that's mourning, too. If you scream at God or punch the wall in anger—that's also mourning.

While grief usually comes naturally, you will have to make an intentional effort to mourn. That's why telling your story is the first central need of dementia care partners. It's an act of mourning essential to your well-being. Other forms of mourning are also necessary. If you don't express your grief, you will end up suffering even more. People who keep their grief inside often find themselves struggling with stress-related challenges, depression, anxiety, substance abuse, and other life-sapping issues. A good rule of thumb: If something is weighing on or bothering you, that means you need to share it outside of yourself.

How are you grieving your loved one's illness? What are some of the most pressing thoughts and feelings you have on the inside right now? Please share.

_____

_____

_____

_____

Have you experienced anticipatory grief? Do you think about future losses, such as your loved one not knowing you, or their death from dementia? Please share.

_____

_____

_____

_____

Have you experienced a sense of ambiguous loss, that your loved one is alive but aspects of them are gone? Please share.

_____

_____

_____

_____

How are you mourning your loved one's illness? What have been some of the outward expressions of your grief? Please share.

_____

_____

_____

_____

_____

A final note on grief and mourning: the society we live in is, in general, grief-avoidant. We don't like to acknowledge or deal with pain and suffering or death and dying. Dementia and the grief of dementia tend to be hidden, marginalized, or passed-over, just as the grief that follows loss through death. As a care partner, you're expected to add in your caregiving duties and the associated mental stress as if they were just another task on your to-do list. This societal attitude makes it harder for you to acknowledge and embrace your own grief (again, what you're feeling on the inside), and it makes mourning (your essential outward expression of grief) even more difficult

You've probably already noticed that some family members and friends you thought would be there for you have not been. They are likely grief-avoidant. Maybe you've experienced somebody changing the subject when you try to talk about the challenges you face as a dementia care partner. They are probably mourning-avoidant. Keeping this in mind might help you understand why others respond to you the way that they do.

WHAT KINDS OF LOSSES DO CARE PARTNERS EXPERIENCE?

In this section I would like to describe the different kinds of loss that dementia care partners experience. Broadly speaking, they are in three areas: personal losses, relationship losses, and loss of peace of mind. Let's explore and reflect on each of these.

PERSONAL LOSSES

As a care partner, you will experience many personal losses in order to provide care for your loved one with dementia, such as:

- Your **personal time and freedom**—the autonomy to do what you want to do, when you want to do it.

- Your **personal health**—the ability to meet your own medical and mental-health needs, including basic necessities such as eating and sleeping.

- Your **occupation**—the ability to pursue or maintain your vocation as well as the satisfaction and income you get from working, or if you're retired or don't have a job, to participate in volunteer activities.

- Your **social activities and recreation**—the ability to spend time with family, friends, and coworkers and enjoy recreational activities or hobbies.

Painted Into a Corner

Mia and Jordan, a couple in their early 80s, had been married for nearly 30 years, a second marriage for both. Prior to retirement, both had busy professional lives and were very independent people.

CARE-PARTNER HARD REALITIES

The Alzheimer's Association (www. alz.org) offers some startling statistics about dementia care partners in the realm of personal sacrifice and burden. There are 16 million care partners, a third of whom are spouses, and two-thirds of whom are adult children. Two-thirds are women, and one-third are daughters. A quarter of dementia care partners are caring for both a parent and children under 18 years old. And family and other unpaid care partners provide 18.5 billion hours of unpaid care valued at $234 million dollars per year, which "values" the care at about $13 per hour. The consequence: those caring for a loved one with dementia have more physical, emotional, and financial challenges.

Mia was an artist, a painter who created impressionistic works in the spirit of Monet and Degas. She was quite passionate about painting, dividing her time between creating paintings (for her own pleasure and to sell), teaching painting to students, and learning from other painters, traveling domestically and abroad to do so. In retirement, Jordan helped Mia by framing her paintings and assisting her in the business aspects of showing and selling her work in galleries and online.

Then Alzheimer's struck Jordan. Early on, he was still able to help Mia. It just took longer. But as time went on, Jordan became more dependent on Mia. Two things occurred that motivated Mia's first counseling visit to me: Jordan lost his ability to drive, and he had become velcroed at the hip to her, wanting to be with her 24/7. Mia was torn. She loved Jordan and wanted the best for him, but she had lost her independence, and the other passion of her life, painting, was being squeezed out. Tearful, tired, and torn, Mia looked at me and said, "I'm losing my life. Is it wrong for me to want to paint?" Of course, I told her it was not wrong to want to paint. In fact, it was important that she continued painting. But in the absence of getting some caregiving help, she would be unable to do so. By bringing in a paid caregiver several afternoons a week, Mia was able to eke out some time in her studio to teach and paint.

Do you identify with Mia's plight? What are some of the personal losses you have experienced as a care partner, such as time and freedom, health, occupation, and social/recreational activities? Please describe.

_____

_____

_____

_____

_____

RELATIONSHIP LOSSES

As a care partner, you will experience an ongoing and progressive loss of the relationship with your loved one with dementia. The nature of the loss depends on the nature of your relationship. The loss felt by a spouse or partner is different than the loss an adult child or sibling will experience, for example. Often, relationship losses are accompanied by a yearning for things to be as they once were.

Relationship losses include the:

- Loss of the **twosome** – the identity you had as two people together in a relationship, of being partners or parent-and-child, helpers, friends, and perhaps lovers, sharing a life. When dementia disrupts your twosome, it changes the individual roles and responsibilities you had in your relationship as well as those things you did together.

- Loss of **intimacy** – the emotional intimacy you shared, and for couples, your sexual intimacy.

- Loss of a **future** together – for couples, the plans and dreams you had for the life you would experience together, and for adult children, the lost relationship with mom or dad as well as your children not having a grandma or grandpa.

A NOTE ON SEXUAL INTIMACY

In the dementia journey, there are many factors that contribute to loss of sexual intimacy. There may be a loss of desire for sex by the person with dementia, their care partner, or both. The person with dementia may no longer remember the couple's bedroom routine or even recognize their partner. They may have the delusional belief that their partner is being unfaithful. Hygiene issues can also be a barrier. No matter the cause(s), sleeping apart and loss of sexual intimacy are often among the most painful losses a care partner can experience.

An Abrupt Ending

Preston and Mary were a longtime married couple who had enjoyed an active sex life throughout their marriage, extending into their senior years. In her mid-70s, Mary had a stroke that left her with some weakness on the left side of her body and some progressive problems with short-term memory and multitasking ability. Despite this, she and Preston adjusted and continued to enjoy intimate relations. Sadly, Mary's memory loss worsened, and she began to have times when she didn't recognize Preston, especially in the late afternoons and evenings. One night, after their typical foreplay, Preston and Mary were about to have intercourse when in the moment, she lost recognition of him and abruptly began screaming, "Stop, stop, you're raping me!" Preston was devastated by Mary's perception that he was violating her. He was able to help her get into nightclothes, reassure and calm her, but that encounter ended their sex life.

Describe the relationship losses you have experienced as a care partner. These may include loss of your identity as a twosome, intimacy, and a future together. Please share.

_____

_____

_____

_____

_____

_____

LOSS OF PEACE OF MIND

As a care partner to someone with dementia, you may constantly worry, and sometimes the worry can be overwhelming. It begins with diagnosis and continues throughout the stages of dementia. To worry is to be anxious about things that have already happened that you can't change, that are happening in the present, and that may or will happen in the future as the journey unfolds.

The ongoing worries of caregiving cause a **loss of peace of mind**. What if errand-running goes badly tomorrow? Was that noise my loved one with dementia getting up and opening the door? What will the test results show? How will the bills get paid this month? What will the holidays be like this year? For dementia care partners, these and a million other worries erode peace of mind and multiply stress.

Perhaps the greatest future worry that both spouses and adult-child care partners have relates to placing their loved one in a care facility. Often, husbands, wives, sons, and daughters alike have promised, "I'll never put you in a nursing home"—a promise that cannot always be honored (Lesson Seven will focus on this difficult issue).

When a loved one's care situation requires them to transition to memory-care or a nursing home, the response of spousal and adult-child care partners is often different. I have observed that spouses typically feel a much greater sense of guilt and regret, which increases their stress, whereas adult children are more likely to feel some relief and actually have less stress. The guilt you may experience as a decision-making care partner can also be accompanied by your own mood changes, including depression and anxiety (we'll talk about this in the next lesson too). Here's one family's story on this topic.

Not on the Same Page

The Douglas family was made up of Ted and Bonita and their three adult children, who ranged in age from mid-30s to early 40s. Ted had Lewy body dementia. About five years into his journey with this disease, Ted was showing all its challenging symptoms—cognitive loss (memory, multitasking, and language difficulties), those relating to Parkinson's (tremor, inability to walk, stiff muscles), sleep and behavior changes (terrorizing nightmares, delusions and hallucinations), and both bladder- and bowel-control problems. Despite the help of a paid caregiver (none of the adult children were local), the emotional and physical strain of caring for Ted became overwhelming for Bonita.

The situation came to a head when Ted was hospitalized for a urinary-tract infection. When it came time for discharge planning, the kids came in from out of town to support their mom, but it became apparent that they and Bonita had different ideas about where Ted would go. They wanted him to go to a facility, to reduce the burden of care for their mom. One of the adult daughters said, "Mom, we can't lose you, too; we'll be orphans." Bonita, on the other hand, felt immense guilt about putting Ted into a facility. "I just can't do that to him. I could never live with myself," she told them.

Ultimately, finances drove the decision. Bonita would have needed two paid caregivers 24/7 to adequately care for Ted's basic activities of daily living in their home. At $20 per hour per person, this represented one-quarter million dollars per year! A memory-care residential facility in the area was half that cost, and that is where Ted went. The kids were relieved by the decision, but even with the excellent care Ted received, Bonita maintained a sense of guilt for the four months that Ted lived before losing his battle with dementia.

Describe some of the ongoing worries of caregiving that affect your peace of mind. Please share.

_____

_____

_____

_____

_____

_____

FAMILY GRIEF AND LOSS

Ultimately, it was the impact of Rebecca's journey with Alzheimer's disease on our family, and the lack of resources available to help us, that compelled me to change careers from oncologist to dementia-focused mental-health counselor. Most of this lesson has focused on the grief and loss you are experiencing as a care partner. We'll now switch gears and examine how dementia affects families.

THE FAMILY IMPACT OF DEMENTIA

It took the wisdom of three grieving young women, my daughters, to help me understand that dementia impacts the entire family and not just the person with the diagnosis and their primary care partner.

In the first half of Rebecca's nine-year journey with Alzheimer's disease, I tried to carry the entire burden of being her primary care partner as well as protect the girls from caregiving responsibilities and the overwhelming sense of loss that I had with her dementia journey and anticipated death. I grieved deeply but did not mourn. I later realized this was a mistake.

Several years before Rebecca lost our identities and no longer recognized us as husband and daughters, we traveled to Florida to attend the wedding of a close relative. It was difficult on Rebecca to travel on an airplane and sleep in a hotel, as it took her out of her daily routine, which was familiar and comfortable to her. The girls, who were all in their 20s, were in the room across from Rebecca's and mine. After getting her tucked in bed one night, mentally and physically exhausted, I sat outside the room, head in hands, for five minutes' peace before going to bed myself.

Erin, Leah, and Carrie saw me there and sat down beside and across from me. They spoke the same message. "Dad, you can't do this by yourself. Mom's Alzheimer's affects us as much as it affects you. We're hurting like you are. We miss her, maybe in different ways than you do, but we miss her just the same. We want to help you but don't know how. You have to tell us what you need. We're worried about your health. There is one thing for sure, we can't lose you too. We just can't."

We then had a good cry together, and afterward, we talked and listened to one another, sharing our feelings of grief and loss about Rebecca's journey. That incident of healthy shared grief and mourning completely changed our family dynamics. Instead of trying to protect the girls from the reality of their mom's disease, I began to turn to them as confidants. I involved all three of them in decisions related to Rebecca, and they took turns coming home to help when I went away for a work-related conference or a weekend off. And when the end of the journey came, as hard as it was, we were all on the same page about carrying out Rebecca's end-of-life wishes,

Families as a whole, sometimes called the family system, **can grieve, mourn, and experience both anticipatory grief and ambiguous loss**. They can experience the three kinds of losses I described earlier — personal losses, relationship losses, and loss of peace of mind. Families can be drawn together during a dementia journey, or they can become conflicted and even torn apart. With this in mind, let's talk just a bit about family conflict.

FAMILY CONFLICT AND CONFLICT RESOLUTION

There is no such thing as a conflict-free family. The bigger the family, the more relationships there are within the family system, and the greater the chance for family conflict. When a family is under stress, the likelihood of conflict increases. Having counseled many families on the dementia journey over the last eight years, I can say with confidence that families who openly communicate with one another on the dementia journey can minimize conflict, reduce individual and family stress, and provide better care for the family member who has dementia.

In a typical family, there is one person who serves as primary care partner, usually the spouse, or if the parent with dementia is single, divorced, or a widow or widower, one of the adult children. When there are multiple adult children, usually there is one who is most involved, whereas the others, for whatever reason(s), are less involved. Sometimes there is bitterness or resentment about the inequality of caregiving roles and responsibilities. If this is the case, the family conflict must be dealt with openly and honestly because of the negative impact it can have on the family system as a whole as well as the person with dementia.

The ideal way to manage family conflict related to a loved one's dementia diagnosis and care is a family meeting. It's helpful to have a meeting leader or mediator, perhaps a medical and/or mental-health professional to provide information and guidance. A family member, such as the unaffected spouse or eldest child, can also lead or mediate. As with any relationship conflict, family challenges that occur in the setting of dementia are usually stressful, but they also can be, and often are in my experience, occasions for positive growth among individuals within the family and the family in its entirety. During Rebecca's journey with Alzheimer's, the girls and I had periodic family meetings, either in person or via Skype or conference call, sometimes in conjunction with her medical doctor.

Describe the impact your loved one's journey with dementia has had on your family so far. Has your family experienced conflict over the care of the person who has dementia? Please share.

_____

_____

_____

_____

_____

_____

Describe an instance where your family resolved a dementia-related challenge in a positive way. If you're thinking instead of an incident that wasn't resolved positively, how might the process have been different? Please share.

_____

_____

_____

_____

_____

_____

THE SANDWICH GENERATION

Jennifer is part of what is now referred to as "the sandwich generation"— the Baby Boomers, Gen Xers, and Millennials who find themselves caring for aging or ill parents as well as their own families. By the way, people who care for grandparents, parents, *and* children at the same time are humorously referred to as "club sandwichers." According to the Pew Research Center, just over one of every eight Americans aged 40 to 60 is both raising a child and caring for a parent.

A Family United

Jennifer was the mother of three upper-elementary and middle-school-aged children. She also worked full-time and was going to graduate school part-time at night to advance her career. When her widowed mom was diagnosed with behavioral variant frontotemporal dementia, Jennifer and her husband decided they would have her move in with them.

Jennifer was a great organizer. She hired several paid caregivers to be with her mom during the weekdays, then between her husband and kids, they were able to cover evenings and weekends. To help reduce her own stress, Jennifer came for individual counseling every couple of months.

She was intentional about talking with her husband about the challenges of having her mom in their home. She also went on regular dates with him, and they had family outings with the kids, without the grandmother, to maintain their family identity. Though Jennifer did not have a moment of spare time or margin in her life, being able to care for her mom in her home meant the world to her.

A FINAL REFLECTION AND LOOKING AHEAD

This was another weighty lesson that focused on the magnitude of the grief and loss associated with your and your loved one's journey with dementia and the importance of both grieving and mourning these losses—which is Central Need 4 of dementia care partners. Before describing what you'll be studying in the next lesson, let's take a moment for some journaling.

What is the one thing you learned from the lesson on grief and loss that stands out the most?

_____

_____

_____

_____

_____

You will now be transitioning to Lesson 6: Stress and Self-Care, which encompasses two important central needs, Central Need 5—Take care of yourself, and Central Need 6—Ask for and accept help from others. You'll learn about three big challenges to your health—depression, anxiety, and stress—as well as the elements of a wellness plan focusing on your physical and mental health, social relationships, and spirituality. Once again, take a minute and repeat the Mindfulness Moment from earlier in this lesson as a way to relax and recharge.

LESSON SIX

Stress and Self-Care

Caregiving is stressful. As a care partner, you know this. You feel the stress, probably every moment of every day. There has been a lot of medical and mental-health research on dementia care-partner stress, the results of which will not surprise you.

Compared to non-caregivers, dementia care partners are more likely to experience fatigue, frustration, despair, depression, anxiety, insomnia, medical problems, and marital strain. Why? It's in part due to the additional roles and responsibilities you have. And, there are only so many hours in a day. Most care partners feel like they're caught between a rock and a hard place of wanting and needing more time for themselves, their family, and the loved one with dementia they're caring for.

"Almost everything will work again if you unplug it for a few minutes, including YOU!"

— Anne Lamott

The Alzheimer's Association describes ten symptoms of caregiver stress — warning signs that indicate you're doing too much, need to take care of yourself, and perhaps need to seek professional help. They are:

- Denial about the dementia and the effects it's having on your loved one

- Anger at the person with dementia, or at others who don't help or understand
- Withdrawal from friends and pleasurable social activities
- Anxiety about the future
- Depression that breaks your spirit and affects your ability to cope
- Exhaustion that makes it difficult to complete your daily tasks
- Sleeplessness caused by a never-ending list of concerns
- Irritability and moodiness that trigger negative words and actions
- Lack of concentration that makes it difficult to perform familiar tasks
- Health problems that begin to take a mental and physical toll

Do you identify with any of the symptoms? Pick the top few you relate to the most, and describe what you are thinking or feeling about them.

_____

_____

_____

_____

_____

_____

The primary focus of this lesson is Central Need 5—Take care of yourself and Central Need 6—Ask for and accept help from others, two things most care partners know they need to do a better job of but usually don't. You'll learn about depression, anxiety, and stress: what they are, how to manage them, and the warning signs when they become overwhelming. The lesson will also teach you about wellness and help you make a wellness plan. Before we jump in, let's take a moment to be mindful. It will help you relax and focus!

MINDFULNESS MOMENT

Think about the ten symptoms of caregiver stress and in particular those you wrote about in the journaling exercise. Perhaps putting pen to paper made you feel even more stressed. A time of stress like this is a good opportunity to take a stress-reducing Mindfulness Moment.

Remember, mindfulness is a state of mind that you achieve by focusing all of your awareness and attention on the present moment and only the present moment, excluding worries of the past as well as the future. The practice of mindfulness gives you a "brain break," inviting you to calmly, nonjudgmentally, and compassionately accept your current thoughts, emotions, and body sensations without feeling as though you need to change them. The Mindfulness Moment includes a short breathing exercise that I hope provides you with a sense of peace that, at least for the moment, everything is OK.

Here we go.

1. Sit in a comfortable chair, put both feet on the floor (or any other comfortable position), clasp your hands over the middle of your belly, and then close your eyes (if desired).

2. Scan your muscles from head to toe and intentionally relax them. Unclench your teeth, let your shoulders sag, and relax your buttock and leg muscles.

3. Take in a slow, deep breath through your nose (count "one one-thousand, two one-thousand, three one-thousand" to yourself as you do so), then slowly exhale through your mouth to the same count, feeling the rise and fall of your belly. Do a total of ten slow, deep breaths like this. Focus solely on the gentle flow of your breath, in and out. Each time you exhale, consciously blow out any negative emotions and stress you feel about your loved one's dementia symptoms and your care partnering.

4. After the tenth breath, slowly open your eyes.

WARNING: DEPRESSION, ANXIETY, AND STRESS AHEAD—FOLLOW DETOUR

Of all the personal challenges that you as care partner face, there are three that will derail you more than any others. The three are depression, anxiety, and stress, an interrelated trio of mental-health challenges that can result in an emotional, physical, and spiritual spiral downward. In this part of the lesson, I will describe the nature of depression (as opposed to sadness), anxiety and panic (versus concern), and chronic (versus situational) stress. In particular, it's important for you to know when the red flag of depression, anxiety, and chronic stress is raised, because it signals your need for help.

DEPRESSION

What is depression? If someone you love dies, and you feel sad (what I refer to as situational sadness), is that the same thing as depression? As a medical and mental-health practitioner, I can say with confidence that they are different, but differentiating between situational sadness and true depression is one of the most difficult diagnoses in all of medicine.

There are **nine symptoms of depression**:

- **Feeling sad**, down, depressed, or hopeless (of note, in older adults and those with dementia, the symptoms **irritability and/or moodiness** can be more common than sadness)

- **Loss of interest** or pleasure in activities one usually finds pleasurable (for example, being around family, such as grandchildren, eating a good meal, and spending time with friends)

- **Feeling tired** and out of energy

- **Sleep disturbance** such as trouble falling asleep, sleeping too much, or waking early

- **Appetite changes** ranging from not being hungry and eating very little to overeating

- **Poor sense of self-worth, or guilt** about letting self and others down

- **Trouble focusing** and concentrating
- **"Idle speed" change** from normal to either restless and fidgety or slow and unmotivated
- **Suicidal thoughts** of being better off dead than alive

As I mentioned in Lesson Four, depression is also associated with worsening of cognitive symptoms, such as poor attention and concentration, short-term memory loss, and multitasking difficulties, some of the very same symptoms of dementia. Not infrequently a care partner will think they are developing dementia, too, when in fact they're more likely experiencing depression with the associated cognitive symptoms.

You might look at this list of depression symptoms and think they can all occur with situational sadness. So, let's differentiate between **sadness**, a normal emotion in reaction to a loss or life transition that will lessen over time on its own or with counseling, and **depression**, a chemical imbalance in the brain that must be treated by counseling, antidepressant medication, or both.

While most of the symptoms of sadness and depression overlap, there are three that are more unique to depression and less common with sadness. The first is loss of interest or pleasure in usual activities. Most of us love to eat, and we love to love and be loved. That is, we are motivated to be in relationship with others. Those with depression do not find joy in anything they do, whether it be a great meal or a day with the children or grandchildren.

A second clue to depression is poor sense of self-worth or guilt. Whereas a sad person might feel bad about a situation, like the death of a friend or relative, someone who is depressed feels as though *they* are bad, even to the point of feeling worthless, often with unending regret and guilt about things they've said or done.

The third thing that is most suggestive of depression as opposed to sadness is **suicidal thoughts**. This symptom often accompanies loss of interest or pleasure and feeling worthless or guilty. When someone feels as though they'd be better off dead than alive, especially if they've made a plan for self-harm that includes the means to end their life, urgent mental-health assessment and intervention is necessary. At the end of Lesson Two, I provided resources to turn to in the event you or someone you love feels suicidal.

To illustrate the concept of sadness versus depression, I want to share Mary's story. Then you'll have an opportunity to journal your thoughts about this topic.

Frazzled and Desperate

From the first time I met Mary, I thought, "This woman has it all together." Mary was in her late 30s, single, and worked as a bank teller, a job this extrovert loved. She was well dressed, always coming for her appointments in stylish clothing, natural-appearing makeup, and a trendy hairdo, the latter being what stood out the most. Mary was the sole care partner for her 75-year-old mother, who had a very aggressive case of Lewy body dementia.

Mary's mom lived with her, and with the help of paid caregivers, Mary was able to manage pretty well. I saw her about once every three months so she could update me on caregiving challenges, problem solve, anticipate what was ahead, and receive some well-deserved encouragement. One morning I saw Mary on the schedule, just a month after her prior visit. When she came into my office, she plopped down wearing a t-shirt and blue jeans, hair unkempt, no makeup, and tears in her eyes. She looked thin, almost gaunt, and exhausted, with dark circles under her eyes.

Mary was frazzled and desperate. With further discussion, Mary said she felt so sad it was as if she was in a deep, dark hole and couldn't climb out. She wasn't enjoying her work, found interacting with customers to be draining and a chore, and was avoiding friends because she just didn't feel like socializing. The trigger seemed to be the incontinence her mom had developed. Mary just didn't want to—in fact, she hated—cleaning her mom's bottom and changing her diapers. This led to overwhelming feelings of guilt and worthlessness as her mother's care partner.

Mary wasn't sure she could go on. Her manageable situational sadness had turned into true depression triggered by a worsening of her mom's dementia. We switched to weekly counseling visits, and her primary-care doctor prescribed an antidepressant for her. Mary responded well to these treatments. We also talked through options for mom's care now that she was incontinent.

Are you experiencing symptoms of depression? Please describe them. Having learned a bit more about situational sadness compared to depression, which do you think you're experiencing and why?

_____

_____

_____

_____

_____

_____

ANXIETY

What is anxiety? How is it different than concern, such as the natural concern you have for your loved one with dementia?

Like depression, anxiety is defined by a set of symptoms. There are **six symptoms of anxiety**:

- Feeling **restless, worried, fearful**, keyed up, or on edge

- Becoming easily **fatigued** and feeling tired

- **Difficulty concentrating**, mind going blank or racing or unwanted thoughts

- **Irritability**

- **Muscle tension**

- **Difficulty falling** or staying **asleep** or waking early

Concern is a normal emotion that comes when you're thinking of the person or situation you're concerned about, but then it goes away. It is constructive to be concerned. In contrast, when you feel anxiety, your mind is preoccupied with a person or situation, and you also experience most or all of the symptoms of anxiety listed above. Being anxious doesn't feel good.

Sometimes anxiety isn't caused by something specific. Often it is caused by generalized negative emotions such as the **fear** of a danger, the **worry** that something bad might happen and you might not be able to cope with it, **frustration** over a blocked desire or goal, **or anger** if you feel you've been wronged. Anxiety is destructive when you think about the same things over and over and are experiencing the symptoms of anxiety as well as stress (which we'll talk about next).

If you compare the six symptoms of anxiety to the nine symptoms of depression, you will see there is some overlap. This is because the chemical imbalances in the brain are similar in anxiety and depression, which is why the two conditions often coexist. When you're experiencing overwhelming anxiety, with or without depression, counseling, medication, or perhaps both are needed.

Are you experiencing symptoms of anxiety? What do you think is causing the anxiety— fear, worry, frustration, and/or anger? Please describe.

_____

_____

_____

_____

_____

STRESS

Stress is not an emotion. It is how your body reacts to negative emotions, such as depression and anxiety, including fear and worry. Like depression and anxiety, there are also symptoms that characterize stress. There are 11 symptoms of stress:

- **Rapid heart rate**, sometimes with palpitations (heart pounding)
- **Sweating**
- **Trembling** or shaking, often uncontrollably
- **Shortness of breath**, even to the point of feeling suffocated
- **Chest pain**
- **Sensation of choking** (not being able to breathe or swallow)
- **Nausea** with or without abdominal pain, even vomiting
- **Feeling dizzy**, lightheaded, or faint
- Having a sense of being **detached** from oneself, or even **out of touch with reality**
- Concern about **losing control** of one's emotions or going crazy
- Fear of **impending doom or dying**

It is usually the symptoms of stress that accompany depression and anxiety that make these conditions so uncomfortable

PANIC ATTACKS

Sometimes overwhelming stress can occur in sudden bursts, called panic attacks. A panic attack is different than feeling anxious and stressed in that it is unprovoked and unpredictable. In other words, there is no trigger; panic attacks just happen. During a panic attack, many of the symptoms of stress are present, especially a fear of impending doom, fainting, or dying. Panic attacks tend to run in families. They are effectively treated with a special kind of counseling called cognitive behavioral therapy and, often, medication. If you're experiencing panic attacks, seek the help of a mental-health professional.

to experience. While our bodies are able to tolerate bursts of stress (sometimes referred to as the fight-or-flight response), **chronic stress** is harmful.

Stress symptoms are caused by the release of two different hormones in the body, **adrenaline and cortisol**. These are important hormones that regulate many different body functions, such as heart rate, blood pressure, energy level, metabolism, and the fight-or-flight response. We can't live without adrenaline and cortisol, yet if we're in a state of chronic stress and our body makes too much of these hormones, there can be devastating effects on our physical and mental health, appearance, and daily functioning.

Chronic stress often has:

- **Effects on mental health and cognitive function**
  Promotes depression, anxiety, fear, and worry; increases startle response (feeling jumpy); causes poor coping and rigid and negative thinking (pessimism); causes poor attention and concentration, and difficulty multitasking; impairs short-term memory; causes trouble learning and remembering (though negative or traumatic memories are often better remembered and recalled)

- **Effects on physical health**
  Increases risk of high blood pressure, heart attack, stroke, elevated cholesterol and triglycerides, and diabetes; depresses immune function, causing more infections (cold sores, lung and kidney/bladder infections, yeast infections); promotes chronic fibromyalgia-like pain (headache, neck, shoulders, low back, muscles); decreases sex drive; causes erectile dysfunction or inability to achieve orgasm

- **Effects on physical appearance and daily functioning**
  Causes chronic feelings of fatigue (even sleep and naps don't help); elevates heart rate; causes excess sweating, shortness of breath, dry mouth, and sun sensitivity; causes more rapid aging (promotes wrinkles, dry skin (sometimes acne), gray hair, hair loss, and dark circles under eyes); changes body shape (stomach larger, arms

The Dementia Care-Partner's Workbook

and legs thinner, sometimes face rounder); increases or decreases appetite; causes heartburn, nausea, and constipation or diarrhea

Wow! Chronic stress can cause so many bad things to happen to you, your brain, and your body. As with depression and anxiety, stress, both short-term and chronic, can be treated with counseling, medication, or both, but lifestyle factors are also important to the management of all of these conditions. The second half of this lesson will focus on self-care and wellness. But first some journaling time about stress.

Reread the section on effects of stress on mental health and cognitive function. Are you experiencing any of the symptoms described? Please share.

_____

_____

_____

_____

_____

_____

Reread the section on effects of stress on physical health. Are you experiencing any of these symptoms? Please share.

_____

_____

_____

_____

_____

_____

_____

Reread the section on effects of stress on physical appearance and daily functioning. Are you experiencing any of the symptoms described? Please share.

_____

_____

_____

_____

_____

_____

What would you say are the top three causes of your stress? Please describe them.

_____

_____

_____

_____

_____

_____

THE NEED FOR CARE-PARTNER SELF-CARE AND WELLNESS

So far in this lesson, we've reviewed the three big personal challenges that you may confront as a care partner: depression, anxiety, and stress. You've also done some journaling about how you are experiencing and dealing with each of these.

I hope you've been able to find some balance in the different roles and responsibilities you have caring for yourself, your family, and your loved one with dementia. However, if you're like most care partners, you're understandably struggling, maybe a little, perhaps a lot.

I've found that most care partners (myself included, as I've shared) are not exactly sure how to care for themselves, how to find the path to wellness. There is a paraphrased quote from *Alice in Wonderland* that says, "If you don't know where you're going, any path will take you there." Please allow me to walk alongside you on a path to a more well you!

What exactly is wellness? Simply, it's being healthy. But more broadly, you can think of **wellness** as a positive state of well-being or health that includes eight interconnected components:

- Physical health
- Mental health
- Social relationships
- Spiritual health
- Community engagement
- Intellectual curiosity and creative thinking
- Occupational contentment and contribution
- Financial stability

These components comprise the "Wellness Wheel" on the next page.

PUTTING YOURSELF FIRST

Perhaps the single most important thing care partners need to do is take care of themselves, and yet the vast majority of care partners don't take the time necessary for self-care. I've been there. I understand. But I want you to think of it in these terms: What if something happened to you? What if you developed a serious illness (perhaps a stress-induced illness, such as a heart attack) and were out of commission for a month or more? What if you died? And did you know that nine out of ten dementia care partners don't have a backup plan for their loved one's care if something happened to them? These are scary statistics! That's why it's so important to have a plan, to take care of yourself, to be well.

SPIRITUAL
Find meaning
in life events,
demonstrate
individual purpose,
and live a life that
reflects your values
and beliefs.

EMOTIONAL
Have a positive
attitude, high self-
esteem, a strong
sense of self, and the
ability to recognize
and share a wide
range of feelings
with others in a
constructive way.

ENVIRONMENTAL
Be aware of the
interactions
between the
environment,
community, and
yourself, and behave
in ways that care
for each of these
responsibly.

FINANCIAL
Live within your
means and learn
to manage your
finances for the
short- and long-
term.

Wellness Wheel

Taking care of each dimension of
the Wellness Wheel can help you become
more aware of the interconnectedness
of each dimension, and how all aspects
of your life contribute to feeling well,
both physically and mentally.

SOCIAL
Build personal
relationships
with others, deal
with conflict
appropriately,
and connect in
a positive social
network.

PHYSICAL
Take care of your
body for optimal
health and
function.

OCCUPATIONAL
Seek to have
a career that
is interesting,
enjoyable,
meaningful, and
that contributes to
the larger society.

INTELLECTUAL
Be open to new
ideas, be creative,
think critically,
and seek out new
challenges.

Modified from University of New Hampshire Health & Wellness website: https://www.unh.edu/health/well/wellness

Look at each of the eight components of the Wellness Wheel. Which aspects of wellness are you struggling the most with? Which component are you experiencing the most success in? Please describe.

_____

_____

_____

_____

_____

If time were unlimited, we could have nine lessons just on wellness, spending one week on what each of the eight components look like for you (identifying strengths, weaknesses, opportunities, and threats), developing an action plan to enhance wellness in each area, then composing your personal wellness plan in week nine. But we don't have time to do that.

So let's concentrate on several of the most important aspects of wellness—those we know are essential for the wellness plan of a stressed dementia care partner. They are **physical health, mental health, social relationships, and spiritual health.** This doesn't mean the other components aren't important. It's more a matter of priority; you probably can't do it all right now! However, if one of the others is particularly meaningful to you, by all means, include it in your wellness plan.

The most important thing you can do to promote self-care and wellness is to make and take the time to do it. **You must be intentional and create time for self-care and wellness.** I believe every care partner needs and deserves at least three to four hours, at least twice a week, for themselves. Although this may be counterintuitive, the more time you spend providing care, and the more advanced your loved one's dementia is, the more time you need for self-care. If you're a full-time care partner, at least every one to three months, you need to be away for a two-day, one-night respite. And, no matter how much or how little time you devote to self-care, you are more than likely going to experience some **guilt** about being away from your loved one. I wish those feelings would go away with the snap of a finger!

PHYSICAL HEALTH

To promote physical wellness, see your **medical doctor or provider** at least twice a year for a check-up. The risk of illness increases with chronic stress (more so if you already have some chronic health conditions). In addition, if you're experiencing symptoms of depression, anxiety, and stress that are worrisome to you, it may be a good idea to see your doctor and make sure that you don't have an underlying medical illness. It's best to err on the side of caution and feel assured that your basic medical health is good.

Also see your **dentist and dental hygienist** at least yearly. Check your **blood pressure** weekly (at home or where a blood pressure machine is available), and report the results to your provider when you see them.

Make time for **exercise**. How much? Aim for 90 to 150 minutes total of moderate-intensity **aerobic exercise** (heart rate increases enough to cause you to sweat) in at least two exercise sessions weekly, but even if you can't achieve this goal, some exercise is better than none. If exercise equipment isn't your thing, a walk or hike outdoors or in nature can make exercise more pleasurable. Consider adding, at least once a week, core **strength training** with yoga or Pilates, and/or weight training. The guidance of a trainer/instructor may be helpful for these activities.

Last but not least is sleep. Most adults need at least seven hours of **sleep** a night, and some as many as eight or nine. Both your brain and body heal themselves of the effects of chronic stress during sleep, hence the popular term **restorative sleep**. If you are having difficulty falling or staying asleep, getting up too early, or sleeping restlessly (you must enter a deep sleep in order for it to be restorative), discuss your sleep challenges with your medical provider, or consider seeing a sleep specialist.

Describe some things you could do to enhance your physical wellness.

_____

_____

_____

_____

MENTAL HEALTH

To promote mental wellness, identifying someone you can talk with (a family member, friend, or mental-health professional) on a regular basis about your everyday challenges as a care partner is crucial to your mental health. Having such a person is key to meeting three of your central needs as a dementia care partner, including Central Need 1—Tell and retell your story, Central Need 3—Adapt to changing relationships, and Central Need 4—Take care of yourself.

Those you choose as your confidants need to be very special people, willing to **companion** you on your journey as a dementia care partner. More than anything else, companioning is about being present and listening, learning and observing, not analyzing or fixing. Just being able to talk about your experiences as a care partner will reduce your level of stress. I sometimes refer to this as "decompression," a metaphor for letting off steam.

If you are experiencing significant symptoms of depression, anxiety, and/or stress, consider seeing a mental-health professional (a licensed professional counselor, social worker, psychologist, or therapist). If you're not already, participate in a caregiver support group, or better yet, a dementia-specific caregiver support group.

Describe some things you could do to enhance your mental wellness.

_____

_____

THERE'S MORE THAN ONE WAY TO RELAX

Taking a Mindfulness Moment is not just for the lessons in this book. In fact, just two Mindfulness Moments a day, every day, can reduce your general stress level and really make a difference in how you feel. A great practice would be to start and finish each day mindfully—that's just a two-minute time commitment! You can add another Mindfulness Moment any time you're feeling really stressed out. Another way to relax that doesn't require a lot of time but has big benefits is progressive muscle relaxation (PMR). With PMR, you tighten, then relax, different muscles in your body, starting at your head and working your way down the body, or vice versa. Here's a script for PMR, similar to the one we use for the Mindfulness Moment:

1. Sit in a comfortable chair, put both feet on the floor (or any other comfortable position), close your eyes (if desired), then take in a slow, deep breath through your mouth, and blow it out slowly through your nose.

2. Close your eyes tightly and keep them closed tightly for a "one one-thousand, two one-thousand, three one-thousand" count, then relax your eyes open, and slowly breathe in and out again.

3. Repeat this same process by tightening and relaxing other muscles throughout your body, top to bottom. You can pick a few muscles or do them all. Breathe normally as you tighten and relax, but always follow the tightening-relaxing of muscles with a slow breath in and out. Here are some other muscles to try: jaw (bite down hard), mouth (exaggerated smile), shoulders (raise them up), back (pull your arms behind your back), arms (flex your biceps), hands (make a fist), stomach (tighten abdominal muscles), bottom (squeeze your buttocks together), thighs (squeeze your thighs together), and feet (heels on floor, pull feet back toward you, then push feet toward floor).

4. End by relaxing every muscle in your body, and take ten slow, deep breaths in and out, closing your eyes for a minute. As with the Mindfulness Moment, I hope this exercise also brings you a sense of peace in the moment.

_____

_____

_____

_____

SOCIAL RELATIONSHIPS

As we discussed in Lesson Four: Adapting to Changing Relationships, human beings are relational in nature, "wired" to love and be loved. Yet as a dementia care partner, you realize, I'm sure, that maintaining social relationships is challenging on several fronts. Lesson Four described various changes in the person with dementia that erode not only your relationship with them, but their relationship with others. This is the root cause of what I refer to as the shrinking world of the person with dementia and their care partners.

Another common force that makes social engagement more difficult is the reluctance of others to be in relationship with someone who has dementia. For many people, it's uncomfortable to be around an adult who is a messy eater or who poops in their pull-up. Both family members and friends become uncertain of what to say or how to behave around a loved one who has changed so much and who doesn't participate in the relationship as much or at all.

For some, being with a family member or friend with dementia causes apprehension because it makes them wonder, "What if that were me?" Or maybe they don't want their last memory of that person to be spoiled. The family members and friends who desire to remain in relationship with you and your loved one despite the dementia will make themselves known. They are the ones who will just show up or offer to come and spend time or help in some way. Others you will need to educate and recruit.

Regardless of the reasons people stay away, both for you as care partner and for your loved one with dementia, the **need for social relationships**

is important all the way to the end of the journey. Recognizing this truth is your first step to wellness in social relationships. You'll also need a caregiving team and the five love languages, applied to you. We'll discuss those next.

Have you noticed changes in your social relationships as part of your loved one's dementia journey? Please describe.

_____

_____

_____

_____

_____

_____

SPIRITUAL HEALTH

The University of Minnesota's Center for Spirituality and Healing website defines spirituality as follows: "Spirituality is a broad concept ... a universal human experience [that] ... includes a sense of connectedness to something bigger than ourselves, and it typically involves a search for meaning in life." It is different than religion, though many of us exercise our spirituality by attending a church, synagogue, mosque, or temple.

Spiritual practices can help provide a sense of peace and calm when the circumstances of life make us feel like we're in the midst of a storm. Praying, a common spiritual practice, is something three out of every four dementia care partners do, and it's been shown to reduce the stress of caregiving as well as decrease symptoms of both depression and anxiety. Mindfulness can also be considered a spiritual practice, as can taking a walk in nature, meditation, yoga, participating in ceremonies or rituals, keeping a gratitude journal, and other activities. For many, a regular time of spiritual nourishment is just as important as physical exercise.

A Helping Hand

One of my best guy friends on Rebecca's journey was Dan. My primary love language, physical touch, was not Dan's. Dan and his wife, Beth, lived just a few minutes away, so when things got really tough, especially when Rebecca was having a challenging day and I was not coping well, I would call them to come over and spend some time, Beth with Rebecca, Dan with me.

Some of the most difficult moments on the journey were when Rebecca became agitated, sometimes uncontrollably. There was one particular instance when I couldn't get her settled and became impatient with her, which made the situation feel out of control and made me feel guilty. I called Dan and Beth to come. When they arrived, Beth helped calm Rebecca while Dan sat with me, placing his hand on my back as I wept and shared the challenges of the day. His hand not only conveyed his love, but it also was very grounding in a situation of uncertainty. Prior to departing, as they always did in such times, Dan and Beth laid hands on both Rebecca and me and prayed, completing the circle of physical, emotional, and spiritual support we needed.

Has spirituality been an important part of your journey as a dementia care partner? If so, please describe.

_____

_____

_____

_____

_____

_____

_____

ASSEMBLING A CAREGIVING TEAM

One of the most important things I share with my counseling clients is the notion that **dementia caregiving is a team sport**. And just like a team captain, you may very well need to recruit members to your team.

In the last two years of Rebecca's Alzheimer's journey, we had 17 people on her team, individuals who in some way committed regular time to be with us. I was the primary care partner and team captain. We had four paid caregivers, the "A-Team," since all of their names ended in "a" (like Rebecca!). Others included our three daughters, Rebecca's mom and sister, a sister- and brother-in-law, two of her best friends and their husbands, and one of the pastors from our church.

Everyone on the team came to our home and was involved in supporting her or me, physically, emotionally, and spiritually, on a daily, weekly, or monthly basis. Some were involved by their own choosing, others because I asked. And for the A-Team, it was their job (though in the process we became family and even two-plus years later, we still get together regularly).

You will need to be intentional and proactive about recruiting members for your team. Others will ask you, "What can I do to help?" or "Call me if there is anything I can do." I encourage you to be bold, share what you need, and ask for help. Most of us are much better at serving than being served. Now is the time for you to receive the grace others extend to you.

Describe the people who are already on your team and what they do to help you and your loved one. If you could recruit others to the team, who might they be and how could they help?

_____

_____

_____

_____

As you contemplate asking others to help, consider doing so verbally, by email or text, or in a note or letter. Here is an example of what such a request might look (sound) like:

> *Dear family member or friend,*
>
> *As you know, Rebecca has Alzheimer's disease. It affects the way she thinks and feels. It changes what she says and does. As her primary care partner, I spend as much time with her as possible and love her as best I can. But with half-time work and graduate school, my time is limited. Sometimes my own physical, emotional, and spiritual energy becomes depleted. Rebecca and I have known you for a long time. We cherish our relationship with you. But we need your help. Would you consider coming and visiting Rebecca once a week, or once a month, just for an hour, spending time with her, sharing comforting words, hugging and loving on her, maybe bringing a chocolate chip cookie or some Ben and Jerry's ice cream? Would you consider having coffee or breakfast with me, maybe monthly, a time when I could talk and you could listen? I am a person who feels loved through touch, so a "man hug" or a hand on the shoulder would be an encouragement to me. And as always, both Rebecca and I continue to covet your thoughts and prayers.*
>
> *With gratitude,*
>
> *Ed*

Not everyone you reach out to will respond affirmatively—or respond at all. That's OK; don't take it personally. People have different reasons for not being able to help, and they may not want to disappoint or burden you with them. What's important is to find those who are willing to be part of the journey, and it's not always who you think.

Do you think you could reach out like this to a family member or friend to seek their help and support, love and encouragement? If yes, what would your letter say? If no, what are the barriers?

_____

_____

_____

_____

_____

_____

Recall what your primary love language is from Lesson Four. Is it words of affirmation, quality time, gifts, acts of service, or physical touch? Although others may sense what your primary love language is, it is best to tell them so they know how best to love you and fill your emotional love tank, just as I did at the end of the letter you just read.

What is (are) your primary love language(s)? Describe ways others could love you using this (these) love language(s) in your role as care partner.

_____

_____

_____

_____

_____

_____

YOUR WELLNESS PLAN

In the prior section, you learned about four aspects of wellness—
**physical health, mental health, social relationships, and spiritual
health.** With that background, you can formulate a wellness plan for
yourself.

Write down one thing you can do to improve your physical health.
Examples include getting a check-up with your primary-care provider,
checking your blood pressure once a week, exercising twice a week for
30 to 45 minutes (or whatever is doable), or going to bed earlier and
getting more sleep. Please describe.

_____

_____

_____

Write down one thing you can do to improve your mental health.
Examples include scheduling time to talk to someone you trust for 30
to 60 minutes weekly or biweekly, making an appointment to see a
counselor or therapist, or signing up for a care-partner support group.
Please describe.

_____

_____

_____

Write down one thing you can do to improve your social relationships.
Examples include spending time with your family free from caregiving
responsibilities, or socializing with a friend, family member, or
coworker you miss and haven't seen for a while. Please describe.

_____

_____

_____

Write down one thing you can do to improve your spiritual health. Examples include saying a daily prayer, attending a place of worship or spiritual group, spending 30 to 60 minutes weekly or biweekly enjoying nature, or having a daily Mindfulness Moment. Please describe.

_____

_____

_____

Great! You now have the core of your wellness plan. What we'll do now is make the plan into a commitment. And to make the commitment feasible, you'll try the wellness plan for one month, see what worked, what didn't, and adjust. OK, here's your wellness plan:

I, _____, commit to doing the following
(your name here)

for the next month because my wellness is important to me,

_____, and my family.
(name of your loved one with dementia)

1. To improve my physical health, I will

   _____

2. To improve my mental health, I will

   _____

3. To improve my social relationships, I will

   _____

4. To improve my spiritual health, I will

   _____

At the end of one month, I will reevaluate.

Signed: _____ Date:_____

Congratulations. Your wellness plan is complete, you've set some feasible goals, and you have a follow-up plan. While you can be accountable to yourself for the one-month reevaluation, also consider finding an accountability partner, perhaps another support- group member, or the person you get together with to talk regularly if that was one of your goals. What will be best for your wellness in the long run is to make the things you've committed to habits. You can do it!

A FINAL REFLECTION AND LOOKING AHEAD

This lesson is so important because it focuses on you—your need for self-care and wellness—and that's why it's Central Need 5 of dementia care partners. Yet most care partners—including me during Rebecca's journey—do not take very good care of themselves. I would like to challenge you to be different, to make and follow through with the wellness plan you just made. You will be glad you did. You will be more likely to be well if you embody the reality that caregiving is a team sport. This is Central Need 6—Ask for and accept help from others, and you will also be glad if you do this as well.

Of the many things we reviewed in this lesson, what is the one thing that stands out the most? Please share.

_____

_____

_____

_____

_____

_____

_____

_____

_____

Next up, Lesson Seven: Getting More Help and Transitioning Care, is a logical extension of this lesson. It explores options for additional help when your loved one's dementia has progressed to the point that you're not certain you can manage on your own. It also discusses transitioning care to a residential setting, like assisted-living, memory-care, or a nursing home, a topic that is often emotionally laden and difficult to even think about. Lesson Seven, like the prior lesson, also focuses on Central Need 6—Ask for and accept help from others., as well as Central Need 7—Prepare for what's ahead.

Let's finish this lesson by repeating the Mindfulness Moment from earlier in the lesson. Perhaps now that you know it is a spiritual practice, it will have more meaning for you.

Getting More Help and Transitioning Care

I hope the last lesson on self-care and wellness convinced you that caregiving is a team sport. We will carry this important thought into the present lesson and add that **dementia caregiving is a marathon, not a sprint**.

"Be smart enough to know when you need help and brave enough to ask for it."

— Ziad K. Abdelnour

A person with dementia, regardless of the type, is on a journey that lasts years—eight to ten on average—not weeks or months. When you have a big project ahead of you, you spend time planning, right? It makes the project go more smoothly. The same is true of the dementia journey. This lesson on getting more help and transitioning care, and the next lesson on legal, financial, and end-of-life issues, describe a number of things that will be helpful for you to consider no matter what stage of dementia your loved one is in right now.

In Lesson Four, we reviewed various behavior changes that occur in the person with early- and middle-stage dementia—changes that likely began to affect your relationship with them. We also looked at strategies to help you respond to and cope with these behaviors. Perhaps you've had opportunities to try some of these tactics. As dementia progresses into the middle and late stages, even more challenging behaviors can occur—more challenging in the sense that you may find yourself thinking, "**If this continues, I don't know if I can manage by myself**," or "**If this gets worse, I don't know if I can keep my loved one at home**."

Let's talk about these challenging behaviors and ways you can get more help if you're raising the white flag!

Please describe a situation in which you have thought, "I don't know if I can manage by myself" or "at home."

_____

_____

_____

_____

_____

_____

_____

MINDFULNESS MOMENT

Thinking about needing more help might be anxiety-provoking for you. Perhaps you have felt that you should be able to do it all but have come to realize you can't. Getting more help might mean sharing the responsibility for your loved one's care with a total stranger, or, if you're thinking about a residential-care transition (what many refer to as "nursing-home or facility placement," though I'm avoiding this phrase intentionally because it has such negative connotations), having your spouse or parent live somewhere else under the care of others.

This is a good opportunity to turn all of your awareness and attention on the present moment, tuning out worries of the past and future, for a stress-reducing Mindfulness Moment. I hope you will experience a "brain break," calmly, nonjudgmentally, and compassionately accepting your current thoughts, emotions, and body sensations without feeling as though you need to change them. So, let's begin the short breathing exercise that frames the Mindfulness Moment.

1. Sit in a comfortable chair, put both feet on the floor (or any other comfortable position), clasp your hands over the middle of your belly, and then close your eyes (if desired).

2. Scan your muscles from head to toe and intentionally relax them. Unclench your teeth, let your shoulders sag, and relax your buttock and leg muscles.

3. Take in a slow, deep breath through your nose (count "one one-thousand, two one-thousand, three one-thousand" to yourself as you do so), then slowly exhale through your mouth to the same count, feeling the rise and fall of your belly. Do a total of ten slow, deep breaths like this. Focus solely on the gentle flow of your breath, in and out. Each time you exhale, consciously blow out any negative emotions and stress you're feeling.

4. After the tenth breath, slowly open your eyes.

WHEN CHALLENGING BEHAVIORS ARISE, START HERE

Before we go over the challenging behaviors of middle- and late-stage dementia, it's very important to always keep a few things in mind when you are confronted by challenging things your loved one does or says.

Since dementia is a slowly progressive disease, if your loved one's behavior changes suddenly (for example, if they become unusually agitated, aggressive, irritable, resistive of care, withdrawn, or sleepy—really anything significantly different from baseline), over hours or several days, **it is essential to rule out medical conditions that might be contributing to the behavior**. A medical doctor or other medical professional, like a physician assistant or nurse practitioner, should be consulted, and certain tests might be necessary to evaluate your loved one. The most common conditions to cause challenging behaviors are infections (lung, kidney, or bladder), dehydration, medication-related issues (too much, not enough, side effects), sleeplessness, pain, and even constipation.

If a medical condition has been ruled out, try to think about other causes or **triggers** for your loved one's new behavior. Has there been a disruption in their daily routine? Has something changed in the environment? People with dementia benefit from a predictable daily schedule and familiar surroundings.

In addition, the **coping strategies** we highlighted in Lesson Four, including patience, "AAR" (acknowledge, affirm, and redirect), "KISSS" (keep it short, simple, and safe), the five love languages, and reminiscence approaches—individually or in combination—can work wonders in calming the challenging behaviors we'll be discussing.

Finally, if you've looked at medical conditions, triggers, and coping strategies and still the challenging behaviors persist, medication can be considered and sometimes is necessary, but behavior-modifying drugs are not without their risks and side effects, such as sedation and an increased chance of falling, among others. And don't forget to partner with the medical and mental-health professionals involved. Behavior management is definitely a team sport!

When all of these options have been exhausted, you may still find you need more help. Let's review the **common challenging behaviors that begin** in middle- and late-stage dementia, as well as other situations that **might require you to get more help at home or consider a residential-care transition**.

CHALLENGING BEHAVIORS AND OTHER COMMON CHALLENGES IN THE PERSON WITH LATER-STAGE DEMENTIA

- **Agitation and aggression**
  Agitation is best described as restlessness, often associated with pacing, repetitive questions, or vocalizations ("Help me, help me", "I

want to go home"), obsessive thoughts and goal-directed behavior, sleeplessness, resisting care, combativeness, and even aggression. I had a retired surgeon as a client several years ago who would wake up at about 2 a.m. to go on rounds. He would get dressed, pace around the house, and walk from room to room to see his patients, then after an hour or two, would go back to bed. Because this disrupted her sleep, the surgeon's wife had a paid caregiver between 11 p.m. and 7 a.m., so she could sleep while the caregiver accompanied her husband on his rounds. This is an example of obsessive thoughts and goal-directed behavior.

Aggression is a more severe form of agitation in which the person with dementia acts out verbally or physically, directed toward themselves or, more commonly, another person, usually a care partner. Aggressive behaviors include yelling and screaming, cursing, spitting, hitting, scratching, kicking, and throwing things. The care partner on the receiving end of these behaviors naturally withdraws from the situation for self-protection. And, after an aggressive exchange, care partners may feel reluctant to interact with their loved one out of fear.

Care partners often ask me, "Why does he attack me when I'm the one who loves and takes care of him?" In the language of attachment theory discussed in Lesson Four, perhaps it's because the loved one with dementia feels safest acting out toward someone they know deep down is securely attached to them, who loves them unconditionally. Or, they may be feeling insecurely attached, so the behavior may be a cry for help or attention, similar to how a child may act out when separated from a parent who makes them feel safe, secure, and loved.

It might help you to understand that in general, most aggressive behaviors are triggered by underlying negative emotions such as anger, worry, fear, loneliness, abandonment, or by physical discomfort of some kind, such as pain, hunger, thirst, the need to urinate or have a bowel movement, or incontinence. (And don't forget about the possibility of a medical condition, especially if aggressive behavior is not typical for your loved one). If you find yourself in this situation, take the opportunity to think about why your loved one is behaving this way, and keep in mind that your natural response (to back away and withdraw from the situation) may be the exact opposite of what they need.

Out of Control and Dangerous

Frank and Shirley, both in their mid-70s, lived in rural western North Carolina. Frank had two 20-year careers, the first in the Army as an infantryman then basic-training instructor, the second as a policeman in the local police department. After retiring at age 65, Frank seemed bored, uninterested in pursuing the things he enjoyed earlier in life, like hunting, fishing, and woodworking. Though he was never an affectionate man, he was always kind and gentle toward Shirley, and would do anything she asked. But in retirement, he seemed indifferent to her and to their adult children and grandchildren, most of whom lived in the area.

Shirley became really concerned when Frank started urinating off the front porch every morning when he awoke, made sexually inappropriate comments to their 14- and 16-year-old granddaughters, and began eating sweets like they were going out of style. She had Frank evaluated at a nearby university hospital, where he was diagnosed with behavioral variant frontotemporal dementia.

One night, Frank snapped when Shirley made a comment about him eating too much dessert. He picked up one of the wooden dining-room table chairs and started swinging it at Shirley. It struck her on the wrist, and she both heard and felt the bones break. Frightened and in pain, she ran out of the house to the next-door neighbors, who called the police. Frank was handcuffed and taken to the local hospital's emergency department. A psychiatrist was called in, who evaluated Frank and recommended he be transported to the university hospital for admission to their inpatient psychiatric ward for medication management of his behavior outbursts.

Has your loved one with dementia experienced agitation or aggression? If so, please describe. What has been the most challenging aspect of this (these) behaviors for you to manage?

_____

_____

_____

_____

_____

_____

- **Hallucinations**

  In Lesson Four, I differentiated between two common behaviors that occur in people with **dementia—delusions and hallucinations**. Again, a hallucination is when someone sees, hears, or feels something that is not there, whereas a delusion is believing something to be true that isn't. Seeing and/or hearing people that are not really there are the most common **visual and auditory hallucinations**. Common visual hallucinations include seeing people (often young children), animals, or bugs. The most common auditory hallucination is hearing voices. Sometimes hallucinations are frightening, sometimes not.

  Hallucinations can occur in all types of dementia, and sometimes they arise from a pre- or coexisting condition like schizophrenia or post-traumatic stress disorder. Visual hallucinations are the hallmark of Lewy body dementia, and when they occur are likely to be frightening to the person or make them feel paranoid, thinking someone (or something) is trying to hurt them. In contrast, the hallucinations of Alzheimer's disease tend to be misidentifications— for example, believing an electrical cord is a snake. Hallucinations are not necessarily problematic unless they are frightening or cause paranoia, in which case they can be accompanied by aggressive behavior toward others.

Has your loved one with dementia experienced hallucinations? If so, please describe them, how they affect your loved one, and how you respond. What has been the most challenging aspect of this behavior for you to manage?

_____

_____

_____

_____

_____

- **Wandering**

  You have probably seen a variable-message sign on the highway issuing a "Silver Alert," which notifies the public that an older person is missing, likely from wandering away from home or a senior residential-care facility. Wandering is a common challenge that can occur at any stage of dementia. It has a variety of causes, such as boredom or restlessness, getting disoriented or lost when walking inside or outside, escaping an unfamiliar or unpleasant environment, or looking for someone or something that may or may not exist (like wanting to "go home"). It's important to try to prevent wandering to the extent possible. However, it only takes a second for someone to slip away, and a loved one determined to leave is going to find a way.

  ### Wandering the Streets

  Lavonne and Leonard were high-school sweethearts who married at 18 and had been together for 70 years. Even after Lavonne had

WANDER-PROOFING

While it is impossible to prevent your loved one from ever wandering, there are some things you can do to try to "wander-proof" them and your home.

- Have them wear an ID bracelet that has their name, address, and diagnosis, as well as your contact information. If they don't want to wear one, offer to also wear one so you match. The ID bracelet is a must for everyone with dementia, regardless of stage. They are available at ROAD iD® (https://www.roadid.com/collections/find-your-id) in a variety of styles and colors, or Google "ID bracelets" or "medical ID bracelets."

- The Alzheimer's Association has a program called MedicAlert® + Alzheimer's Association Safe Return®, a 24-hour nationwide emergency response service for people with dementia who wander or have a medical emergency. For a fee, they provide ID bracelets and 24-hour assistance everywhere in the U.S. (https://www.alz.org/help-support/caregiving/safety/medicalert-safe-return).

- If your loved one is prone to wandering, consider having them wear a trackable GPS device (several are available on Amazon.com).

- Hide the car keys, or if your loved one is no longer driving but you have their car at home, store it elsewhere, give it away, or sell it to remove the temptation.

- Install window and door locks and chimes (available through home-security companies) as well as childproof doorknob covers. Also consider getting a Knox® Rapid Access System (Knox Box). It's a key box that allows emergency medical services and the fire department to unlock your front door in an emergency rather than break the door down. (www.knoxbox.com).

- Camouflage exterior doors and highlight interior doors in your home.

- Place pressure-sensitive mats on the bed and chairs (available at local medical supply companies and Amazon.com).

- Ask the neighbors to be on alert in case your loved one wanders.

- Make sure you have a current picture of your loved one just in case.

suffered a mild stroke, they were able to stay in their home with the assistance of a paid companion who came three days a week to help Lavonne shower and do some cooking, cleaning, and household chores for the happy couple. In the evenings, Lavonne liked to read, while Leonard preferred to work in his studio, where he enjoyed making ceramic pots.

One evening, Leonard received a phone call from a neighbor, who saw Lavonne walking up the street looking lost. He went outdoors and found her about a block away. When he asked what she was doing, she said, "I'm going home." The same thing happened twice more over the next week, and one of the times Lavonne was in her nightgown.

Leonard took Lavonne to see their geriatrician, who diagnosed her with vascular dementia and put her on some medication. It didn't seem to help, and the wandering problem worsened. Leonard had to keep his eyes on Lavonne 24/7, because every time he turned his head, she was trying to leave the house. One night, at 3 a.m., the doorbell rang. At the front door was Lavonne, covered by a blanket with nothing on underneath, accompanied by two policemen who had found her wandering naked four blocks from their house. Uncertain he could continue to keep Lavonne safely at home, Leonard began exploring options either for them to move to an assisted-living facility together, or for Lavonne to move into memory-care.

Has your loved one with dementia wandered? If so, please describe. What has been the most challenging aspect of this behavior for you to manage?

_____

_____

_____

_____

The Dementia Care-Partner's Workbook

- **Sexual behaviors**

 Sexual behaviors are some of the most distressing and challenging to deal with in people with dementia. They include internet pornography use, phone sex and sexting, exposing themselves or masturbating, inappropriate sexual comments or touch, sexual demands, soliciting a prostitute, extramarital affairs, and even forced sex. Such behaviors are much more common in men than women. Care partners may be reluctant to talk about sexual behaviors, especially spouses who may feel obligated to meet their husbands' sexual demands. When daughters or granddaughters are subjected to unwanted comments or touch, it can understandably cause rifts in family relationships.

 Despite the challenges, sexual behaviors can be talked about, understood, and prevented or effectively managed with a team approach. Here's an example:

 ### Coming to the Aid of an Aide

 For nearly 20 years, Suzanne had been a certified nursing assistant (aide) for a home health agency. She had encountered a lot of challenging clients, but Marvin, an 86-year-old widower, took the cake. He was bed- or chair-bound from severe arthritis, and incontinent from late-stage Alzheimer's disease.

 Marvin lived with one of his adult daughters. She had a job that allowed her to work from home. Each weekday, she had a home-health agency send an aide to help get dad up, bathed, dressed, and fed breakfast and lunch to allow her to work with minimal disruption.

 When Marvin's regular aide called in sick one day, the agency sent Suzanne. While she was giving Marvin his bed bath, he reached up and touched her breasts. She sternly moved his arm away and asked him not to do that again. Moments later, he grabbed her crotch. At that point, Suzanne covered Marvin and contacted the agency, who sent out their nurse supervisor.

Marvin's daughter, Suzanne, and the supervisor met to discuss what had happened. Marvin's daughter said her dad had never done anything like this before. Although this had not happened with Marvin's previous aides from the agency, the agency supervisor said they would have to dismiss themselves from Marvin's care if he continued to harass the aides, which greatly upset Marvin's daughter.

The home-health agency owner was a good friend of mine. He called and asked if I'd be willing to intervene. To better understand what happened, I asked Suzanne to walk through the morning's events. She said her bed-bath routine was the same for Marvin as all her other clients: she removed all his clothing, and had him lie on the bed, completely uncovered, while she washed him head to toe without saying much or anything at all. The groping occurred while she was washing his genitals.

Together we brainstormed a change in routine for Marvin. First, she would wash his upper body, keeping the covers over Marvin from the waist down. Second, she would cover his upper body and uncover him from the waist down, keeping a towel over his genitals, and wash everything but his genitals. When it came time for his genitals to be washed, she'd have him do it himself while she stepped back. Third, she would narrate what she was doing to Marvin throughout the bathing process. If this approach didn't work, the agency had a male aide they could send. Fortunately, these changes stopped the unwanted behavior and Suzanne actually became a regular aide for Marvin.

- **Resisting or refusing care**

  Resisting or outright refusing care is another common challenge faced by dementia care partners. This can range from more passive and benign things—like not wanting to change clothes day to day or get into pajamas at night, or refusing to take a shower—to more active and important things, such as refusing to eat, drink, or take medications.

  When I was raising teenagers, a wise mentor once told me to "pick and choose your battles." This wisdom also applies to dementia care. People with dementia lose a lot of autonomy as the disease progresses. If they won't change into their pajamas, consider just letting them sleep in their clothes. If they won't get dressed, you might have them spend the day in their pajamas. If they refuse essential medications, think about crushing the pills and putting them in juice, apple sauce, or ice cream (check with the pharmacist to make sure it's OK).

  In my experience, people with dementia are more likely to resist their family-member care partners than a paid caregiver, especially with certain basic activities of daily living like bathing or toileting. Often they prefer to not have their spouse or adult child involved in things that compromise their dignity. If this is the case for you, consider having a paid caregiver come into your home to help with basic ADLs.

  ### Gut Punch of a Lesson

  Patricia was in her mid-40s and cared for her mom in the family home her parents had raised her in for the initial eight years of her mom's Alzheimer's journey. When her mom became incontinent, Patricia transitioned her to a nursing home, which fortunately was near the fast-food restaurant Patricia managed and spent long hours at during the day and evening. On her salary, Patricia couldn't afford paid caregivers 12 hours a day, six days a week. The facility was less expensive, and it provided 24/7 coverage.

I counseled Patricia for an unusual reason: whenever she visited, her mom would become agitated and punch her in the stomach! Patricia was unsure why her mom would do this, as they had always had a very close relationship. I asked Patricia to describe her daily visits to mom: when she went, what she did and said, and how her mom responded to her in general during the visits. It turned out that when she first arrived, Patricia would always change her mom's diaper, whether it needed changing or not, and in the process, her mom would grow agitated and hit her. Once the process was over, the mom was angry at Patricia, turned away from her, and wouldn't interact. Patricia was puzzled why her mom so aggressively resisted her care, which was done with the best of intentions.

Patricia and I brainstormed a different routine for her visits to mom. Not infrequently, people with dementia will not want their spouse or adult children to help with toileting, whether wiping or changing diapers or pull-ups. For Patricia's mom, she was the one who changed Patricia's diapers, not vice-versa! We also discussed her mom's love languages (physical touch, gifts) and also the music she enjoyed.

Patricia's new routine was quite different. When she arrived, she had one of the aides change her mom's diaper. Then she'd enter the room with a Hershey's chocolate bar in hand (her favorite) and play her mom's most-loved music on her phone, which they'd listen to for the hour Patricia had for her visit. During this time, she would also rub her mom's back, arms, and legs with lotion. Patricia's subsequent visits with her mom went great, and were punch- and pain-free!

- **Sundowning and day-night reversal**
  Sundowning, sometimes called **late-day confusion**, refers to worsening changes in personality, mood, cognitive function, and behavior that begin in the late afternoon (when the sun starts to go down) and continue into the evening. It is most often seen in

Alzheimer's but can occur with any of the dementias. The changes and behaviors most likely to occur are fatigue and apathy, depression and anxiety, confusion and disorientation, restlessness and agitation, pacing and wandering, aggression, delusions and hallucinations, and resisting or refusing care. Although the exact cause of sundowning is unknown, factors such as mental and physical fatigue from the day's activities and disruption of the biological clock, or circadian rhythms (such as our day-night and wake-sleep cycles), are thought to contribute.

Related to sundowning, and sometimes occurring with it, is **day-night reversal**, which is when the person with dementia is awake at night and sleeps during the day. Although day-night reversal is not harmful in and of itself, it can create challenges for care partners and the caregiving routine. For example, if you have to be up with your loved one all night because they're not sleeping and prone to wander, and you work during the day or have other daytime responsibilities that prevent you from sleeping, after 48 to 72 hours of minimal sleep, you'll be exhausted and ineffective as a care partner. As we discussed in Lesson Six, restorative sleep is an essential component of your self-care and wellness. If day-night reversal is compromising your sleep, it's time to consider a plan that keeps your loved one safe and you sleeping at night.

Begin by discussing the situation with your loved one's medical provider. Make sure there are no medical causes of the problem, such as a bladder infection that results in frequent urination during the night. Medication side effects can also cause nighttime wakefulness. A common example is the drug donepezil (Aricept®). Two of its side effects, insomnia and vivid dreams, could be contributing factors, and a simple switch to taking it in the morning could help. Sleeping medications can also be beneficial. Lifestyle changes, like a late afternoon or early evening walk, or listening to music for an hour before bedtime, might promote sleepiness too. If all else fails, consider adding a nighttime caregiver so you can sleep while they keep watch of your loved one. Day-night reversal is one of the more common reasons to add a paid caregiver to your caregiving team.

Has your loved one with dementia demonstrated sexually inappropriate behaviors, refused care, experienced sundowning, or had sleeping issues? If so, please describe. What has been the most challenging aspect of this (these) behavior for you to manage?

_____

_____

_____

_____

_____

_____

- **Other challenging issues**

  There are several other challenging issues of late-stage of dementia that can raise the question of whether more help is needed in the home or if a residential-care transition is necessary. The most common of these is **urinary and fecal incontinence**. As alluded to in several of this lesson's stories, sometimes a person with dementia doesn't want their loved one being "rear admiral," and at other times, a family care partner may not want this responsibility.

  A related issue to incontinence is urinating or defecating in places other than a toilet or bedside commode. Common places include a hallway near the bathroom (they just don't quite make it), in a trash can, or in the corner of a room. Sometimes smearing feces on the floor or walls will occur.

  Other issues that typically happen when the person with dementia approaches the end of life include refusal to do certain essential things, such as getting out of bed, drinking fluids, eating food, and/or taking medications.

Any or all of these other situations can be strong motivators to consider getting more help or a residential-care transition.

HOW DO YOU DECIDE WHEN YOU NEED MORE HELP?

There are many factors that will enter into your decision about when you need more help as well as the kind of help you need. Some of the more common factors are listed below.

Regardless of why you decide you need more help, the first step is to get more information. In the next section of this lesson, various supplemental care options are described, ranging from help while keeping your loved one at home all the way to residential care. If your gut is saying, "If this continues, I don't know if I can manage by myself" or "If this continues, I don't know if I can keep them at home," it's time to at least educate yourself about the options.

Here are the most common things to consider when you feel you need more help:

- The **stage of the disease, the type of dementia**, and the **symptoms**. When your loved one is in the middle stage of their dementia, they're needing help with most or all of their instrumental activities of daily living (ADLs), and they're beginning to need help with their basic ADLs. If they're in the late stage, they need help with most or all of their basic ADLs. Later-middle-stage or late-stage dementia is typically when care partners feel they need help caring for their loved one. It also depends on the type of dementia. Those with frontotemporal dementia often have behavioral challenges that are harder to manage without help, like the ones described in this lesson, even in the early stage of the disease. For people with Lewy body dementia, the Parkinson's-disease-like issues (tremor, unsteady walking, and rigid muscles) may necessitate getting help sooner. Delusions and hallucinations, especially with paranoia, as well as incontinence also present significant care challenges with Lewy body and other dementias.

- **Not enough or no help from family and friends**. If you feel like you need more hours to get everything done in a given day, or you feel like you routinely have to accomplish two days of work in one day, you probably need more help. You might be experiencing **caregiver burnout,** in which you feel depleted physically, mentally, and spiritually. Maybe you're spending so much time caregiving that you're losing precious time with your loved one as their husband, wife, son, daughter, or whatever special relationship you have with them. As you've learned, dementia caregiving is a team sport. If you don't have others to help you and you're at the limit of what you can do by yourself, it's time to get more help.

- **Not enough money**. You may have come to the decision you need more help, but the financial resources are just not there to afford a paid caregiver. We'll talk more about paying for care in the next section of this lesson as well as in the next lesson. Several of the resources described in the next section of this lesson are low- or no-cost. In general, if financial resources are very limited or nonexistent, you'll still be able to find more help for your loved one, but your options will be more limited, and you're more likely to be stuck with a caregiving situation that you or your loved one may not prefer.

AN ADL REFRESHER

In Lesson Three we covered the definition of instrumental activities of daily living (ADLs) and basic ADLs. Here's a quick list as a reminder.

INSTRUMENTAL ADLs

Cooking

House cleaning

Taking medication

Laundry

Shopping

Managing finances

Communication

Transportation

BASIC ADLs

Bathing

Dressing

Transferring

Toileting

Feeding

OPTIONS FOR MORE HELP WHILE YOUR LOVED ONE STILL LIVES AT HOME

If you're at the point of considering more help and would like assistance exploring your options, consider hiring a **geriatric care manager**. Geriatric care managers are usually social workers who specialize in working with seniors, including those with dementia, and they know the resources for more help in your area. Although they charge an hourly fee, in my experience their knowledge and expertise is well worth the cost. More information on geriatric case managers and their services, as well as identifying individuals in your area, is available at the Aging Life Care Association (www.aginglifecare.org).

ASSISTANCE THAT ALLOWS YOU TO KEEP YOUR LOVED ONE AT HOME

- **No- or low-cost community care**

  Your community may have organizations and/or programs at no or low cost that can help you and your loved one with dementia. This may include volunteers who provide companionship, usually for briefer periods of time (several hours or days per week), services such as small-scope remodeling or building projects (for example, widening a doorway or installing a handicapped-accessible entry ramp), transportation for errands or doctor's appointments, and precooked meal delivery.

  In the U.S., a good resource to identify such options is your Area Agency on Aging (AAA). The AAA is a nationwide network of more than 600 offices that serve geographic areas or an entire state. They provide resources to seniors in a number of important areas. However, AAAs do not provide hands-on care, do legal work such as writing powers-of-attorney or wills, or help with Medicare or applications.

  If your loved one is a veteran, many resources provided by AAAs are also provided specifically for older veterans through your local or regional Veteran's Administration (https://www.benefits.va.gov/persona/veteran-elderly.asp).

- **Home-health agencies**

Home-health agencies are the backbone of home-based care when family members cannot provide all the care needed for a loved one with dementia or the care needs exceed what they can or want to provide. According to the American Association for Retired Persons, one in three families caring for a senior in their home will require paid help.

Services provided by home-health agencies include skilled-nursing care (care requiring the expertise of a registered nurse or licensed practical nurse), personal care (usually provided by a certified nursing assistant, or CNA), and companionship (keeping person company, light housework and/or meal preparation, provided by minimally trained individuals). Some home-health agencies also offer physical therapy, occupational therapy, and speech therapy.

For those with dementia, paid home-health care is usually provided by a CNA. There are more than 1.5 million CNAs in the U.S., and the need for them will increase as the Baby Boomers continue to age (there are over 75 million of us!). CNAs make somewhere between minimum wage (currently $7.25 nationally, though it's higher in many states) and $18 per hour. The average is probably in the range of $10 to $15, depending on experience and geographic location. To this rate, home-health agencies add an hourly agency fee, somewhere in the range of $6 to $10, so the total cost of a CNA to families is $16 to $25 hourly. Assuming an eight-hour shift at $20 per hour, five days a week, that's $160 per day, $800 per week, or just under $44,000 per year. If 24/7 care is needed, the cost would be $175,000 yearly through an agency!

Medicare and health insurance generally do not cover the cost of CNA care for those with dementia, although this is beginning to change, whereas most long-term care insurance policies do at some level. Skilled nursing and physical, occupational, and speech therapy are much more expensive but usually are covered by Medicare and insurance, at least for a period of time.

Of course, you can hire a CNA on your own instead of using a home-health agency, which would reduce your costs because you would not be paying the agency fee. However, keep several things in mind. Most agencies check references, do criminal background checks, and require drug testing before they hire a CNA. Some long-term care insurance policies require you to use an agency in order to receive the in-home caregiver benefit. What's more, if you don't feel the CNA an agency provides is a good fit, they'll find someone else for you, usually very quickly, without you having to handle the letting-go of the original person they sent. And, the agency takes care of scheduling for you. For example, to staff 24/7 coverage, at least four or five CNAs are needed when you factor in evening and weekend coverage as well as sick and vacation time.

- **Adult daycare**
Adult daycare centers are non-residential facilities that are available for seniors, including those with dementia, who require daytime supervision while their family care partner is working or taking time for respite. They are staffed with companions, CNAs, and/or volunteers, and provide oversight, support with instrumental and basic ADLs, meals (typically breakfast and/or lunch), social activities and engagement with other participants, light exercise, and in some instances, services of a physician, dentist, podiatrist, barber or beautician, and care-partner support groups. There is usually a fee for adult daycare, though it is less expensive than a paid caregiver and there may be a sliding scale or special assistance to help offset the cost.

- **Respite care**
If you are committed to keeping your loved one at home but need a break, respite care may be a good option. Respite care either involves someone coming into the home to care for your loved one while you're away, whether a family member, friend, or paid caregiver, or having your loved one stay in a residential-care facility (assisted living or memory care) during the time of your absence. The cost of respite care is usually not covered by medical insurance or Medicare but may be if respite is provided in a hospice setting or with certain long-term care insurance policies.

Based on where you are in your loved one's journey with dementia, what are your thoughts and feelings about the various options described that allow you to keep them at home? Please share.

_____

_____

_____

_____

_____

FULL-TIME RESIDENTIAL CARE

Considering a transition into full-time **residential care** is one of the most emotional and challenging issues you may face when caring for your loved one with dementia. Perhaps the promise was made that "You'll never go into a nursing home." You may be feeling guilty or that you're abandoning your loved one for even considering such a transition. Although these feelings are normal, they are unpleasant nonetheless. Since this is such a big decision, it may be a good time to arrange a family meeting that includes your loved one's healthcare providers so you better understand where things are and what lies ahead.

A Memory-Care Dance

Marla was a 55-year-old elementary teacher who had been named her school district's teacher of the year two years before her word-finding problems started. Initially she couldn't think of the word she wanted to say, but as time went on, she had more trouble completing sentences as well as understanding what others were saying to her. Marla was diagnosed with primary progressive aphasia (PPA), a less-common form of frontotemporal dementia that primarily affects language function. People with PPA may, over time, also develop coexisting Alzheimer's disease or behavioral variant FTD.

Sadly, Marla's disease progressed rapidly. Within two years, she was disoriented, couldn't talk at all, was very unsteady on her feet, and had become incontinent. Her husband, Troy, still worked, and none of their

HELPFUL HINTS FOR FAMILY MEETINGS

Family meetings typically require 60 to 90 minutes. Consider who might participate in the meeting. Usually it involves the person with dementia's doctor, spouse, and adult children. The meeting may or may not include the person with dementia.

Here is a typical agenda for a family meeting at the point in the journey when residential care is being considered.

1. Introduction of members present, their role in the person with dementia's care, and what they hope to discuss in the family meeting.

2. Summary of the person with dementia's current status, including things like type of dementia, stage of disease, current and anticipated symptoms and challenges (cognitive, medical, mental health, other) and life expectancy, if appropriate.

3. Discussion of options for care—for example, keeping the person home versus transition to residential care. What are the options? What are the advantages and disadvantages of each one?

4. Decision on next steps—examples include engaging the services of a geriatric care manager, meeting with an elder-law attorney, interviewing home-health agencies and paid caregivers, visiting residential-care communities, and so on.

At the end of the meeting, set a timeline for when next steps will occur and who will carry them out, when a decision on the best option for care should be made, and if appropriate, when a follow-up meeting will take place.

three adult children lived locally. And Troy was really struggling trying to help with Marla's toileting and showering.

Within several miles of Marla and Troy's home was a residential-care community that had both assisted living and memory care. The admissions coordinator evaluated Marla and thought she was most appropriate for memory care. She moved in and adjusted quickly to her new environment. Troy visited her daily after work and on both weekend days. Marla and Troy loved music and dancing. Troy's visits would always include a time where they would sit on a couch in the memory-care lounge, holding hands and listening to their favorite music (tunes from the 60s and 70s) on Sirius-XM. Marla would usually fall asleep with her head on Troy's shoulder, humming along to the music, but sometimes she and Troy would slow dance to the music.

Here are the options for transitioning your loved one to full-time residential-care. Note that these options may exist as individual, stand-alone facilities or as combined facilities, which are often called **continuing-care retirement communities (CCRC)**. CCRCs provide all levels of care, either in multiple buildings on the same campus or on different floors or wings of the same building. CCRCs offer the convenience of your loved one not having to move in the event of a transition from one level of care to another, such as assisted living or memory care to a nursing home, which is common.

- **Independent-living communities**
  Independent-living communities, sometimes called **55+ communities**, are for individuals or couples who are able to function independently but prefer to be in a setting with others their age. Various housing types are often available (for purchase or rent), ranging from apartments (efficiency, one-, or two-bedroom) to condominiums, townhomes, and single-family homes. Depending on the size of the community, independent-living communities often include other features, such as restaurants or a dining room, retail

stores, a barbershop or salon, planned activities, and a shuttle. Cost varies widely depending on geography, the type of accommodations, amenities offered, and level of luxury. Most independent-living communities allow residents to have help in the home, even 24/7 care, if one or both people require additional care. Some of these communities even employ CNAs.

- **Assisted-living facilities**
  Assisted-living facilities are for individual seniors or senior couples who are mostly, but not completely, independent. An assisted-living facility is an option for those with mild cognitive impairment or dementia who are dependent with their instrumental activities of daily living (for example, meal preparation and taking medications) and may also require some assistance with certain basic activities of daily living, such as taking a bath or shower. The accommodations in assisted-living facilities are usually efficiency or one- or two-bedroom apartments. Nursing and CNA staff are stationed on each floor of assisted-living facilities to assist residents, and the ratio of residents to staff varies depending on the facility and shift, ranging from five-to-one all the way up to thirty-to-one. Planned activities and meals are provided. Cost varies (ranging from $2,500 to $7,500 or more monthly) and is highly dependent on geography, private versus shared room, and facility quality. Assisted-living facility costs are not typically covered by private insurance, and they are not covered by Medicare. Some assisted-living facilities offer low-income housing, and financial assistance may be available through community programs. Your Area Agency on Aging or local department of social services can help you explore options.

- **Memory-care facilities**
  Memory care is essentially an assisted-living facility for those with dementia who are prone to wander or exhibit some of the challenging behaviors discussed earlier in the lesson, and need the security of locked doors to protect their safety as well as specially trained staff. The vast majority of memory-care facilities only allow

the person with dementia, but not their spouse, to reside there. Cost varies but is typically on the higher end of what one would pay for an assisted-living facility, and insurance and Medicare don't provide coverage. In recent years, a greater emphasis has been placed on so-called **person-centered care**, where the day-to-day care routine revolves around the person with dementia as an individual rather than the schedule and routine of the staff. An example of this is Abe's Garden® in Nashville (www.abesgarden.org).

- **Nursing homes**

  When someone requires around-the-clock oversight and care because they're not independent enough to be in assisted living, but they don't have medical or physical conditions that would necessitate hospitalization or care in a skilled-nursing facility or rehab, then a nursing home may be the most appropriate option for care. The most common services provided by the nurses and CNAs in a nursing home are dispensing medications and **custodial care**, which includes assistance with basic activities of daily living such as bathing, getting dressed, and eating. The majority of nursing-home residents are the **frail elderly**, defined as seniors who are weak and fatigued, minimally physically active, walk slowly, and have experienced unintentional weight loss (more than ten pounds in the prior year, especially loss of muscle mass). Frail elderly people are at increased risk for declining health, greater dependence in ADLs, falls and other causes of poor mobility, hospitalization, and death. Medical insurance, Medicare, Medicaid, and long-term care insurance may cover all or part of the cost of a nursing home, though the benefit may be time-limited. The daily cost begins at $150 and can be considerably higher, with an average of about $225 to $250, and significant increases seem to occur every year. For someone with dementia, if they are frail because of age and/or their disease and are not a wandering risk, residential care is usually provided in a nursing home rather than memory care.

- **Skilled-nursing facilities**

  Often referred to as "sniffs" for short, skilled-nursing facilities are for people who require medical care but don't need to be in a hospital. Inside, skilled-nursing facilities look similar to hospitals, however. By definition from Medicare and Medicaid, every person's care in a skilled-nursing facility must be supervised by a physician, and a nurse must be available 24/7. Medical care is administered by a nurse (for example, antibiotics, wound care, feeding tube, urinary catheter, or colostomy care). Other services are also available in skilled-nursing facilities. Physical, occupational, and speech therapies, for example, are usually available for one hour a day, five days a week (in contrast to rehab facilities, where therapies are more intensive; see below). Activities of daily living assistance is the responsibility of CNAs. Usually, a person's stay in a skilled-nursing facility is temporary. The transition to a skilled-nursing facility often occurs after someone has been hospitalized but is not quite ready to return to independent living or their assisted-living facility. For example, a person with dementia might need to be in a skilled-nursing facility if they develop an infection of some sort and require intravenous antibiotics for ten days. Medical insurance, Medicare, and Medicaid may cover the cost of a skilled-nursing facility, although the duration of the benefit is usually time-limited, up to 100 days. The daily cost of a skilled-nursing facility room varies widely, from $150 to $750, with an average of about $250 to $300.

- **Rehabilitation facilities**

  A rehabilitation facility ("**rehab**") looks physically similar to a skilled-nursing facility, has physician oversight and nurses/CNAs as staff, but differs in several ways. Rehab is for those who have more physical rather than medical limitations following injury or illness and hospitalization, and who have the potential for recovery (for example, following a hip replacement, stroke, traumatic brain injury, or motor vehicle accident). Services typically provided in rehab include physical, occupational, and speech therapy, for at least three

The Dementia Care-Partner's Workbook

KEEPING PACE WITH PACE

PACE, or Programs of All-Inclusive Care for the Elderly, are programs in the U.S. that provide comprehensive health services for those 55 years of age and older who are frail enough to meet the state's criteria for nursing-home-level care. According to the National PACE Association, "The typical PACE participant is similar to the average nursing-home resident ... an 80-year-old woman with eight medical conditions and limitations in three activities of daily living. Nearly half ... of PACE participants have been diagnosed with dementia. Despite a high level of care needs, more than 90 percent of PACE participants are able to continue to live in their community."

There are 134 PACE programs in 31 states, the largest of which has 2,500 enrollees. PACE programs provide services that include medical checkups, exercise, dietary monitoring, programs to increase strength and balance, and the like. PACE programs organize their services in a "PACE Center," which have a day center, doctor's offices, nursing care, social services and rehabilitation services (physical, occupational, and speech therapy), and administrative staff, all in one site. Members attend centers up to seven days a week (two days a week on average), depending on their care needs and individualized care plan. Services provided by a PACE program are paid for by Medicare, Medicaid, and private health insurance. To see if you have a PACE program in your area, contact the National PACE Association at (703) 535-1565, info@npaonline.org, or www.npaonline.org.

hours a day, five days a week. Sometimes both medical insurance and Medicare or Medicaid cover the cost of rehab, which is in general at the higher end of what a skilled-nursing facility would be. For people with dementia, rehab or skilled-nursing care may be appropriate following a fall with hip fracture that has been surgically fixed, for example, or after a fall with head injury, for recovery following a stroke, or for those with Parkinson's disease or Lewy body dementia who have worsening of their physical function. Where a person with dementia would be transitioned to after a hospital stay depends on their ability to participate in therapy. If they can manage one hour a day, five days a week, skilled nursing is appropriate, but if three hours a day, five days a week is doable, then rehab would be the choice.

- **Hospice care**
  Hospice care is for individuals who are at the end of life, defined as an anticipated life expectancy of six months or less. Care is provided by a team of specially trained people that usually includes doctors, nurses, CNAs, social workers, counselors, and chaplains. The focus of hospice is to keep the person comfortable and free from distressing symptoms (so-called **palliative care**) while meeting their physical, emotional, and spiritual needs. Hospice care can be provided in a variety of settings, including the home, assisted-living facilities, memory care, skilled-nursing facilities, nursing homes, or freestanding hospice facilities. The cost of hospice is usually covered by medical insurance, Medicare, or Medicaid.

After reading about all these options for residential care, you might be wondering, "How do I find the best place for my loved one?" If you're not using the help of a geriatric case manager, good ways to identify options include asking family members, friends, and healthcare providers for recommendations, doing a Google search (don't forget to check Google ratings), and checking government facility ratings (https://www.medicare.gov/nursinghomecompare/search.html).

When you've narrowed your options down to a manageable number, I recommend that you visit each one, take a tour, and speak with their intake coordinator, several staff members, and even a few residents. If possible, I would further encourage you to take your loved one along on the tours. Your gut, and their response, will tell you if a certain place is a good fit for them or not. When I've toured residential-care

HELPFUL HINTS WHEN YOUR LOVED ONE IS IN A RESIDENTIAL-CARE FACILITY

Some people believe that once their loved one has transitioned to a residential-care facility, their worries will be over. Unfortunately, that's not entirely true. Research actually shows that care-partner stress and burden often increases with a residential-care transition. What's more, in my experience active and regular care-partner engagement with the facility staff is also necessary to ensure high-quality care.

If your loved one is in a residential-care facility, there are things you can do to make sure they get the best care possible. I have had counseling clients in a variety of settings, ranging from the county nursing home to the Cadillac of memory-care units, and all received excellent care when care partners followed these suggestions:

- Have a presence. If possible, you or another family member or friend should visit daily or almost every day, so the staff become accustomed to seeing you. Vary the time you go, so you see and are seen by nurses and CNAs on the different shifts.

- Get to know the staff. Learn the names of the staff. Let them get to know you, and ensure you get to know them. Be kind and friendly. Also help them get to know your loved one. Put up a poster board with pictures and facts about family, former occupation, hobbies, and likes and dislikes. This will encourage the staff to engage your loved one in dialogue about their life (a reminiscence approach).

- Express concerns you have about your loved one's care. If you're visiting in the evening, tell the CNA, "I'm leaving now. You'll check on him regularly, won't you? He's been restless tonight." Or, "When I came this morning, his pull-up was soaking wet. How often are you changing him?" Let your concerns become their concerns.

- Have a regular care-plan review. Everyone in a residential-care setting is required to have a care plan. You should know what that

(continued...)

plan is, have input into it, and review the plan on a regular basis. When you have such a meeting, ask to have the charge nurse and a social worker present, as well as the physical, occupational, and/or speech therapists if your loved one is in skilled nursing or rehab. Bring a list of your questions or concerns, and don't forget to share praises for overall care or individual staff whenever it's deserved. If you're a long-distance care partner, this can be done via conference call or Skype, too.

Following these suggestions won't guarantee your loved one gets the best care possible, but it will definitely be a big step in the right direction.

---

facilities myself, I always ask the head nurse how long she and the CNAs working on the unit have been there. Staff who have been there for years rather than weeks and months usually indicates a well-run facility.

Based on where you are in your loved one's journey with dementia, what are your thoughts and feelings about the various options for transitioning them to residential care? Please share.

_____

_____

_____

_____

_____

_____

_____

A FINAL REFLECTION AND LOOKING AHEAD

This lesson has provided what must feel like an overwhelming amount of information regarding challenging behaviors and the myriad options available when you need more help. Not surprisingly, many of your central needs have been addressed by this lesson, including the need to tell and retell your story (Central Need 1), educate yourself (2), adapt to changing relationships (3), take care of yourself (5), ask for and accept help from others (6), and prepare for what's ahead (7). You are well on your way to becoming a better and better-equipped care partner! Before we move on to the next lesson, let's pause for a moment for some journaling.

Of the many things you learned about in the lesson, what is the one thing that stands out the most?

_____

_____

_____

_____

_____

_____

The next lesson, Lesson Eight: Legal, Financial, and End-of-Life Issues, is a logical extension of this lesson. It's about preparing yourself, your loved one, and your family by having important legal documents in place, figuring out how to pay for the many care options that are available, and making end-of-life decisions. Once again, the focus is Central Need 7—Prepare for what's ahead. Let's finish this lesson by having you repeat the Mindfulness Moment with which you are now so familiar.

Legal, Financial, and End-of-Life Issues

During the ten-week care-partner support groups my colleagues and I lead, this week's lesson on legal, financial, and end-of-life issues is the one participants routinely identify as the most practical. I hope you will feel the same way. Interestingly, these three subjects (which are all, to some extent, legally related) are often what family care partners put on the back burner because they seem less relevant to the day-to-day care of their loved one with dementia. In reality, these are all issues that need to be on the front burner, because not planning for them can have huge negative consequences for both your loved one's care and for you and your family.

"Caution: Dates on calendar are CLOSER than they appear."

— Tony Robbins

So let's dive into these topics, but first, I want to share a story of why planning ahead is so important.

A 104-Degree Crisis Averted

Daniel retired in his mid-50s from a 30-year career as an auto mechanic for a large Toyota dealership. It was a job he loved, and he made and saved enough money to retire on the early side.

Daniel had a strong family history of Alzheimer's disease, and he was worried he would develop it in his 60s, just as his mother and grandmother had. It turns out he was right. He was diagnosed with dementia in his early 60s, but not Alzheimer's. He had a rare form of dementia called progressive supranuclear palsy (PSP). His symptoms were pretty typical of that disease, including extreme fatigue and apathy, muscle stiffness, especially in the neck, double vision with an aversion to bright lights, and his biggest challenge, imbalance, with a lot of falls, usually backward (a big clue to doctors that the diagnosis was PSP).

I primarily counseled Daniel's wife, Penelope, and saw her about every three months. She was a very competent care partner who always wanted to know what Daniel's next PSP symptoms were going to be and how she could best prepare for them. Daniel reached the time in his journey when he lost the ability to walk, became incontinent, and was having enough difficulty swallowing that he suffered repeated bouts of aspiration pneumonia (caused by the saliva, liquids, and solids he ingested getting into his lungs). The pneumonia required treatment with antibiotics.

At that point, Daniel's life expectancy was just a few months. I shared this with Penelope, which prompted a discussion of end-of-life issues. One of the questions she had was at what point might she choose not to have Daniel's pneumonia treated? When he retired, Daniel and Penelope went to an elder-law attorney and had a living will made. Daniel indicated he did not want any extraordinary measures taken to prolong his life if he was unable to make decisions for himself and was at the end of life. So, Penelope made the decision that the next time Daniel developed a fever and other symptoms of aspiration pneumonia, she would not have him treated with antibiotics.

The very next day, Daniel developed shaking chills and a fever of 104 degrees. He was bed-bound and unresponsive, breathing rapidly and shallowly. Penelope called me, and we discussed the high likelihood that Daniel had another case of aspiration pneumonia (or some other kind of infection). I asked if she was comfortable with yesterday's decision not to diagnose and treat the probable infection, which she was. I also shared that an untreated infection could result in sepsis (when the infection enters the bloodstream and can result in damage to the major organs), which is usually a relatively painless way to die.

Twenty-four, 48, then 72 hours passed. Daniel slept through these three days, and at the end of the third day, his fever broke and he woke up enough to open his eyes and squeeze Penelope's hand. He had several more bouts of aspiration pneumonia in the days that followed, and died a few weeks later.

Ordinarily, a high fever from aspiration pneumonia would cause panic and concern. By educating herself and planning ahead, Penelope was able to manage the situation without going into crisis mode.

Are you the primary care partner for your loved one with dementia? If you are, what is the back-up plan for your loved one's care if something temporarily incapacitated you, like pneumonia requiring a week in the hospital and a week's recovery at home? Or if you died, what is the back-up plan? If you're not the primary care partner, answer the back-up plan question just the same.

_____

_____

_____

_____

_____

_____

MINDFULNESS MOMENT

Is the story of Daniel and Penelope, or perhaps concerns about legal, financial, and end-of-life issues, causing you to feel stressed? If so, I apologize! My hope is that some planning ahead now will decrease your stress in the long run. In the meantime, this time of stress you may be experiencing is a good opportunity for a stress-reducing Mindfulness Moment.

Remember, mindfulness is a state of mind that you achieve by focusing all of your awareness and attention on the present moment and only the present moment, excluding worries of the past as well as the future. The practice of mindfulness gives you a "brain break," inviting you to calmly, nonjudgmentally, and compassionately accept your current thoughts, emotions, and body sensations without feeling as though you need to change them. The Mindfulness Moment includes a short breathing exercise that I hope provides you with a sense of peace that, at least for the moment, everything is OK.

Here we go again.

1. Sit in a comfortable chair, put both feet on the floor (or any other comfortable position), clasp your hands over the middle of your belly, and then close your eyes (if desired).

2. Scan your muscles from head to toe and intentionally relax them. Unclench your teeth, let your shoulders sag, and relax your buttock and leg muscles.

3. Take in a slow, deep breath through your nose (count "one one-thousand, two one-thousand, three one-thousand" to yourself as you do so), then slowly exhale through your mouth to the same count, feeling the rise and fall of your belly. Do a total of ten slow, deep breaths like this. Focus solely on the gentle flow of your breath, in and out. Each time you exhale, consciously blow out any negative emotions and stress you feel about your loved one's dementia symptoms and your care partnering.

4. After the tenth breath, slowly open your eyes.

LEGAL ISSUES

There are a number of very important **legal issues** for you to consider as care partner to a loved one with dementia. In general, it is best to have an **elder-law attorney** (or an attorney very familiar with elder-law-related issues) assist you with these things. In this section, we'll focus on the four most common legal issues that arise when a loved one has dementia: durable power of attorney, guardianship, HIPAA, and driving.

WHAT IS AN ELDER-LAW ATTORNEY?

Many care partners I have encountered have been reluctant at first to see an elder-law attorney. Some already had a will or power-of-attorney in place from their general-practice or estate-planning lawyer. Others just didn't see the need. However, a certified elder-law attorney has specialized training, knowledge, expertise, and experience about dementia and working with families on the dementia journey that other lawyers may not.

Elder-law attorneys handle all the legal matters affecting older adults, including issues related to health care, long-term-care planning, guardianship, retirement, Social Security, Medicare/Medicaid, and more. In the Memory Counseling Program at Wake Forest Baptist Health, we refer nearly every family we see to an elder-law attorney, or if cost is an issue, we have an Elder Law Clinic at the Wake Forest University School of Law that provides services for free. Elder-law attorneys often belong to an organization called the National Academy of Elder Law Attorneys. Their website (www.naela.org) has a link to help you find an elder-law attorney in your area. Or, if you have a general-practice or other lawyer, they should be able to direct you to an elder-law attorney they know and work with. Family members and friends can also be helpful in the search for an elder-law attorney.

DURABLE POWER OF ATTORNEY

The **durable power of attorney (DPOA)** is a crucial document that should be the very first of the legal, financial, and end-of-life tasks you deal with. It is a document that names who will make decisions on your loved one's behalf if they become unable to due to incompetence or incapacitation. This person is referred to as your "agent." Every adult in the family should have a DPOA, regardless of age or health status, since any of us can become incapacitated at any time. Since dementia is a disease that affects cognitive function, and since both competence and capacity, in the legal sense, are cognitive issues, a definition of **legal capacity/competence** is important.

In brief lay terms, legal capacity refers to the ability to make good decisions, whereas competence is the ability to act on those decisions. In cognitive terms, it's the ability to exercise good judgment by understanding the pluses and minuses (benefits versus risks) of a decision, a process that requires the brain's executive function to be intact, and carry out the actions resulting from decisions that are made. Research suggests that a **Mini-Mental Status Exam (MMSE)** score of at least 20 is necessary for capacity/competence. In legal terms, it's the ability to understand, weigh the options, remember, and communicate a decision, contract, or binding agreement that is personal or financial in nature.

Who you choose or help your loved one choose to serve as their agent in the DPOA is a very important decision. If you are the person with dementia's spouse or long-term partner, it would typically be you. If you are an adult child of the person with dementia, it might be you or someone else in your family. Regardless, the person designated in the DPOA should be someone all of you really trust, who will look out for your (and all family members') best interests, will honor your wishes, and won't abuse the power granted to them as DPOA. If for some reason that person can't act as DPOA, then the document should name at least one (or even several) back-up DPOAs. For example, I have one family in which the father, who is 86 years old and has early-stage

Alzheimer's disease, named his wife as DPOA followed by a series of successor DPOAs, including (in order) his brother, daughter, and elder-law attorney.

Besides who you choose as DPOA, three other things are important. First, if your loved one still has capacity/competence, they can revoke their DPOA or name others to serve in that capacity if desired. Second, it is best to have the DPOA made when your loved one still has capacity/competence. And third, the DPOA document should be stored somewhere both safe and accessible to the primary care partner and any other successor DPOAs who are named. Many states have a public registry (for example, North Carolina's county registers of deeds) as the depository for DPOAs, and the documents are also available online.

HEALTHCARE POWER OF ATTORNEY

The healthcare POA is a written document, typically generated at the same time as the DPOA and another document, the living will, which I'll discuss later in the lesson. The healthcare POA spells out who you want to make decisions about your medical care, including but not limited to end-of-life issues, in the event you are not able to. Your healthcare POA should be someone you trust, preferably who lives nearby, to carry out your medical and end-of-life wishes. Typically, it is your spouse, partner, or one of your adult children, but it could also be someone who is not related but lives close to you. It can, but does not have to be, the same person as your durable POA. You might want to name an alternate too. Usually you would not name your doctor, or a staff member if you live in a residential-care setting, as your healthcare POA (many states ban this by law).

GUARDIANSHIP

There are situations in which a person with dementia lacks capacity/competence, does not have a living, close, or involved family member (or is in a second marriage with adult children from the first marriage), and has no DPOA in place but needs someone to make medical and sometimes financial decisions on their behalf. In this case, there might

ELDER ABUSE

Another reason to consider guardianship and involve APS is when elder abuse may be occurring. According to the World Health Organization (WHO), elder abuse is "a single, or repeated act, or lack of appropriate action, occurring within any relationship where there is an expectation of trust which causes harm or distress to an older person." Elder abuse can take various forms such as financial, physical, psychological, and sexual. It can also be the result of intentional or unintentional neglect or abandonment. The WHO estimates that one in six people 65 years or older is subject to elder abuse. If you suspect your loved one with dementia is being abused, contact your county APS office.

be a need to ask a court to appoint an objective, impartial individual to represent the person with dementia. If the court finds that the person does need a guardian to help them understand the legal process and express their views, they would appoint a family member (if available) or impartial attorney to serve in this capacity. This advocate is referred to as the **guardian ad litem**.

A **guardianship hearing** is a court proceeding in the county-court system that occurs in the presence of a judge but is more of an informal process. Someone must file for **guardianship** in order to have a guardianship hearing. This may be a social worker in the county Adult Protective Services (APS) department, a family member, or an attorney, depending on the situation.

In the guardianship hearing, evidence is presented, which the judge uses to determine the person's capacity/competence and to choose the best guardian for them. When there is some contention associated with this process—for example, if adult children from a prior marriage have different desires for their parent with dementia than the person with dementia's current spouse, then the court will select the person they feel would do the best job as guardian. In some states, it is possible to request that the guardianship dispute go to mediation. This is an informal process in which a trained mediator helps the parties try to reach an agreement about the person with dementia's guardianship. Mediation can help the family members reach a flexible solution, while maintaining family relationships. You can see from the complexity of the guardianship process why it makes sense to appoint a DPOA while the person with mild cognitive impairment or early-stage dementia is still considered competent.

A Contentious Guardianship Situation

Benjamin was a lifetime bachelor in his mid-70s who developed short-term memory loss 15 years before coming to my geriatrics department for an evaluation. He had two brothers but was always accompanied only by his older brother and his older brother's wife, Ruth, who lived locally. Benjamin was diagnosed with Alzheimer's disease.

Despite his diagnosis, Benjamin was able to live independently at first, in an independent-living community, with the help of his brother and Ruth. About five years after his diagnosis, his brother passed away. Ruth continued to support Benjamin, who by this time was steadily deteriorating and needed to be moved initially to assisted living, then memory care, and eventually into a nursing home, where he needed total care.

Benjamin paid for his care with his own financial resources, which were managed by a financial planner he had worked with for years. Ruth wrote the checks for Benjamin's residential care and other medical-care costs and living expenses.

One day, when Benjamin was approaching the end of life, his younger brother and his spouse appeared from out of town, unannounced.

They told Ruth they wanted to be the decision-makers for Benjamin's care, and they were the rightful heirs to whatever money would be left after his death.

Benjamin did not have a DPOA in place. Ruth sought the counsel of an attorney, who petitioned the court for a guardianship hearing with the intent of Ruth becoming Benjamin's legal guardian. At the hearing, evidence was presented showing Benjamin was in fact incompetent and lacked decision-making capacity. Both medical and financial records showed that over the prior ten years, Benjamin's older brother and Ruth handled all of Benjamin's affairs. There was not a single documentation that the younger brother or his wife had ever accompanied Benjamin on a doctor's visit, and under oath, they said prior to their recent appearance, they had not had contact with Benjamin in years. The judge ruled that Ruth, not the younger brother, should be Benjamin's guardian.

HEALTH INSURANCE PORTABILITY AND ACCOUNTABILITY ACT

The **Health Insurance Portability and Accountability Act** of 1996, or **HIPAA**, was a federal statute that guaranteed health-insurance portability in the event you moved from one state to another. It is best known for its provision to safeguard the confidentiality of your medical information as well your actual paper or computerized medical records.

The passage of HIPAA resulted in a lot of safeguards being put in place in doctors' offices and hospitals, or anywhere you might have medical information stored. Because of HIPAA, your medical records (as well as the personal information that is also part of your medical records) must be secured in a safe place (locked in the case of paper records, encrypted for computerized records), kept confidential, and disposed of properly.

You have likely been asked to sign documents related to HIPAA when you've interacted with the medical system. Pertinent to this lesson, the most important document your loved one with dementia might sign is the HIPAA authorization form, sometimes referred to as the **HIPAA**

authorization or release form. When they sign a HIPAA authorization or release, they can then specify who their medical providers can share their medical information and medical records with. It will usually be family members.

Having a signed HIPAA authorization form gives you as care partner the ability to discuss your loved one's medical conditions with doctors and get vital feedback about what occurred in a doctor's appointment if you were not present. This is extremely helpful for adult children caring for aging parents in general. Like the DPOA, your loved one's HIPAA authorization should be stored in a safe and accessible place for those who may need it. Since you usually sign the authorization at the doctor's office or local hospital, they may also keep copies of the document.

Do you have any questions about DPOA, guardianship, or HIPAA at this point? If so, please write them down to ask someone, such as your attorney, local Area Agency on Aging, or one of the other resources mentioned earlier in the lesson.

_____

_____

_____

_____

_____

_____

DRIVING

One of the most contentious challenges you may face as dementia care partner is assessing and monitoring your loved one's ability to continue to drive safely, both for their own safety and for the safety of other drivers as well as pedestrians. I have included it as a legal issue because of the potential legal consequences of unsafe driving.

In the United States, with the exception of large urban areas with well-developed public transportation systems, driving gives us personal freedom and autonomy to be independent—to get from here to there throughout the day when we want to. We take this for granted until someone tries to take our privilege to drive away. Then we may become very protective of and defensive about it.

But driving is one of the most complex tasks the brain performs. Referring back to Lesson Three, we see that driving involves all five of our cognitive functions—attention and concentration, planning, problem-solving, multitasking, memory and learning, language, and visuospatial function. Impairment of one or more of these as a result of dementia will impair a person's ability to

SAFE OR NOT SAFE TO DRIVE?

Are you concerned about the driving safety of your loved one with MCI or dementia? Here are two simple questions that might help you decide if further assessment of their driving is warranted.

1. When you are in the car with them, do you always drive?

2. Would you be reluctant to let young children, such as your loved one's grandchildren, ride in the car with them?

If you answered "yes" to either question, then your gut is telling you that further assessment is warranted!

drive safely. Other brain functions, like vision, hearing, and motor skills (arms/hands and legs/feet responding in a coordinated way as they should) are also necessary for safe driving.

If and when you have concerns about your loved one's driving safety, here are several things for you to think about:

- Driving safety is related to the stage of the disease. Many people with mild cognitive impairment remain safe to drive, whereas those with middle- and late-stage dementia are not. In early-stage dementia, some might still be safe to drive, but many will not. Generally speaking, the lower a person with dementia scores on a cognitive-function test like the MMSE, the less safe their driving is going to be. However, there is not a specific MMSE score that can absolutely predict safe or unsafe driving ability.

- The most thorough assessment of driving safety is an **occupational-therapy driving evaluation**. Some occupational therapists (OTs) have special training to evaluate driving safety using a combination of paper and pencil tests (like the MMSE or Montreal Cognitive Assessment, and/or others) and a road test. An OT driving evaluation must be ordered by a medical provider (doctor, physician assistant, nurse practitioner) and is generally not covered by your health insurance. The OT will determine if the person can drive without restrictions, or with some restrictions (for example, local driving, during the daytime, on roads with speed limits of 45 or less), or is unsafe to drive, in which case they require the person to surrender their driver's license to the state **Division of Motor Vehicles (DMV)**. You might wonder if the written and road tests provided by your DMV are comparable to an OT driving evaluation. In my opinion, and I believe most in the profession would agree, they are not as thorough, as they do not include the paper and pencil cognitive tests, and the evaluator does not have the background and training in assessing driving safety in people with dementia.

- If you are confronting the issue of driving safety with your loved one, it works well to allow your medical provider to be the team captain of the process. They will be able to integrate all the components of the driving-safety assessment into a decision for your loved one. When a medical professional deems someone unsafe to drive, it has been my experience that half the time they will willingly give up their license. The other half of the time there will be some resistance to the recommendation. "I've been driving for 50 years" and "I've never gotten into an accident" are typical responses. If your loved one is one of these resistors, let the doctor, not you, be the bad guy. It's better they be the one to receive your loved one's wrath, not you, although you are likely to be the one who has to physically remove the keys (including hidden ones!) from your loved one's possession or have the car removed from the home, both difficult tasks.

From a legal perspective, there are two big driving-safety issues that warrant your consideration, **criminal liability** and **civil liability**. A person who drives unsafely might break the law, resulting in criminal liability ranging from a speeding violation to unintentional vehicular manslaughter. The former, punishable by a ticket and a mail-in fine, is much different than the latter, which would require an appearance in criminal court before a judge, necessitating legal counsel and possibly resulting in jail time, a substantial fine, or both.

The other issue, civil liability, is the legal process by which a person who has been injured, or whose property has been damaged, or both, can seek financial compensation from the individual(s) who caused that damage. Let's say a motor-vehicle accident occurred that totaled the other driver's car and caused injury to their neck from whiplash. In the process of investigating the accident, their insurance company may request the medical records of the driver who caused the injury. If that person has a diagnosis of early-stage Alzheimer's disease, particularly if the issue of driving safety has been documented somewhere in the medical record, a civil lawsuit could ensue. Civil lawsuits are heard in civil court, also in front of a judge. They require legal counsel to represent the driver and can result in a significant financial settlement to the victim. Besides the possibility of physical harm, the potential for civil liability is often the greatest consideration at play when you are deciding whether or not a person with dementia should drive.

Is your loved one still driving? If so, write down any concerns you have about their driving to ask their medical provider about.

_____

_____

_____

_____

_____

_____

FINANCIAL ISSUES

After reading the section on legal issues, perhaps you're feeling like you need a law degree to navigate the journey as a dementia care partner! This next section won't make you feel too differently, but it will provide more helpful information on financial topics and issues, which include wills and trusts, and the cost of and paying for long-term care.

WILLS AND TRUSTS

Wills and trusts are legal documents that spell out who you want your assets—money, real estate, and personal property—distributed to (your heirs) upon your death, as well as who you want to be the person who makes sure that the distribution happens according to your wishes, also called the **executor** (who may or not be one of your heirs, or could be your elder-law attorney or even a corporation like a bank that helps execute a will).

Every adult should have a will or trust. If you have limited assets with straightforward instructions to distribute those assets, a **simple will** with a family member as executor should be adequate. After you die, the executor's main responsibility is to **probate** the will, meaning they make sure the money, real estate, and property are given to the people you intended, including paying state and federal taxes and transferring deeds for the land as necessary. The more specific you are in your will, the easier it will be for your executor to probate the will. Usually, the attorney who drafts your will also assist the executor in the probate process.

If you have significant assets and/or your instructions for distributing them are complicated, then a **trust** may be a better choice than a will (and sometimes, you might need both a will and a trust). Your elder-law or estate-planning attorney can help you decide what's best. A trust is more expensive than a simple will.

A trust:

- Describes how your assets will be distributed after you die.

- Takes effect immediately when you're still alive, with you (or someone you designate) as trustee (similar to executor in a simple will), rather than upon your death.

- Includes the name of the person to succeed the trustee (you or your designee) if you become incapable of being trustee, or when you die, called the successor trustee, who oversees your trust and its assets (your money, real estate, and personal property).

- Often reduces state and federal taxes, such as gift taxes.

- Distributes assets to your heirs without going through probate, eliminating the time and expense associated with probate (can be up to ten percent of the value of your total estate).

- Better protects your assets from creditors, guardianship, and lawsuits.

There are two types of trusts, revocable and irrevocable. What's best for you or your loved one—a simple will, a revocable trust, or an irrevocable trust—is something you should also discuss with your elder-law or estate-planning attorney. Along with your durable power of attorney document and designating who your DPOA is, having your will or trust in place should be on your short list of things to do sooner rather than later.

COST OF LONG-TERM CARE

The cost of your loved one's care over the course of their dementia journey may very well be the issue that causes you the most worry, and rightfully so. With an average lifespan of eight to ten years from the time of diagnosis, people with dementia often require costly care that can be a financial drain for many families. The cost of care varies depending on several factors, such as the care needs of the person with dementia, how much care the family chooses to provide, whether or not the person with dementia has long-term care insurance, and their financial resources.

For illustration purposes, let's contrast two families, the Smiths and the Millers, each of whom took over the care of Grandma Sadie from the age of 88 to 92, which is when she died. At 88, Sadie was widowed and diagnosed with early-stage Alzheimer's disease. She had been living in a one-bedroom apartment in a senior complex, but she had been struggling with her instrumental activities of daily living. Her doctor had told her she couldn't drive anymore, so she couldn't shop for groceries or pick up prescriptions without someone driving her. She also wasn't able to prepare her meals any longer, she got confused about which pills to take, and her bills weren't getting paid on time. It was time for her family to step in.

Let's see how the Smiths and Millers cared for their Grandma Sadie, and how much it cost them.

- **The Smiths**

  The Smiths are a family of four, with Mr. Smith (full-time men's clothing salesman), Mrs. Smith (at-home mom), and two high-school-aged children, plus Grandma Sadie (mom's mom), who has long-term care insurance and $175,000 in the bank from her late husband's retirement savings and sale of their home. When Sadie was no longer able to live alone, the Smiths decided to have her move in with them. She stayed in a spare bedroom. Mrs. Smith was able to provide most of her mom's care for the first two years. She took Sadie to an adult daycare program three half-days a week to give herself some personal time, and in the evening and on weekends, her husband and kids helped care for her. After two years managing this way, Sadie then needed help with basic ADLs, such as getting dressed, bathing, and going to the toilet. She also wasn't sleeping well at night, tending to get up and wander. The Smiths hired paid caregivers, one to cover the 11 p.m. to 7 a.m. shift, then another for 7 a.m. to 11 a.m. Otherwise, among all of the family members, they were able to meet Sadie's care needs for another two years. Then she fell and broke a hip. The Smiths decided to have hospice come into their home, in keeping with Sadie's end-of-life wishes for comfort care. She died about one week later. The cost of Grandma Sadie's care was $261,500.

- **The Millers**
A family of four with Mr. Miller (disabled veteran, unable to work), Mrs. Miller (a full-time secretary), and two high-school-aged children, plus Grandma Sadie (Mr. Miller's mom), who did not have long-term care insurance and had $60,000 in the bank. When Sadie was no longer able to live alone, the Millers thought residential care would work best, since Mr. Miller was disabled, Mrs. Miller worked, and the kids

GRANDMA SADIE SMITH'S COST OF CARE

How much did the Smiths spend on Grandma Sadie's care?

FIRST TWO YEARS:
- Adult daycare
$50 for 4 hours for 730 days = $36,500

SECOND TWO YEARS:
- Paid caregiver
$25/hour for 12 hours for 730 days = $219,000 (long-term care insurance policy paid $125 per day or $91,250, so net cost to Grandma Sadie was $127,750)

- Medical supplies
Including pull-ups/diapers, walker, wheelchair, shower chair, and the like = $6,000 (long-term care policy covered cost of $250 wheelchair)

- Hospice
Covered by Medicare and Grandma Sadie's supplemental medical insurance = $0

COST:
- Total: $36,500 + $219,000 + $6,000 = $261,500

- Covered by long-term care policy: $91,250 + $250 = $91,500

- Covered by Grandma Sadie's savings: $261,500 - $91,500 = $170,000

- Cost to Smiths = $0

were busy with school and after-school activities. They found a residential-care community that had assisted living, memory care, as well as a nursing home for low-income individuals. After the first year in assisted living, when Sadie's assets were exhausted, the Millers applied for Medicaid on Sadie's behalf. After another year in assisted living, Sadie began to wander, so for the next year, she was moved to memory care. However, Sadie's care needs then increased. She was now requiring help with basic ADLs, such as getting dressed, bathing, and going to the toilet. She also wasn't sleeping well at night, and was getting more and more unsteady on her feet. So, the decision was made to move her to the nursing home, where she lived for the next two years. One night, while trying to get up and go to the bathroom, Sadie fell and broke a hip. Sadie was hospitalized and underwent hip replacement, honoring

GRANDMA SADIE MILLER'S COST OF CARE

How much did the Millers spend on Grandma Sadie's care?

FIRST TWO YEARS:

- Assisted living
  One year, $5,000 per month for 12 months = $60,000 (paid for by Grandma Sadie's assets)

- Memory care
  One year, $7,500 per month for 12 months = $90,000 (covered by Medicaid)

SECOND TWO YEARS:

- Nursing home
  Two years, $6,000 per month for 24 months = $144,000 (covered by Medicaid)

- Hospitalization
  Hip-replacement surgery = $75,000 (all but $7,500 covered by Medicare and Medicare supplement)

COST:

- Total: $60,000 + $90,000 + $144,000 + $75,000 = $369,000

- Covered by Grandma Sadie's assets = $60,000

- Covered by Medicare + Medicare supplement and Medicaid = $301,500

- Cost to Millers = $7,500

her wishes to have aggressive medical care "till the end." Following surgery, Sadie developed a kidney infection, and despite antibiotics, died one week later. The cost of Grandma Sadie's care was $369,000.

You might be alarmed by the cost of Sadie's care in the illustrations provided. In both cases, it's six figures, over a quarter-million dollars for the Smiths, one-third million for the Millers. For the Millers, most of the cost was borne by Medicaid, which is the rule rather than the exception when it comes to paying for long-term care. Medicaid covers the cost for six in ten nursing-home residents. Though the cost of care was less for the Smiths, their total cost didn't include the value of the unpaid care they provided in their home.

PAYING FOR LONG-TERM CARE

You might be wondering how you will afford to care for your loved one. This is an area where the help of a professional might be very beneficial, such as an elder-law attorney, or as we discussed in the last lesson, a geriatric-care manager, and/or a financial planner.

Here is a list of some financial resources you can explore as you think about current and future costs of your loved one's care (some will apply, others won't).

- **Medicare and Medicare supplemental insurance** (or personal medical insurance if the person with dementia is younger than 65) will pay for most of the medical costs (but not long-term care costs) for a typical person with dementia 65 years of age and older. Medicare has four parts: Part A (covers inpatient hospital stays, skilled nursing, hospice, and home care [with limitations]), Part B (covers doctor visits, surgery, lab tests, and medical equipment), Part C (covers eye exams and eyeglasses, hearing exams and hearing aids [with limitations]), and Part D (covers prescription drugs). A Medicare supplement will cover some of the things not paid for by Medicare Parts A-D, such as copayments and deductibles.

- **Long-term care insurance** policies vary widely in what they do and don't cover. If your loved one has long-term care insurance, ask their insurance agent to provide a written summary of what the policy covers, or sit down with the agent to understand this information. It is likely that the financial assistance from a long-term care insurance policy will be helpful when your loved one reaches the middle stage of their disease. The American Association of Retired Persons (aarp. org) provides a comprehensive guide to long-term care insurance that is worth checking out.

- Veterans with dementia have special **benefits through the Veterans Administration** (VA)—for diagnosis, medications, caregiving, and residential care. If your loved one is a veteran, contact your local VA regional office, medical center, or clinic for specific information and services, or go to the following VA website: https://www.va.gov/ geriatrics/Alzheimers_And_Dementia_Care.asp.

- Other sources of income that may help pay for the cost of dementia care include **Social Security Disability Income** (SSDI) and **Social Security Income** (SSI). Someone diagnosed with early-onset dementia (less than age 65) qualifies for immediate SSDI and SSI under the Social Security Administration's Compassionate Allowance program, and you can apply online (https://www.ssa.gov/ compassionateallowances/).

- Some **community agencies and programs** may provide a limited amount of financial assistance. Refer back to Lesson Seven in the section on this topic for further information.

- One's **personal assets**, such as retirement savings, are likely to be needed to help pay for the cost of care since none of the resources listed above pay for the entire cost.

- If the person with dementia has no personal assets to use, or if they've been exhausted, then you may need to consider applying for **Medicaid**. Medicaid is a dual state and federal program that helps pay some of the cost of medical care for people with limited assets and income. Medicaid also pays for some things that Medicare only covers for a short period of time, like residential care in a nursing home, and home-health care in some settings. The government requires that the person with dementia's assets are spent (or if the person with dementia is part of a couple, half of the couple's assets are spent) before Medicaid will pay, though selling your home or vehicle is not required. There are other assets that one is also allowed to keep, and if the person with dementia is married, the "asset protection" rules in Medicaid are even more generous. This is so the spouse who remains at home is left with a certain amount of assets. The rules are complicated and they do change, so you should not make financial decisions with the aim of obtaining Medicaid without expert advice, from someone such as your elder-law attorney or an attorney who specializes in the Medicaid application process.

Do you have concerns about how you are going to pay for your loved one's care? If so, please write them down to ask someone, such as your care manager, attorney, or financial planner.

_____

_____

_____

_____

_____

_____

END-OF-LIFE ISSUES

If your loved one has recently been diagnosed with dementia, and you're at the beginning of the caregiving journey with them, you understandably might find it hard to read this section of the lesson on end-of-life issues. Yet, dementia is an incurable disease for the present time, and we all will have to consider these issues at one time or another.

Most of us want to live as long as possible and as well as possible. This notion is embodied in the title and theme of a recent book called *Live Long, Die Short: A Guide to Authentic Health and Successful Aging.* Author Roger Landry talks about how to live life to its fullest until just before we die, then die as quickly and gracefully as possible. Still, talking about the end of life, whether yours or someone else's, is neither enjoyable nor easy. But it is important, especially when you have a loved one with dementia.

As an oncologist who specialized in brain-tumor treatment, as well as a mental-health counselor to those on the dementia journey, I have spent more than 30 years talking to people confronting end-of-life issues. I've found that whether it's brain cancer or dementia, those who are diagnosed know that they have a bad disease that will probably shorten their life expectancy. They may not know when they will die, but they do know what they'll die from. And they're willing, sometimes even relieved, to be able to talk about it.

As I've shared, Rebecca died nine years after she was diagnosed with Alzheimer's disease. Though she didn't like talking about her diagnosis, once she learned her memory problems were due to Alzheimer's, she wanted to talk about the end of her life. She made it very clear to me (as I wept, listening to her every word) that when the end came, she didn't want anything done to prolong her life: no intravenous fluids, no feeding tube, no respirators, no cardiopulmonary resuscitation, "none of that folderol," as she put it. (Folderol was one of her favorite words; it means "foolish nonsense.") During her dementia journey, I prayed every day for her. My first prayer request was for her cure, and my second was that my daughters and I would know when she had come to the end of her life, so we'd be able to honor her wishes. I hope my story will serve as a gentle reminder for you to discuss end-of-life issues with your loved one as early in their journey as possible, when they are still able to provide input.

WHAT ARE THE MOST IMPORTANT END-OF-LIFE ISSUES?

There are a finite number of important end-of-life issues that should be addressed. They are:

- **Whether or not to administer fluids**

  When someone can't or won't take any liquids, dehydration will occur, and eventually, it will be a contributing factor to their death. While a person can go for a month without eating, generally one can only live about a week without drinking. In addition to swallowing fluids, they can also be given intravenously (IV) and through a feeding tube—either one that goes through the nose and down to the stomach (nasogastric feeding tube), which is a bedside procedure, or one that goes directly into the stomach through the overlying abdominal skin (gastric feeding tube or G-tube), which is a surgical procedure. Generally, if you or your loved one decide against fluid administration when they can't or won't take fluids, you would decline both IV fluids and fluids through a feeding tube.

- **Whether or not to be fed**

  When a person is dying, their need for food dramatically declines. This might be due to a slowing of their metabolism, inactivity, or both. Not being able to feed your loved one when they're dying may be troubling to you. Societally, and sometimes culturally, we view feeding someone as an act of love and nurturing. When a person is no longer able to feed themselves or be fed by another, if they are to continue being nourished, it must be done using liquid nutrition, either through an IV, a process called total parenteral nutrition, or through a G-tube. In either case, the person is being hydrated while they're being fed. Typically, if you decide to decline fluids, you'd also choose not to be fed. A person dying of dementia could be kept alive for weeks or months if they are hydrated and fed.

- **Whether or not to perform CPR or use a respirator**

  For the heart to beat and circulate blood, and for the lungs to breathe and take in oxygen, the brain (specifically, the brainstem) must be functioning. There are numerous reasons why a person with dementia could have their heart or lungs stop working, such as an infection, abnormality of electrolytes like sodium, potassium, or calcium, or the neurodegenerative disease process damaging the brainstem, among others. If the heart stops or is beating in a way that doesn't adequately circulate blood, and/or the lungs stop breathing, CPR must be initiated, often the heart must be shocked, and usually a breathing tube must be inserted into the lungs and hooked up to a breathing machine (respirator). However, the decision can be made not to take these measures.

For someone with dementia, the decision to perform CPR, shock the heart, and put them on a respirator depends on several factors. First and foremost is the disease stage. If they are in the late stage of the disease and dependent on others for their basic ADLs, especially if bed-bound, usually you would not perform CPR or consider a ventilator. However, for someone who is in the early or middle stage of the disease, particularly if they have a reversible cause to their heart or lung problems, such as infection or an electrolyte disturbance, then it is reasonable to opt for CPR and if necessary a ventilator.

On the other hand, I have worked with families over the years who have decided no matter what stage of dementia their loved one is in, or what the cause of the heart and lung issues, they will not agree to CPR or a ventilator. This is also quite reasonable given that dementia is still an incurable disease.

- **Whether or not to treat an infection with antibiotics**
People with dementia are at increased risk for both respiratory-tract (lung) infections like pneumonia and urinary-tract infections of the bladder or kidney. The decision process for treating an infection with antibiotics is much the same as the CPR and ventilator decision, in that it is primarily dependent on the disease stage. If the choice is made not to treat an infection, death from an overwhelming infection, called sepsis, can be dignified and peaceful.

- **Whether or not to have surgery for a hip fracture**
A fall and hip fracture in an older adult, particularly in those affected by dementia, is one of the most emotionally and medically challenging things that can occur on the dementia journey. As care partner, you may feel responsible for the fall, even if you weren't present when the fall occurred. Yet I tell all families on the dementia journey that their loved one will fall, likely more than once. So, it's not *if* they will fall, it's *when*, and what the consequences of the fall will be.

At some point in their life, one in three people over the age of 65 years will experience a fall. Of those who do fall, two-thirds will fall again. The majority of falls and hip fractures occur on a trip to or from or in the bathroom. In general, if a person with dementia is still ambulatory—that is, still walking—prior to their fall and hip fracture, then surgery followed by rehabilitation (physical and occupational therapy) is usually recommended. However, the likelihood of dying within six months of a fall and hip fracture is an alarming 25 percent, and half or more of people never walk again or achieve the same level of independence as they had before.

For the person with dementia who is not walking, the decision not to pursue surgery is very reasonable. Although their life expectancy is usually short in this circumstance, perhaps a month or two, they can be kept pain-free and comfortable with medication.

- **Where to die: home, hospital, or hospice**
This is a difficult question to discuss, and yet nearly all of us have a strong preference for where we hope to be when we take our last breath. With the availability of home-based hospice care, more and more people are choosing to die at home, in familiar surroundings, with loved ones (including pets) surrounding them. For those who don't want to be at home, they can likely be hospitalized at the end of life, or choose an inpatient hospice, which may be located within a hospital or may be a freestanding facility in the community. Hospice offers a more homelike environment. If this is a question you would

like your loved one with dementia's input on, asking it as early as possible in the journey, though challenging, is best.

- **What to do with the body after death**

  On the surface, this is the cremation versus burial question, but for the family who has been on the dementia journey, there is also the question of whether or not to have an autopsy just of the brain to determine or confirm the type of dementia that caused the death. Whether death comes following a slow, progressive decline, or it comes quickly, following a fall or infection, family members who didn't plan ahead usually wish they had. You can pre-plan (and if desired, pre-pay) for the funeral (including writing the obituary and eulogy) while your loved one is still alive—a process that can be both highly emotional and healing. Helpful information about planning a funeral is available on the Center for Loss and Life Transition website (https://www.centerforloss.com/grief/funerals-and-ceremonies/). The Alzheimer's Association also has information about brain donation on its website (www.alz.org/alzheimers-dementia/ research_progress/brain-donation).

Have you discussed some of these issues with your loved one or as a family? Pick one or two of these end-of-life questions, perhaps the most challenging one(s), and write down the decisions you would make about it (them) at this point in time. Please share.

_____

_____

_____

_____

_____

_____

Based on your response to the question above, what questions do you have for your medical provider about your loved one's end-of-life issues? Please share.

_____

_____

_____

_____

_____

_____

_____

LEGAL DOCUMENTS RELATED TO THE END OF LIFE

There are three legal documents, collectively referred to as "advance directives," that are specifically related to end-of-life issues (a fourth one, the healthcare power of attorney, was discussed earlier in the lesson). They spell out the answers to the questions described in the prior section of this lesson in the event your loved cannot answer them at the time. Whether you need one, two, or all of these is something you should discuss with an elder-law attorney and the medical doctor caring for your loved one.

Each state has its own advance directives forms. You can download them for free through the American Association for Retired Persons (AARP) website at aarp.org and enter "advance directives" in the search box. Copies of the living will should be available in the home (posting them on the refrigerator is helpful, as emergency medical personnel will look for them there if they need to come into the home), added to the hospital medical chart, and placed on file at the residential-care facility.

- **Living will**—A written document used when the person is still alive but facing a disease like dementia or end-of-life issues and is unable to make decisions or speak for themself. It expresses the person's wishes about fluid administration, being fed through a tube, CPR, shocking the heart, respirator use, antibiotics, and virtually any other situation that may occur in a home, hospital, or residential-care setting (for example, morphine use at the end of life).

- **Do not resuscitate**—A **do not resuscitate order** (**DNR**) is an order written by a doctor or medical provider (like a physician assistant or nurse practitioner) in the hospital or residential-care setting specifying that in the event your heart stops and/or you stop breathing, you will not have CPR, the heart won't be shocked, or a breathing tube will not be inserted (a process called **intubation**) and hooked up to a breathing machine. Synonyms for DNR include **DNR/ DNI** (do not resuscitate/do not intubate), **no code** (in many hospitals, when a patient needs resuscitation or intubation, a team of people is alerted by issuing a "code blue, room XYZ" over the intercom system), or **desire for a natural death**. The DNR is part of what's written in the living will, but here it is written as a medical order as well.

- **Physician's orders for life-sustaining treatment**—This document, also referred to as **POLST**, is a DNR order that, in addition to covering CPR and intubation, specifies other end-of-life care options such as fluid administration, feeding, and antibiotics. Like the DNR, an order for these other things must be written in the person's hospital or residential-care facility chart. It goes by several other names, as well, depending on state of residence, including **MOST** (medical orders for scope of treatment), **MOLST** (medical orders for life-sustaining treatment), **POST** (physician orders for scope of treatment), and **TPOPP** (transportable physician orders for patient preferences).

Does your loved one have a living will, healthcare power of attorney, DNR/DNI, or POLST (or equivalent) document in place? If yes, what end-of-life decisions have been specified by the document? If they don't have one or more of these documents in place, what are the barriers preventing this from happening? Please share.

_____

_____

_____

_____

_____

_____

_____

SAYING THINGS AT THE END OF LIFE, AND LIFE AFTER DEMENTIA

I've included this brief section in the lesson for very personal reasons. As I shared back in Lesson One when I told Rebecca's story, she lost recognition of our daughters and me literally overnight. Though I believe she know how much I loved and appreciated her, had I known what would happen that terrible day, I would have made a point of sitting her down one day long before that to tell her **thank you** for being such a wonderful wife and amazing mother to our daughters and how much I truly loved her. This is my biggest regret of her journey, our journey, our family's journey with her Alzheimer's disease. I was able to say goodbye to her on the morning of her death. In fact, when we knew her death was imminent, we had as many family members and friends come and say **goodbye** as we could.

In the end, just the girls and I surrounded Rebecca and said goodbye. And I remember thinking over and over, "How am I (how are we) going to live without her?" Well, life has gone on, but it was forever changed by Rebecca's death for all who loved her. I was very fortunate to have had a compassionate mental-health counselor who walked alongside of me in Rebecca's last years of life and through grieving her physical death. I still think of her each and every day, and I expect to for the rest of my days.

Looking back, there aren't too many things I would have done differently. I'll always remember two things my middle daughter, Leah, said during the journey, simple yet helpful bits of wisdom I've shared with many clients I've companioned on their dementia journeys: "You're doing a good job" and "You can only do the best you can do, and no better."

What are some things you would like to say to your loved one before the end of their life? Please share.

_____

_____

_____

_____

_____

_____

A FINAL REFLECTION AND LOOKING AHEAD

I hope you've found this lesson to be both helpful and practical. It can also be a very emotional lesson, particularly when thinking about the end-of-life issues. At its core, it's a lesson about preparing for what's ahead, which is Central Need 7 of dementia care partners and a very important one indeed.

Based on everything covered in the lesson, what is the one thing in the areas of legal, financial, and end-of-life issues related to your loved one's dementia journey you feel the most prepared for? Please explain.

_____

_____

_____

_____

_____

What do you feel the least prepared for? Please explain.

_____

_____

_____

_____

_____

_____

In the next lesson, Lesson Nine, we will be talking about existential and spiritual questions you may have, questions that often come up during the present lesson on legal, financial, and end-of-life issues. These are the so-called "why" questions, such as "why him" or "why her," that are sometimes directed at God. Anticipating the challenge and emotion of this lesson, spend a minute repeating the Mindfulness Moment you engaged in earlier in the lesson. Believe it or not, you have just two more lessons to go in your support group or self-study. Here's a virtual pat on the back for your endurance!

LESSON NINE
Existential and Spiritual Questions

Over the last eight years, I've counseled hundreds of families on the dementia journey. Almost all have asked what I refer to as the "**why questions**." The person with dementia may ask "Why me?" You as a care partner may ask "**Why him?**" or "**Why her?**" If you have a belief in God or a higher power, you may ask the questions of them, and you may have further existential questions, such as "Does God exist?", "If God exists, how could He allow this to happen?", "What is the meaning of life?", "Is there such a thing as the 'soul'?" and "Is there an afterlife?"

"Bad things happen to good people all the time. It sucks. It's not fair, but then, much of life isn't fair. It's how you live that matters. It's how you deal with the bumps in the road."

— Maya Banks

These kinds of questions are **existential** and **spiritual** in nature, since they deal with the existence and character of God or something bigger and infinite. They are questions of faith that naturally come up when bad things happen to good people. They are questions that arise when we feel empty, powerless, and have no control—when we're unsure if we can endure what's on the road ahead. Yet, they are questions that do not necessarily have absolute, right or wrong, or even satisfying answers. Perhaps they don't have answers at all. Yet we are as human beings are naturally inclined to ask them, sometimes over and over when trials and tribulations occur on the dementia journey.

During Rebecca's nine-year journey with Alzheimer's disease, I prayed daily that she would be miraculously cured. That prayer was never answered. While there were many discouraging moments along the way, there was one particular day that I was downright angry, questioning whether God really existed and upset by the pat, "churchy" answers that some people gave me in the particular situation I was in.

It was about six months before Rebecca died, and one morning I heard her daytime caregiver scream out to me, "Come quickly, Rebecca is having a seizure." I ran into the bedroom and sure enough, Rebecca was rigid, biting her tongue, with blood oozing from the corner of her mouth. She was also incontinent—all symptoms of a grand mal seizure. We had an anti-anxiety medication in the house called lorazepam, which also is a fast-acting seizure treatment. I pried her mouth open and put two of the pills under her tongue. Then I held her rigid body. Her lips were turning blue because she was hardly breathing. I told her I loved her, not knowing if this would be the end. It wasn't.

After what seemed like an eternity but was probably just two or three minutes, she relaxed and started breathing. The caregiver and I helped her into bed, where she slept the entire day. Rebecca was never the same after that seizure. In retrospect, I could see that it was, in fact, the beginning of the end. I was deeply shaken. The level of stress I felt during the seizure episode could not have been higher. Though I honored Rebecca's living will not to have any extraordinary measures to prolong her life (hence, no call to 911, no ambulance trip to the emergency department), she (we) survived the experience.

That night, I slept fitfully. On my nightstand was a baby monitor with the camera fixed on Rebecca's face and the volume loud enough that

I could hear her every breath. She had her nighttime caregiver sitting right next to her, but I needed to see and hear her. The next morning I woke, went into the bathroom, and splashed water on my face to try and wake up. Something wasn't right. The eyelids of my left eye would only partially close, leaving my eye partially exposed as I splashed water onto it. The left side of my mouth drooped, and I drooled out of the left corner of my mouth. When I tried to talk, my speech didn't sound quite right. And the skin behind my left ear felt numb.

My thoughts raced. Was I having a stroke? I didn't think so, as there were no other stroke symptoms. Did I have a brain tumor? Not likely; there were no other symptoms of that either. Or was this Bell's palsy, paralysis involving one side of the face, the cause of which is uncertain but thought to be viral or stress-induced (which is what it turned out to be)? I went back into my bedroom and flung myself

WHEN GOD GAVE ME MORE THAN I COULD HANDLE

As a Christian, during Rebecca's journey I was often told, particularly when I shared with others the stories of her seizure episode and my subsequent Bell's palsy, something like, "God will not give you more than you can handle." I did not find this comforting and was unsure why others felt compelled to say this to me. Central Need Five—Take care of yourself—includes the importance of being companioned as a care partner (see Lesson Six). The most essential component of being companioned is being listened to, being heard (which is Central Need 1—Tell and retell your story). What I needed at that point in the journey was to talk and have someone listen to and empathize with me— about Rebecca's seizure and my Bell's palsy and well as the new challenges she and I now faced—not religious platitudes. I'll share a bit more of my faith perspective at the end of the lesson.

on the bed in defeat. This was the last straw. I broke down and wept uncontrollably. Though I viewed myself as a person who was physically and emotionally strong, with a deep faith, in that moment I felt like it was Alzheimer's disease: 1, me: 0. "God," I cried out, "how could you allow this to happen to me? How could you allow this to happen to us? Why Rebecca? Why our family? What have we done to deserve this?" There was only a deafening silence.

Have you asked any of the "Why questions" as care partner to your loved one with dementia? If you have, please put them down here and expand on them. What are you thinking and feeling? Have your "why" questions changed over time? Which "why" questions are most pressing on your heart and soul right now? Please share.

_____

_____

_____

_____

_____

_____

Has someone shared "empty words" with you, such as "God will not give you more than you can handle"? If so, how did this make you feel? How did you respond? Please share.

_____

_____

_____

_____

_____

Has your loved one's dementia journey challenged or strengthened your faith or spirituality? Please share your thoughts about this.

_____

_____

_____

_____

_____

_____

When it comes to the "why" questions, one particular couple's story comes to mind. What I remember most is how the person with Alzheimer's disease reacted so differently to his diagnosis than his wife did.

Opposite Reactions to the Same Diagnosis

Roger Parnell was a retired fireman who had a strong lineage of firefighters and police officers on his father's side of the family and a strong history of Alzheimer's disease on his mother's side. When he started experiencing memory loss and some difficulty multitasking at the age of 75, he sought evaluation. Not surprisingly, the diagnosis was Alzheimer's disease. I recall sitting right in front of Mr. Parnell and his wife when they returned to my office to discuss test results and hear the diagnosis. "Mr. and Mrs. Parnell, I have something very difficult to tell you both. All of the tests we did point quite consistently in the same direction. The diagnosis is Alzheimer's disease. I'm so sorry." The facial expressions of both of the Parnells changed immediately to sadness. Tears welled up in their eyes. She spoke first, staring blankly ahead and said, "There is no God." It was different for him. He looked me square in the eye with a look of resignation and said, "Doctor, why *not* me?"

Mr. and Mrs. Parnell had completely opposite reactions to his diagnosis of Alzheimer's disease. Which one of them do you relate more to and why?

_____

_____

_____

_____

_____

_____

MINDFULNESS MOMENT

The lesson covers some very thought-provoking and challenging topics. In the process of self-reflection, you may be asking some deep questions, to yourself, to others, perhaps to God. Times of deep introspection, however you experience them, are good opportunities for a stress-reducing Mindfulness Moment. Remember, mindfulness is a state of mind that you achieve by focusing all of your awareness and attention on the present moment and only the present moment, excluding worries of the past as well as the future. The practice of mindfulness gives you a "brain break," inviting you to calmly, nonjudgmentally, and compassionately accept your current thoughts, emotions, and body sensations without feeling as though you need to change them. The Mindfulness Moment includes a short breathing exercise that I hope provides you with a sense of peace that, at least for the moment, everything is OK.

Here we go again.

1. Sit in a comfortable chair, put both feet on the floor (or any other comfortable position), clasp your hands over the middle of your belly, and then close your eyes (if desired).

2. Scan your muscles from head to toe and intentionally relax them.

Unclench your teeth, let your shoulders sag, and relax your buttock and leg muscles.

3. Take in a slow, deep breath through your nose (count "one one-thousand, two one-thousand, three one-thousand" to yourself as you do so), then slowly exhale through your mouth to the same count, feeling the rise and fall of your belly. Do a total of ten slow, deep breaths like this. Focus solely on the gentle flow of your breath, in and out. Each time you exhale, consciously blow out any negative emotions and stress you feel about your loved one's dementia symptoms and your care partnering.

4. After the tenth breath, slowly open your eyes.

OK, let's continue on.

THE SEARCH FOR MEANING

WHY ASK WHY?

When something bad happens to someone you love, it's natural to feel lost and frustrated as you try to understand "why." It's OK if you never come to a resolution of "why," because it's often the process of exploring, of undertaking the search for meaning, that may be most helpful for you.

In general, following your natural search for meaning wherever it leads you and making time for spirituality are important because they help you cope with the most challenging matters of human existence—why is there pain and suffering, why are there diseases like Alzheimer's and the other dementias? Whether you are religious or not, spiritual practices like prayer or meditation can give you a place to turn when you're feeling overwhelmed or hopeless and lacking the momentum to go on. Spiritual practices may or may not lead you to satisfactory answers to your "why" questions, but they do tend to help people come to terms with the fact that we often can't fully understand the mysteries of life and death. For all of these reasons, the need to explore existential and spiritual questions and find meaning is the eighth central need of dementia care partners.

ONE PHILOSOPHER'S VIEW OF WHY AND HIS SEARCH FOR MEANING

Viktor Frankl was a Jewish psychiatrist from Vienna, Austria, who was imprisoned in Auschwitz and other Nazi genocide camps during most of World War II. His wife and children, as well as his parents, lost their lives in the Holocaust. Despite starvation, physical and psychological torture, and little to live for, Frankl survived, and from his experiences wrote a book called *Man's Search for Meaning*, acclaimed as one of the ten most influential books ever written. Frankl went on to become a world-renowned therapist. The first part of his book (which I highly recommend for care partners to read) details the horrors he and others endured living in the subhuman conditions of a concentration camp. The second part (especially meaningful for medical and mental-health professionals) describes his counseling philosophy, called logotherapy (derived from the Greek word for meaning, *logos*), which is how you can find meaning, and how you can respond, when bad things happen to you or someone you love.

Frankl believed that all people experience **difficult circumstances** they cannot change, and no matter what their circumstances are, people are able to find **meaning and purpose** in those circumstances by changing how they view them. He said, "When we are no longer able to change a situation, we are challenged to change ourselves." And what is that change in self? It's the ability to find meaning and purpose, even if what we're encountering is painful.

If his philosophy was applied to what you're experiencing right now, Frankl would not necessarily attempt to answer your "why" questions, though he would encourage you to ask them. Rather, he would have you focus on the meaning and purpose your life has now that you are a care partner for a loved one with dementia. Perhaps you find meaning and purpose in recognizing your ability to be a care partner, even though you never saw yourself having this role. Maybe you find

WAYS TO FIND AND CREATE MEANING ON THE DEMENTIA JOURNEY

Here are some ideas for meaning-making.

- Create a scrapbook or write a biography about the person with dementia. The website Alzlive has a free downloadable template to help you do this (https://www.alzlive.com/resources/books/a-template-for-creating-your-loved-ones-biography/).

- Donate money to a dementia-focused nonprofit organization for research and education. There are nonprofit associations, foundations, and societies specific to the common forms of dementia (Alzheimer's disease, frontotemporal dementia, and Lewy body dementia).

- Participate in your local annual Alzheimer's Association's Walk to End Alzheimer's (https://www.act.alz.org/site/SPageServer/?pagename=walk_homepage)

- Volunteer in an organization that helps those with dementia, such as an adult daycare center. For example, at the Tab Williams Adult Day Center in Winston-Salem, North Carolina, parents of young children can volunteer for the Kindermusik program, in which children age seven and under participate in an intergenerational music class with seniors (www.kindermusik.com), and teens as well as adults can volunteer for the Music and Memory program, equipping a senior with an iPod containing their favorite music (www.musicandmemory.org).

- Engage a person with dementia in the arts, such as dance (https://www.forsythwoman.com/camel-city-creates-christina-soriano-dance-dementia/) and painting and drawing (https://www.aarp.org/health/dementia/info-2018/dementia-alzheimers-art-therapy-new.html).

- Companion another dementia care partner and be a compassionate listener for them.

Of course, there are many other examples, but I hope this gives you some ideas.

meaning and purpose in trying to be the best care partner possible, even though it's a really hard job. Maybe you find meaning and purpose in learning to love someone you were not very close to before they developed dementia. Perhaps it's something else. In the box on page 253, I've listed some ways people with dementia and their family care partners can find and create meaning. I feel confident you, your loved one, and your family could add to the list!

Tarshira's Ministry

Tarshira was in her early 50s when she lost her husband of 30 years to Parkinson's disease dementia. She was a nurse by training, was active in the health ministry of her large church, and wanted to do something after losing her husband that would help others on the dementia journey. With the blessing of her pastor, she decided she would volunteer some of her time to visiting church members affected by dementia, whether at home or in a facility of some sort. Several months into doing this, Tarshira recognized a huge need. Many families needed caregiving help they couldn't afford. She expanded her ministry to involve others. In addition to the visits, she and the other volunteers she recruited also began providing up to three hours respite for dementia care partners free of charge once per week. Church members of all ages wanted to be involved, from teens to seniors. Several other churches in the area loved Tarshira's program so much they started something similar. Tarshira had found a way to make meaning out of her late husband's awful disease.

Think about your role as care partner to a loved one with dementia. What meaning or purpose has that role brought to your life? Please describe.

_____

_____

_____

Before I describe Frankl's advice for finding meaning in your life no matter what you're enduring, I want to tell you the story of somebody with dementia who embodied Frankl's philosophy,

Brad's Search for Meaning

Brad was in his mid-50s, nearly 30 years into a career with a large computer software company. He had a lot of responsibility, which included managing a team of software engineers and the projects they were responsible for. Once a very organized and detail-oriented person, Brad started to struggle. He couldn't assign roles and responsibilities to team members in a logical manner. The quality of his own work deteriorated. After seeking medical evaluation, he was diagnosed with mild cognitive impairment and told he was already transitioning to early-stage Alzheimer's disease.

Brad applied for and was granted long-term disability. While it provided some income replacement, Brad had adult children in college and graduate school and a house that wasn't quite paid for. The disability checks weren't enough. Brad's wife, Melinda, a high school teacher who hadn't worked for a number of years, had to return to the classroom.

All of a sudden, life was totally different for Brad. He was home full-time managing the household, while Melinda was away all day at work and creating lesson plans and grading papers in the evening. He didn't quite know what to do with all of the extra time he had. He seemed lost without goals or direction. Then, something changed: how he viewed his extra time. Rather than seeing it as something that was dragging him down, he started to think of it as a gift, an opportunity to do something he'd never had the time to do previously.

Brad had always been a lover of nature, particularly the diversity and beauty of trees, and nobody had ever written a book about the trees native to the area where he and Melinda lived. He began spending many of his days hiking trails in the local state park, categorizing and describing all of the trees he encountered. He discovered hundreds of different tree species! His plan was to self-publish the book and sell copies of it at a nominal cost at the state park's visitor center for others to enjoy.

Brad found the park ranger and Melinda to be willing helpers in this venture, since his cognitive symptoms were an ongoing challenge for an undertaking such as this. Brad knew his MCI and eventually the Alzheimer's would get the best of him, but for the time being, he had found meaning and purpose, and was confident his book would be something that he'd leave behind as a treasure to those who loved nature and trees as much as he did.

Brad's story illustrates the psychological concept called **post-traumatic growth**, which refers to a positive change that's a direct result of a traumatic event that occurs in your life. The trauma doesn't occur in order for something positive to happen; however, given that something traumatic did happen, the experience can be used to create something positive. In a religious context, God does not cause someone to develop dementia in order for something good to happen; rather, I believe God can help people flourish and grow in spite of the dementia.

With that in mind, and both Brad and Tarshira's stories, let's get back to Frankl. Here are the three ways he described to find meaning and purpose in life, when bad things happen to good people. They are:

- **What you give back to the world.** By this, Frankl meant what you create, how you treat others, the legacy you leave behind. What you give back might be through family, your job, or perhaps hobbies. From a legacy standpoint, it's what you'll be remembered for, hopefully generations from now. For Brad, in the story you just read, what he gave back to the world included his role as husband to Melinda and father to his children, his career as a software engineer, and his tree book. These are things he did well and what he hoped others would remember him for. For Tarshira, it was her ministry, something that others would likely remember both her and her husband for. And keep in mind that legacy isn't just about what people will remember you for. It's also about the ripple effects you create in the world, that ripple goodness and love out to other people, who then are more likely to act with goodness and love in the world themselves. To give back you don't necessarily have to be personally remembered; you just have to start ripples.

Let's apply this to your loved one. What did they create through family, career, and/or hobbies? How did they treat others? What will their legacy be? Please describe.

_____

_____

_____

_____

_____

_____

_____

_____

- **What you experience in or from the world.** The second way Frankl said you can find meaning is through the things you find unique and beautiful in the world, and how you experience them. Perhaps you love art or nature, and spend time drawing, painting, or admiring the artwork of others, or hiking in the beautiful countryside to soak up the sights and sounds of nature. Brad loved trees, a love which he became passionate about sharing with others through his book

What did your loved one uniquely experience in or from the world, even if they no longer remember it anymore? Please describe.

_____

_____

_____

_____

_____

_____

- **Your attitude toward the inevitable suffering that happens in this world.** Frankl believed that all human beings will experience suffering of some sort, and that even in the worst of circumstances, they can find meaning. Living in a concentration camp stripped of freedom, family, and a sense of self, he still maintained hope and managed to survive, sometimes barely. One of the most frequently cited quotes of Viktor Frankl is the following: "Everything can be taken from a man but...the last of human freedoms—to choose one's attitude in any given set of circumstances, to choose one's own way." Despite a rough start to his long-term disability, Brad ultimately chose to make the best of his time off, but it required an attitude adjustment. His positive attitude helped others, especially his wife and adult children, think more positively about his Alzheimer's journey. Similarly, for Tarshira, rather than remaining bitter about her husband's Parkinson's disease and the dementia caused by it, she chose to transform something that was tragic into a ministry of kindness and compassion that served and helped others.

What has been your loved one's attitude toward their diagnosis of dementia? Perhaps they have been in denial, or had a negative attitude, or maybe they've been able to think of it more positively. Please share.

_____

_____

_____

_____

_____

_____

_____

REFLECTIONS BACK ON MY OWN CARE-PARTNERING JOURNEY

As a way to wrap up this lesson, I want to share something I wrote in the last lesson of my prior book, *Keeping Love Alive as Memories Fade: The 5 Love Languages and the Alzheimer's Journey*. It was written in January of 2016, the year Rebecca died, but several months before her seizure and my Bell's palsy. Even as I reflect back on these words now, several years after Rebecca's death, they still represent where I stand in my faith journey. It is my hope that these words are meaningful and helpful to you.

"I have also learned to trust God. The best way I can explain this is with a driving metaphor. A car has both a windshield to look through when driving ahead, and a rearview mirror to show what is behind. When I look into the rearview mirror and see the life I've shared with Rebecca, from the sweetness of our relationship to the joy of our children and now grandchildren, my response is one of gratitude, recognizing that the good things in life are indeed a blessing from God.

"Looking through the windshield at what's ahead, I see a road that has twists and turns, darkness and uncertainty. It is the journey down the path not chosen. My heart tells me that the God I praise looking in the rearview mirror is a good God, whereas I question the character and power of the God that is ahead. My head says there cannot be two Gods, a good one and a bad one; they must be one and the same. It is out of this struggle that my faith has been strengthened, and trust, the noun, has given rise to trust, the verb.

"And like Rebecca, I have seen good come from this journey of hers with Alzheimer's disease. My daughters, Erin, Leah, and Carrie, and I are closer than ever. We have learned to hold one another up. We depend on one another. Other relationships have also been strengthened with family members, friends, and coworkers. Their love has been poured out willingly and freely. The Memory Counseling Program, now a program of Wake Forest Baptist Health, did not exist five years ago, and would not exist had Rebecca not developed Alzheimer's disease. This counseling program has now served hundreds of individuals, couples, and families impacted by dementia through counseling sessions and support groups."

Recall from Lesson Five the definition of a paradox: a contradictory statement about something or someone that is actually true. The last paragraph of what I just shared with you is yet another paradox of the dementia journey: that my soulmate and life partner could die of Alzheimer's disease, and yet some good would come of it.

Thinking about your loved one with dementia, yourself, and the dementia journey, could you go so far as to say something good has come from it? Please explain.

_____

_____

_____

_____

_____

_____

_____

A FINAL REFLECTION AND LOOKING AHEAD

One of my favorite parts of writing this book has been researching and picking a favorite quote to put beneath the lesson title at the beginning of each lesson. This lesson was challenging not because there were so few quotes, but just the opposite—there were so many. Below are five other quotes related to the existential and spiritual issues discussed in this lesson:

> *"I am learning to trust the journey even when I do not understand it."*
> — Mila Bron

> *"Trust that everything happens for a reason, even when you're not wise enough to understand it."*
> — Oprah Winfrey

> *"Someday you will look back and understand why it happened the way it did."*
> — Boniface Z. Zulu

> *"Sometimes...bad things happen to inspire you to change and grow."*
> — Robert Tew

> *"When something bad happens, you have three choices. You can either let it define you, let it destroy you, or you can let it strengthen you."*
> — Dr. Seuss

> *"Sometimes what we think is a setback is really a setup for God to do something great."*
> — Joel Osteen

Which one of these quotes stands out to you the most? Why? Please explain.

_____

_____

_____

_____

_____

_____

Try to find a different quote that resonates with you, or think of your own, that is existential and/or spiritual in nature and reflects what you're feeling right now. Please share.

_____

_____

_____

_____

_____

_____

In the next lesson, Lesson Ten, your final lesson of the _Workbook_, you will have a chance to retell your story now that you have learned so many more things about being a dementia care partner over the last nine lessons. Once again, take a minute and repeat the Mindfulness Moment from earlier in this lesson before wrapping up this thought-provoking and challenging lesson on Central Need 8 of dementia care partners: Explore existential and spiritual questions to find meaning.

Retelling Your Story Starting Today

Whether you're part of a care-partner support group or have been studying the lessons in *The Dementia Care-Partner's Workbook* on your own, you've made it to Lesson Ten, the final one. I hope you've learned a lot from the book, but you may be feeling as though you have so much more to learn and so little time to do it. If so, you've joined the ranks of most dementia care partners, who feel as though they could or should be spending more time with their loved one with dementia, doing more for or with them, as well as spending more time on self-care and meeting the needs of other family members and friends. It is with all of you in mind that I chose the quote for this lesson: "The path of wisdom is a lifelong journey."

"The path of wisdom is a lifelong journey."

— Author Unknown

By working through the contents of this workbook (as well as selectively working back through certain lessons or sections as the need arises), you made the choice to be a more educated, wiser care partner (kudos!), which is a process, not an event.

In this last lesson of the workbook, you will have the opportunity to reflect back on what you've learned by revisiting each of the eight central needs of dementia care partners. In the process of doing this, you'll be given some questions to journal about which will help you retell your story, or at least pieces of it. Then you'll have a chance to look forward, at what you anticipate is on the road ahead.

To jumpstart this process, I want to share a story about a care partner who very reluctantly joined one of our support groups, but in the long run, was very glad she did.

Confessions of a Reluctant Suppor-Group Participant

Sue Ann, to my surprise, had not missed a single week of our ten-week care-partner support group. She had reluctantly agreed to participate, telling our dementia counseling center coordinator she was way too busy to come given the caregiving responsibilities she had for her 80-year-old husband with Alzheimer's disease.

For the initial two lessons, Sue Ann came in, sat down, didn't interact with the other group members, and was silent throughout the session. After that, she changed. She would actually come about 15 minutes early and chat with the other care partners about her husband, his Alzheimer's symptoms, and her challenges taking care of him. Her behavior in group was also different. Each week, Sue Ann would share things she'd journaled about in her workbook. She was engaged in group discussions, and in the last few weeks of group, even began asking probing questions of the classmates she had come to know.

For the very last support-group meeting, we always have an exercise during which group members share about what they've learned and what they will miss now that the ten group sessions have come to an end. Sue Ann volunteered to share first. "When I first came to this group, I was angry and didn't want to be here," she said. "I was angry that such a group even existed. Who in their right mind would want to go to an Alzheimer's caregiver support group? After the first session or two, I realized what has turned out to be the biggest blessing of all to me from the group—that I am not alone, I am not the only woman in

Winston-Salem taking care of someone with dementia. I also realized that I was angry—at my husband, for getting Alzheimer's, at God, for letting this happen to us, at our kids, for not being more involved in their dad's care. By being in this group, I'm now aware my anger was unreasonable. It's not his fault, or God's, that he got this terrible disease. And the kids, why I've hardly told them anything about what's going on; how could they help? I thought I'd be the last person in here to say these words, but I'm going to really miss this group." Sue Ann was tearful by the time she finished saying these things. She and the ladies around her shared some hugs and echoed similar feelings.

Sue Ann is a regular at our monthly maintenance care-partner support-group meetings (refer back to the workbook's Introduction for a description of maintenance groups). In fact, she rarely misses. She has also come to the counseling center for some individual sessions, one time bringing her adult children for a family meeting, so several of them are now helping Sue Ann with their dad's care. Sue Ann's husband is slowly declining, but she's more accepting, and she has gained a lot of insight about herself as she's become a more wise care partner.

Having read the lesson introduction and Sue Ann's story, describe how you are feeling about wrapping up your support group or self-study. Please share.

_____

_____

_____

_____

_____

_____

MINDFULNESS MOMENT

You might identify with some parts of Sue Ann's story, or maybe you are having some different emotions about yourself as a care partner or about wrapping up your study of *The Dementia Care-Partner's Workbook*. Since this is the last formal Mindfulness Moment you'll experience in the book, remember that you can be intentional about these timeouts whenever you are feeling the stress of being a care partner. If mindfulness is a practice you've embraced as part of your wellness plan, the "Resources" section of the workbook has recommendations on several books and apps that may be of interest to you.

Remember, mindfulness is a state of mind that you achieve by focusing all of your awareness and attention on the present moment and only the present moment, excluding worries of the past as well as the future. The practice of mindfulness gives you a "brain break," inviting you to calmly, nonjudgmentally, and compassionately accept your current thoughts, emotions, and body sensations without feeling as though you need to change them. The Mindfulness Moment includes a short breathing exercise that I hope provides you with a sense of peace that, at least for the moment, everything is OK.

Here we go.

1. Sit in a comfortable chair, put both feet on the floor (or any other comfortable position), clasp your hands over the middle of your belly, and then close your eyes (if desired).

2. Scan your muscles from head to toe and intentionally relax them. Unclench your teeth, let your shoulders sag, and relax your buttock and leg muscles.

3. Take in a slow, deep breath through your nose (count "one one-thousand, two one-thousand, three one-thousand" to yourself as you do so), then slowly exhale through your mouth to the same count, feeling the rise and fall of your belly. Do a total of ten slow, deep breaths like this. Focus solely on the gentle flow of your breath,

in and out. Each time you exhale, consciously blow out any negative emotions and stress you feel about wrapping up your support group or self-study of *The Dementia Care-Partner's Workbook*.

4. After the tenth breath, slowly open your eyes.

LOOKING BACK: REVISITING THE EIGHT CENTRAL NEEDS OF DEMENTIA CARE PARTNERS

In the introduction to this book, I shared the "Eight Central Needs of Dementia Care Partners"—eight things that my experiences as Rebecca's care partner and as a care-partner support-group leader had taught me were important to each and every person who cares for a loved one with dementia. As a reminder, here they are again:

The Eight Central Needs of Dementia Care Partners

- **Central Need 1**—*Tell and retell your story*
- **Central Need 2**—*Educate yourself*
- **Central Need 3**—*Adapt to changing relationships*
- **Central Need 4**—*Grieve your losses*
- **Central Need 5**—*Take care of yourself*
- **Central Need 6**—*Ask for and accept help from others*
- **Central Need 7**—*Prepare for what's ahead*
- **Central Need 8**—*Explore existential and spiritual questions to find meaning*

Back in Lesson One, you told your story, the story of your loved one's diagnosis with dementia, the story of you as their care partner. Now, if you've been reading and filling out this workbook along with a support group, it's likely ten or more weeks later. Lots of things have happened since then. Your loved one has changed, and you have changed. As a way of sharing about these changes and retelling your story (**Central Need 1**), we're going to revisit the other central needs to refresh your memory about what we covered in each lesson. So let's dive in!

CENTRAL NEED 2—*Educate yourself*

Central Need 2 is about educating yourself about dementia and the brain. Although every lesson has had an educational component, the foundation for what you learned in lessons three through nine was based on the content in lessons two and three. In Lesson Two: Basics of Alzheimer's Disease and Other Dementias, you learned about what dementia is, how it is diagnosed, and the symptoms of mild cognitive impairment, Alzheimer's disease, and the other more common forms of dementia—vascular, frontotemporal, and Lewy body. In Lesson Three: Brain Structure and Function, you learned about the different brain lobes and what they do, and about the five cognitive functions of attention and concentration, memory and learning, executive function (multitasking), language, and visuospatial function (balance). You also learned about three other brain functions related to cognitive function—personality, mood, and orientation. The concept of Activities of Daily Living (ADLs) was also presented, including the instrumental ADLs and basic ADLs. Then you learned about the stages of dementia—early, middle, and late stage. With this as background, please answer the following questions.

What is the one thing you learned about dementia or the brain from Lessons Two and Three that has been the most helpful to you? Just pick one! Please share.

_____

_____

_____

_____

_____

_____

What changes have you seen in your loved one's disease since you started this workbook? You can describe changes in their symptoms, cognitive function, ADLs, stage, or something else you choose. How do you feel about the changes you've witnessed? Please share.

_____

_____

_____

_____

_____

_____

CENTRAL NEED 3—*Adapt to changing relationships.*

Central Need 3 is about adapting to change. Because Alzheimer's disease and the other dementias are neurodegenerative diseases, things are always changing—we hope very slowly, but they tend to get progressively worse over time. In Lesson Four: Adapting to Change, you learned about changes in your loved one that tend to erode and alter relationships, sometimes by disrupting attachment bonds and causing separation distress, such as apathy, lack of insight and denial, loss of empathy, depression and anxiety, repetitive and persistent behaviors, lost identity, delusional thinking, and disinhibited behavior. We also reviewed strategies for adapting to those changing relationships by trying to be more patient, use techniques like AAR (acknowledge, affirm, and redirect) and KISSS (keep it short, simple, and safe), the five love languages, and reminiscence approaches, including music. With this as background, please answer the following questions.

What is the one thing you learned about behavior changes and adapting to changing relationships from Lesson Four that has been the most helpful to you? Just pick one! Please share.

_____

_____

_____

_____

_____

_____

Describe a challenging behavior in your loved one that you've adapted to well. What is the behavior? How did you adapt? Please share.

_____

_____

_____

_____

_____

Describe a challenging behavior in your loved one that you've not been able to adapt to very well. What is the behavior? How have you adapted so far? What changes could you make that might help things go better? Please share.

_____

_____

_____

_____

_____

CENTRAL NEED 4—*Grieve your losses*

Central Need 4 is about grief, which is what you think and feel on the inside about your loved one's dementia diagnosis and being a care partner, and mourning, which is the outward expression of your grief and a necessary part of your well-being. Lesson Five: Coping with Grief and Loss focused on the kinds of losses you can experience as a care partner, including personal losses (your time and freedom, health and occupation), relationship losses (as a couple, parent-child, and/or family), and lost peace of mind. As a dementia care partner, your grief and loss experiences are similar to those following the death of a loved one. With this as background, please answer the following questions.

What is the one thing you learned about grief and loss as a dementia care partner from Lesson Five that has been the most helpful to you? Just pick one! Please share.

_____

_____

_____

_____

_____

_____

Describe your grief, what you think and feel on the inside about your loved one's dementia diagnosis and being a care partner. Please share.

_____

_____

_____

_____

_____

_____

CENTRAL NEED 5—*Take care of yourself*

Central Need 5 is about you and your wellness as care partner on a journey that challenges your physical, mental, and spiritual health, which was described in Lesson Six: Stress and Self-Care. You learned about three big challenges to your health—depression, anxiety, and stress—as well as the elements of a wellness plan focusing on your physical and mental health, social relationships, and spirituality. With this as background, please answer the following questions.

What is the one thing you learned about stress and self-care from Lesson Six that has been the most helpful to you? Just pick one! Please share.

_____

_____

_____

_____

_____

_____

What things are you doing to take care of yourself physically, mentally, and spiritually? Please describe.

_____

_____

_____

_____

_____

_____

CENTRAL NEED 6—*Ask for and accept help from others*

Central Need 6 is about two simple yet extremely important notions about caring for a loved one with dementia—it is a team sport, and it's more of a marathon than a sprint. Yet most care partners try to do too much themselves and are reluctant to ask for and accept the help of others. In the latter part of Lesson Six: Stress and Self-Care, you learned that you can be intentional and proactive about forming a caregiving team for your loved one with dementia—that there are family members and friends who want to be there for you and help, and it's not always who you think. With this as background, please answer the following questions.

What is the one thing you learned about asking for and accepting help from others in the latter part of Lesson Six that has been the most helpful to you? Just pick one! Please share.

_____

_____

_____

_____

_____

_____

Who is one person you could add to your team, and in what way(s) would you have them help? Please share.

_____

_____

_____

_____

_____

_____

CENTRAL NEED 7—*Prepare for what's ahead*

Central Need 7 is about the need to solve both existing challenges and anticipate and plan for future ones. In Lesson Seven: Getting More Help and Transitioning Care, you learned about agitation and aggression, hallucinations, wandering, sexual behaviors, resisting or refusing care, sundowning and day-night reversal, and incontinence, any one of which may be more than you can manage at home on your own. The options for more help that were presented include home health, adult daycare, assisted living, and memory care, among others. In Lesson Eight: Legal, Financial, and End-of-Life Issues, we reviewed power of attorney documents, wills and trusts, HIPAA (Healthcare Insurance Portability and Accountability Act), driving safety, how to pay for care, and common end-of-life challenges, which address potential medical and legal problems and ways to plan ahead to avoid them. With this as background, please answer the following questions.

What is the one thing you learned about solving problems and planning ahead from Lessons Seven and Eight that has been the most helpful to you? Just pick one! Please share.

_____

_____

_____

_____

_____

What are your thoughts about bringing a paid caregiver such as a certified nursing assistant into your home to help you, and/or about the possibility of transitioning your loved one to assisted living, memory care, or a nursing home, whichever is the most applicable to their situation? Please share.

_____

_____

_____

_____

CENTRAL NEED 8—*Explore existential and spiritual questions to find meaning*

Central Need 8 is about asking questions of an existential and spiritual nature and is the topic of Lesson Nine: Existential and Spiritual Questions. Such questions include, "Why did he (or she) develop dementia?" These are hard questions, but for many, are normal and necessary to ask, even if there are no answers. With this as background, please answer the following questions.

What is the one thing you learned from Lesson Nine on existential and spiritual questions that has been most helpful to you? Just pick one! Please share.

_____

_____

_____

_____

_____

Think again about Dr. Viktor Frankl's philosophy: even if what you're encountering in life is painful, you still have the ability to find meaning and purpose in it. Share what's on your mind and heart about the meaning and purpose you find in life at the moment as care partner to your loved with dementia. Are your feelings different now than they were when you started this workbook? Please share.

_____

_____

_____

_____

_____

_____

LOOKING FORWARD—WHAT'S AHEAD ON THE JOURNEY?

This workbook has taken seven years to plan and nine months to write. I thought long and hard about what to include, and was blessed to have the input of my counseling colleagues. If I had the ability to know each of you who have used _The Dementia Care-Partner's Workbook_, we could sit down together, talk about where your loved one is in their dementia journey, and what lies ahead for you as their care partner. Every person with dementia has a unique journey, and your experience as their care partner is equally unique.

As a way of sharing some parting wisdom and advice with you, I will leave you with eight things, based on the eight central needs, I wish I had known before Rebecca's journey that would have made me a better care partner and helped me take better care of myself too. And then I'll have three final questions for you.

EIGHT THINGS I WISH I'D KNOWN WHEN I WAS A CARE PARTNER

- **CENTRAL NEED 1—_Tell and retell your story._** Find someone you trust and make the time to talk about your caregiving experiences on a regular basis. It really helps to be able to decompress about the challenges of being a dementia care partner. This can be a family member or friend, and/or it can be a counselor or therapist. If you have a support group available to you, sign up! You get a different kind of experience being part of a group that you don't get talking with someone one-on-one.

- **CENTRAL NEED 2—_Educate yourself._** Learn as much about dementia and caregiving as you can. Understanding why your loved one says or does the things they do, or doesn't say or do certain things, will help you respond out of knowledge rather than emotion. That being said, there are times you will respond with emotion—too much, in fact—and you have to learn to forgive yourself for that

- **CENTRAL NEED 3—*Adapt to changing relationships.*** Relationship changes, especially when the changes bring challenges, are so hard emotionally, cognitively, spiritually, and often physically. Try not to focus on who your loved one isn't and what they can't do; rather, focus on who they still are (and always have been) and what they can do. In that regard, when they're having a great day (or week or month), you have a great day right along with them. You've got to "make hay while the sun shines"!

- **CENTRAL NEED 4—*Grieve your losses.*** The grief you're experiencing is real and it's normal, but it hurts. The losses are profound and run deep. Expressing your grief outwardly is not an option, it's a must. Cry. Yell and scream. Do what you must to mourn. The only way to the other side of this grief is to walk through it, not around it.

- **CENTRAL NEED 5—*Take care of yourself.*** Oh this is so hard. Most care partners put their needs and wellness last on the list. Yet there are so many people who depend on you, it should be just the opposite. And don't forget about sleep. A good night's rest is one of the nicest and most important things you can do for yourself.

- **CENTRAL NEED 6—*Ask for and accept help from others.*** When Rebecca was diagnosed with Alzheimer's, her doctor said to us both, "You've served others your whole life. You're entering a new season of life where others will need to serve you. This is going to be a hard change to make." He was right. I accepted help later in the journey than I should have, especially from my daughters. I should have gotten over my reluctance to ask others for help sooner than I did. The paid caregivers who helped Rebecca in her last three years of life became family.

- **CENTRAL NEED 7—*Prepare for what's ahead.*** Of the many things I felt unprepared for as a care partner, the challenging behaviors from the middle and late stages of the journey were the most difficult problems for me to solve. For Rebecca, these included agitation, aggression, profound depression with despair, resisting care, sundowning, and incontinence. If I had had a better understanding of what these things were, and why they occur, dealing with them would have been easier on and better for Rebecca, and less stressful for me. However, right after her diagnosis, Rebecca did bring up her end-of-life wishes. She told us what she wanted and didn't want, and my daughters and I were able to carry out these wishes at a time when our focus was on companioning her as her soul transitioned into eternity.

- **CENTRAL NEED 8**—*Explore existential and spiritual questions to find meaning.* I'll be very honest and say that for nine years, I asked those "why" questions of God on a daily basis, and to this day, they're still unanswered. And yet, somehow, I've emerged with a stronger faith and a deeper trust. It's truly a paradox. I can't imagine that a journey like this could not be filled with existential and spiritual angst, and I would encourage you to freely question as I did.

The subtitle of *The Dementia Care-Partner's Workbook* suggests it will guide you in three areas—understanding, education, and hope. Having completed the workbook, in the context of the bits of wisdom and advice that I just shared, please answer these last three questions.

How has your understanding of dementia changed since you started the workbook? Please share.

_____

_____

_____

_____

_____

Thinking about the journey ahead of you, what information or foresight do you wish you had that you don't? Please share.

_____

_____

_____

_____

_____

_____

What are new ways in which you are experiencing hope because of participating in a support group that used _The Dementia Care-Partner's Workbook_ or through your own study of the material?

_____

_____

_____

_____

_____

PARTING WORDS

You did it! You've come to the end of the book. If you have a moment to provide some feedback, I would love to hear from you and promise that your comments will be used to make the next edition of the workbook even better than this one. You can contact me by email (drshaw@empatheducation.com) or through my website (www. empatheducation.com), which also has information about my availability to come speak in your community or for your organization. And as you continue your journey down the path not chosen, I will hope and pray for your strength, courage, and wisdom.
Ed

ACKNOWLEDGMENTS

To Dr. Alan Wolfelt, longtime friend and colleague, for the opportunity to publish this book with Companion Press and for his encouragement over the years to pursue my dream of becoming a "real" grief counselor. To my Companion Press editor, Karla Oceanak, for her instruction, guidance, and patience walking with me though the process. Thank you so much. To Nicole Duggan at Companion Press, for her early input, final manuscript review, help, and encouragement, with gratitude. To Debbie Barr and Gary Chapman, for inspiring my faith and encouraging me to answer "the call" to be a writer.

To my amazing Memory Counseling Program colleagues, for their input on the support-group curriculum and for leading groups over the years, as well as for their insights conceptualizing the workbook: Casey Johanson, Beverly Ingram, and Samantha Culler, with special thanks to Alyssa Botte for her thoughtful comments on the penultimate draft of the manuscript. And to my other Wake Forest University and Wake Forest Baptist Health colleagues, past and present, who have contributed in some way to the support-group program and curriculum, including Jonathan Adams, Rabeena Alli, Bill Applegate, Hal Atkinson, Sara Bailey, Markela Batts, Tina Brunelli, Brian Calhoun, Phil Clarke, Jo Cleveland, Abbie Eaton, Carol Ebron, Marinda Freeman, Sam Gladding, Daniel Hall, Christina Hugenschmidt, Nathaniel Ivers, Renee Minx, Mollee Reitz, José Villalba, Bonnie Sachs, Ben Williams, Julie Williams, Jeff Williamson, Joe Wilkerson, Cathy Wilson, Kim Wilson, Mia Yang, and Rachael Zimmer.

To Dr. Kaycee Sink, friend, colleague, and dementia doctor extraordinaire, for her thorough and thoughtful medical review of the manuscript, with deep appreciation. To attorney Kate Mewhinney, with gratitude for reviewing the lesson on legal issues.

To my heroes in the field, Teepa Snow, Lisa Gwyther, Dr. Peter Rabin, Dr. Ronald Petersen, and Dr. Gary Chapman, with great admiration for their work and appreciation for their willingness to review this book.

And to my wife, Claire, for loving, supporting, and listening to me through the writing of this book, especially keeping me on task and being the detail-oriented proofreader that I am not!

RESOURCES

Here is a selection of helpful resources about dementia and caregiving. It's not an exhaustive list; rather, I've selected three to six resources (in a few instances, more) in a variety of areas that you may find helpful.

BOOKS

- *Keeping Love Alive as Memories Fade: The 5 Love Languages and the Dementia Journey.* Deborah Barr, Edward G. Shaw, and Gary Chapman. 2016.

- *The 36-Hour Day.* Nancy L. Mace and Peter V. Rabins. 6th edition. 2017.

- *The Alzheimer's Action Plan: What You Need to Know—and What You Can Do—About Memory Problems, from Prevention to Early Intervention and Care.* P. Murali Doraiswamy and Lisa P. Gwyther. 2009.

- *Creating Moments of Joy Along the Alzheimer's Journey: A Guide for Families and Caregivers.* Jolene Brackey. 5th Edition. 2008

- *Healing Your Grieving Heart When Someone You Care About Has Alzheimer's: 100 Practical Ideas for Families, Friends, and Caregivers.* Alan D. Wolfelt and Kirby J. Duvall. 2011.

- *Grace for the Unexpected Journey: A 60-Day Devotional for Alzheimer's and Other Dementia Caregivers.* Deborah Barr. 2018.

WEBSITES

- The Alzheimer's Association: www.alz.org

- The Alzheimer's Foundation of America: www.alzfdn.org

- The Dementia Action Alliance: www.daanow.org

- African Americans Against Alzheimer's: www.usagainstalzheimers.org

- Alzheimer's Disease International: www.alz.co.uk

- Lewy Body Dementia Association: www.lbda.org

- The Association for Frontotemporal Degeneration: www.theaftd.org
- The National Institute on Aging: www.nia.nih.gov
- The National Institute of Neurologic Disorders and Stroke: www.ninds.nih.gov

DEMENTIA EDUCATIONAL PRODUCTS, PODCASTS, AND TED TALKS
- Teepa Snow and the Positive Approach to Care: www.teepasnow.com
- The Fight Against Alzheimer's and Dementia (TED Talk, Samuel Cohen): https://www.ted.com/talks/samuel_cohen_alzheimer_s_is_not_normal_aging_and_we_can_cure_it?referrer=playlist-the_fight_against_alzheimer_s
- Johns Hopkins Medical Podcasts on Alzheimer's and Dementia: https://podcasts.hopkinsmedicine.org/category/podcasts/health-topics/alzheimers-disease-and-dementia/
- Embodied Labs Virtual Reality Training for Alzheimer's Disease and Lewy Body Dementia: www.embodiedlabs.com

MINDFULNESS
- *Mindfulness for Beginners: Reclaiming the Present Moment for Your Life.* Jon Kabat-Zinn. Sounds True, Boulder, CO, 2016.
- *Wherever You Go, There You Are: Mindfulness Meditation in Everyday Life.* Jon Kabat-Zinn, Hyperion, New York, NY, 2005.
- *Dancing With Elephants: Mindfulness Training for Those Living With Dementia, Chronic Illness or an Aging Brain.* Jarem Sawatsky. 2017.
- Apps: Mindfulness Daily (www.mindfulnessdailyapp.com) and Aura (www.aurahealth.io).

OTHER
- Powerful Tools for Caregivers: www.powerfultoolsforcaregivers.org

Presentations, Trainings, and Consulting by Dr. Shaw

To contact Dr. Shaw about speaking engagements, training opportunities, or consulting for your organization, visit his website www.empatheducation.com or email him at **drshaw@empatheducation.com.**

I WOULD APPRECIATE YOUR FEEDBACK!

Whether you are a care partner in a support group or using *The Workbook* for self-study, or you are a professional support-group leader or a lay facilitator, I would love your feedback! Here are a few suggested questions to guide your response, or feel free to provide comments and suggestions however you see fit.

1. What did you find most helpful about *The Workbook*?

2. What did you find least helpful about *The Workbook*?

3. What additions would you suggest to make *The Workbook* more helpful?

4. What other support-group materials would you find useful to support care partners or those with dementia?

5. Tell me a bit about your story and, if appropriate, the organization you work for.

Please email your thoughts to me at **drshaw@empatheducation.com.** Thanks so much!

About the Author

Edward G. Shaw, M.D., M.A., is dually trained as a physician and mental-health counselor. He was the primary care partner for his late wife, Rebecca, who was diagnosed with early-onset Alzheimer's disease in 2008, at age 53. She died in 2016 after a nine-year battle. He was a practicing academic radiation oncologist for 23 years, specializing in the treatment of adults and children with brain cancer. In 2010, inspired by Rebecca's journey, his medical interest shifted to dementia diagnosis and treatment, and with his additional training in mental-health counseling, he founded the Memory Counseling Program in 2011, part of Gerontology and Geriatric Medicine and the Sticht Center for Healthy Aging and Alzheimer's Prevention at Wake Forest Baptist Health in Winston-Salem, North Carolina. The program serves individuals, couples, and families affected by Alzheimer's disease or another form of dementia. Ed is also the founder of Empath Education, a company whose mission is to provide empathy-based education to people with dementia, their care partners, and healthcare professionals who work with older adults, including those affected by Alzheimer's disease or another form of dementia. With Dr. Gary Chapman and Deborah Barr, he co-authored the book *Keeping Love Alive as Memories Fade: The 5 Love Languages and the Alzheimer's Journey*, which describes his moving personal story of caring for Rebecca coupled with an innovative use of the five love languages in dementia counseling. Ed resides in Winston-Salem with his wife, Claire. He has three adult daughters, Erin, Leah, and Carrie, a son-in-law, Darian, two grandsons, Paul and Isaiah, and a stepson, Patrick.

A Leader's Manual for Dementia Care-Partner Support Groups

By Edward G. Shaw M.D., M.A.
Alan D. Wolfelt Ph.D., C.T.

A Leader's Manual for Dementia Care-Partner Support Groups is for both professional mental-health

caregivers and laypeople who facilitate support groups for those who provide daily care to loved ones with Alzheimer's or another form of dementia.

This manual includes ten detailed meeting plans based on the curriculum used at Wake Forest Baptist Health's Memory Counseling Program, where Dr. Shaw is founder and director. The lessons dovetail with Dr. Shaw's book for group members, *The Dementia Care-Partner's Workbook*—which is part educational primer, part guided-journaling tool.

The *Leader's Manual* also includes practical information on how to start a group, where to meet, ways to publicize the group, choosing the optimum number of participants, screening members, handling challenging participants, and more. Lesson-specific handouts, assessment instruments, evaluation forms, and a printable certificate of participation are also included.

Price: $19.95 • 8.5 x 11 • Downloadable PDF
Find at www.centerforloss.com

Companion
P R E S S

All publications can be ordered by mail from:

Companion Press
3735 Broken Bow Road
Fort Collins, CO 80526
Phone: (970) 226-6050
Fax: 1-800-922-6051
www.centerforloss.com

Healing Your Grieving Heart
When Someone You Care About has Alzheimer's

By Alan D. Wolfelt, Ph.D. and Kirby J. Duvall, M.D.

Navigating the challenging journey that families and friends of Alzheimer's patients must endure, this heartfelt guide reveals how their struggle is as complex and drawn out as the illness itself. Confronting their natural but difficult process of grieving and mourning, this crucial addition to the popular 100 Ideas series covers the inevitable feelings of shock, sadness, anger, guilt, and relief, illustrating the initial reactions people commonly feel from the moment of the dementia's onset.

Authors Dr. Wolfelt and Dr. Duvall suggest healthy and productive ways to acknowledge and express these feelings along with tips and activities that fulfill the emotional, spiritual, cognitive, physical, and social needs of those who care about someone afflicted with this debilitating disease. Special consideration is also shown for caregivers, whose grief is often complicated by the demanding physical attention that patients require.

ISBN: 978-1-617221-48-4

Price $11.95 • softcover • 242 pages

Companion
PRESS

All publications can be ordered by mail from:

Companion Press

3735 Broken Bow Road
Fort Collins, CO 80526

Phone: (970) 226-6050
Fax: 1-800-922-6051

www.centerforloss.com

Companioning the Bereaved
A Soulful Guide for Caregivers

By Alan D. Wolfelt, Ph.D.

This book by one of North America's most respected grief educators presents a model for grief counseling based on his "companioning" principles.

For many mental-healthcare providers, grief in contemporary society has been medicalized—

perceived as if it were an illness that with proper assessment, diagnosis, and treatment could be cured.

Dr. Wolfelt explains that our modern understanding of grief all too often conveys that at bereavement's "end" the mourner has completed a series of tasks, extinguished pain, and established new relationships. Our psychological models emphasize "recovery" or "resolution" in grief, suggesting a return to "normalcy."

By contrast, this book advocates a model of "companioning" the bereaved, acknowledging that grief forever changes or transforms the mourner's world view. Companioning is not about assessing, analyzing, fixing, or resolving another's grief. Instead, it is about being totally present to the mourner, even being a temporary guardian of his soul. The companioning model is grounded in a "teach me" perspective.

ISBN 978-1-879651-41-8

Price $29.95 • 191 pages • hardcover

Companion
P R E S S

All publications can be ordered by mail from:

Companion Press
3735 Broken Bow Road
Fort Collins, CO 80526
Phone: (970) 226-6050
Fax: 1-800-922-6051
www.centerforloss.com